CarriBolles

Tracing the Moon

A Memoir of a Woman's Journey in India

Kumari Ellis

BALBOA
PRESS
A DIVISION OF HAY HOUSE

Balboa Press books may be ordered through booksellers or by contacting:

Balboa Press
A Division of Hay House
1663 Liberty Drive
Bloomington, IN 47403
www.balboapress.com.au
1 (877) 407-4847

Because of the dynamic nature of the Internet, any web addresses or links contained in this book may have changed since publication and may no longer be valid. The views expressed in this work are solely those of the author and do not necessarily reflect the views of the publisher, and the publisher hereby disclaims any responsibility for them.

The author of this book does not dispense medical advice or prescribe the use of any technique as a form of treatment for physical, emotional, or medical problems without the advice of a physician, either directly or indirectly. The intent of the author is only to offer information of a general nature to help you in your quest for emotional and spiritual well-being. In the event you use any of the information in this book for yourself, which is your constitutional right, the author and the publisher assume no responsibility for your actions.

Printed in the United States of America.

ISBN: 978-1-4525-1327-0 (sc)
ISBN: 978-1-4525-1328-7 (e)

Balboa Press rev. date: 2/28/2014

Acknowledgements

There are always so many people to thank in life, those who make our day easier in some way, small or great. In this respect there are many people I can mention and indeed, to realize this inspires a feeling of gratitude. In terms of writing this memoir I firstly would like to mention my friend and writing teacher Sarah Armstrong. Under her guidance this project came to life, some years ago now, and along with the members of our writing group whose encouragement allowed the ideas to take shape. Sarah has continued to mentor with regular manuscript assessments, and through her probing and suggestions a deeper layer of story emerged.

Several friends have recently read the completed manuscript and it has been their response that has encouraged me to self-publish. Thank you Sheia, Lynda, Bita and Amanda. Thanks also to Najma Ahern and Gabrielle Nagel for your patient technical support. The mandali, who you will meet in this book, have been so willing to be included in parts, and also have contributed photos to be included. Thank you and I love that after all these years five of the six of us are still very much in communication.

Likewise the community of friends here in the northern rivers of NSW and around the world, that gathered in Lucknow, and still have such a strong presence in my life, I am deeply grateful.

Thank you to Wroth for always believing in this project. Thank you to Ma Yoga Pratima, your editorial skill is greatly appreciated. Thank you to Gatya Kelly for the book cover design, and to Chandi Devi for the back cover photo of the moon rising over Arunachala, the sacred mountain in southern India.

Contents

CHAPTER ONE

—◦◦◦◦◦◦—

London

'Since before time, I have been free. Birth and Death are only doors through which we pass. Sacred thresholds on our journey.' Thich Nhat Hahn

O n a full-moon night I witnessed a death. Twilight had just given way, as if the hour herself supported this surrender. I entered Henry's room to change the morphine drip; I knew his life was drawing to a close. Always pale, his skin had a translucent glow, as if reflecting the angels already near.

At his bedside four friends chanted quietly. Henry was a Buddhist and his community kept vigil by his side. Melissa was there too, sitting by his side as she had over the years, his long fingers entwined in hers. Henry's persistent cough, five years earlier, had confirmed his diagnosis and revealed his preference for men. Their son was six years old. Yesterday Jack had sat on his mother's lap staring at his dad – his thin face so like Henry's, wet with lost tears. Now Jack was with his grandmother, who had once been Lady in Waiting to the Queen.

With each of Henry's admissions to our ward, this Buddhist community filled the room with ancient sound. When I first heard the murmured cadence of ancient prayers, I had stood at his doorway with goose bumps rising up my arms.

Henry told me the Buddha taught that life is just a fleeting event, one blink among many as we journey through the worlds. Henry's surrender to his approaching death touched me deeply. None of the many patients I'd seen over the years had such a sure sense of calm acceptance.

'His breathing's changed. He just closed his eyes.' Tears spill down Melissa's face. I laid my hand on his heart that was still beating but erratic, a distant drum roll somewhere far away. His breath came in shallow gasps. I had made friends with death, working on this ward, yet when it was there before me I felt my stomach tighten, my own heart beat stronger. I wanted to be part of this moment too and ignored the phone ringing at the nurses' station just outside the door, and the beeping of a machine telling me that a drip needed changing.

'I just left. I had to get away, to find a meaning in it all,' Henry had told me when we first met, his eyes shining in a face stretched tight. 'I found a monastery in Japan after travelling the world. It was on an island and somehow that spoke so much to me. After a small boat delivered me to the shore, I walked through a forest then up a hill to the monastery. It was springtime and all the cherry blossoms were in bud.' He had sat on the bed with his eyes glazed over as if he was transporting himself back to that blossom-strewn monastery. And it may have been then that the seed took root in my own soul, as if I too knew there was more, that a journey awaited me, and my destiny included a spiritual search of my own.

'I found peace there. Peace for the acceptance of my diagnosis, peace in my sexuality and the sure knowing I would die. Judith, we all will die, every one of us. I have had to face it fair and square.' He had looked deep into my eyes. Henry was tall and thin and gave the appearance of already touching heaven.

Henry was not the first patient to challenge my beliefs about the soul and the mysterious journey of death. I'd seen dozens die, mostly young men, some of them afraid as they breathed their last. Yet Andrew, a committed Quaker, had held his partner's hand as he passed, and journeyed with him towards the light until his breathing and consciousness was no more. Later he had told me that he too had sensed the light, a great white expanse, and felt that Tim, his beloved for many years, was at peace. And Andrew too held that peace even in grief. Belief seemed to me to be an important part in it all. Henry inspired me to inquire more deeply of the eastern religions I was already drawn to, the words of Thich Nhat Hahn, J Krishnamurti and the writings of Joseph Campbell.

As I read, I wondered what could be understood about death, except that it is our shared destiny – the one and only certainty from the moment we take our first gasping breath. It was the immense grief of those left holding thin entwined fingers as final breaths receded that affected me deeply. How would lives recover with the burden that grief seemed to bring? Mothers in shock and dismay, blank faces and forced cheeriness. Death insisted I search my own heart, my own beliefs, and I felt an urgency in me to understand what this life is all about. Before death comes knocking at my own door.

We became easy friends, Henry and I, as his admissions became more frequent. One day, he told me that he'd stayed six months in the Japanese monastery. 'We chanted for peace, within ourselves and for the whole world. The teachings of the Buddha were painted on the faces of the monks. Serenity surrounded me. For the first time ever I felt at peace.' And he fixed his wide blue eyes on me before his face erupted in a smile.

'Has that peace stayed with you?' I asked as I changed a bag of blood during a short admission for a blood transfusion.

'Yes. It is like the base line, the rhythm for my being. Sometimes the melodies become more of a challenge and then I practise more diligently.' He sat up and crossed his thin legs. 'I chant. I sit still. I remember again that peace is all around me, always, no matter what the circumstance. Life can throw many challenges – better to be prepared in your mind.'

As the admissions became more frequent and as he became thinner than I thought possible, he was calm, always ready with his gentle smile, sitting up cross-legged on the starchy sheets until he no longer could.

Then it was his last day. After changing his drip I found another nurse to take charge of the ward keys and told her I wanted to stay with Henry as he died.

I returned to his room and slipped in as quietly as I could. Henry's pale face was ashen grey, his cheekbones sunken, his eyes slightly open. I wondered for a moment if he had already passed. I reached for his hand, cool and waxy. His pulse was a thin whisper. His breathing, a shallow rattle all day, now came in gasps with long pauses in between. The chanting continued unbroken. Henry's fingers slipped from Melissa's hand. After a few minutes he sighed deeply. It was the full moon in May.

As death reached down, a presence filled the room. Henry slipped free and life and death stood side by side. In that briefest moment, I held eternity. I felt a pure unadulterated love, and it was as if everything – thought, time itself – ceased to be. Consumed by this presence I found only silence. An absence of everything I had previously known. The sense of my self expanded to include it all – this body still warm but already vacant, other patients in nearby rooms, the flowers in the vase, and the oblivious world outside the window. Reality slowly returned and my feet again felt rooted to the floor, my hand heavy as it rested on the chair where I sat. I looked at his body, and the immediate absence of him seemed so sudden, so complete. What was it that gave Henry his soul, his life? Surely it was more than the simple act of breath? Perhaps the presence *was* God and it was his spirit I had felt so strongly. God's spirit, Henry's spirit, felt vaster than the world I knew.

*   *   *

I cycled home through London's streets. It was late but taxis swooped in to collect couples arm in arm and pubgoers mingled on the street. It was a warm night, with a lingering fragrance of summer. I rode my bike carefully, slower than usual, to savour every moment. The normality of life unchanged was poignant – rumbling buses, beeping horns, and a siren wailing in the distance. The night was clear and the full moon's brilliance fell all around.

My cosy houseboat on the Thames had never felt so welcoming. I lifted my bike over the steps to the floating mooring. The full high tide surged and as I paused a moment to find my balance I was struck by the illusion that we believe life to be stable, yet it is just like this: moving planks on a swollen river.

The other boats were in darkness. No cheery 'hello!' or offers of a tea from this little community of river dwellers. My boat was moored at the end of the floating jetty, furthest out into the river. I stepped across the gangway to the bow. Pots of geraniums and petunias trailed from the roof in the moonlight. Once inside the tiny living space I closed the door and put the kettle on the stove. I collapsed on the lounge, my thoughts utterly consumed by Henry and the wonder of his death. Melissa and I had bathed his body together and then zipped it tight in a body bag as the law required. Not much more than a bundle of bones stretched with skin. Melissa had been calm, her tears all spent. For many years she had known this moment would come but as she ran her finger along the zipper of the body bag, she said: 'Nothing, nothing can prepare you for this. Jack now has no father.' Her look of utter sadness brought my own tears. I made no effort to hide them. Now I wonder that perhaps I should have held them back and remained professional. But something had touched me in the moment of his death that gave me no choice.

The whistle of the furious kettle pulled me back to the present. I sat out on the bow with a mug of camomile tea. My boat bobbed with the swell as the last party boat passed by. The moon spilt molten white through the black water.

The brief meeting with peace I'd felt at Henry's death was now distant and dilute but the flavour was still with me – a sharpening of the senses, a clarity and spaciousness in my mind. Later I would realise that in the moment of Henry's death I had seen the landscape of God – the oneness where life and death play hand in hand.

*   *   *

God had been in my orbit ever since I spun to life in my mother's womb. I was born in Sussex to missionaries recently returned from the

Philippines. Ours was a home of prayers at bedtime, church twice on Sundays and prayer meetings throughout the week. Family holidays to a seaside town in Wales where the church beach mission gathered on the sands. A born-again Christian household caught me in a web of rules. I prayed to God as if my life depended on his mercy. God was to be feared, Jesus the only way for redemption. Promises of heaven, threats of hell – we were sinners all unless we repented. But when my mother brushed my hair, hard so it hurt, I knew, with a certainty, that she had it wrong about God. I always knew. Then as I witnessed Henry – his graceful acceptance, his serenity in such suffering, his own belief far from that of Christianity – I knew again with a final certainty that the God of my childhood was not for me.

Stars breathed barely visible light and the moon hid behind patchy cloud. I threw the last of my tea into the river and retreated from the night. Sleep seemed far away. A subtle thrum of energy coursed through my veins. I had felt something extraordinary take seed in me and I wanted to know what it was.

I thought of the pilgrims I had seen when backpacking in India. I had stood on the banks of the river Ganges and watched them bathing as the sun rose pale and promising over their holy river. The image had stayed with me. As I climbed into bed I remembered the sound of temple bells and the mysterious holy men in their orange robes, gazing far away from the chaos of life all around them.

Six months later I handed in my notice at work, sold my boat, and in mid-January I boarded an Air India flight with a one-way ticket to Bombay.

CHAPTER TWO

In the beginning

'We shall not cease from exploration, and the end of all our exploring will be to arrive where we started and know the place for the first time.' T.S. Eliot

'Mandi! Mandi! Mandi!' The driver shouts his destination for all to hear. The day is new, the air sharp. The still-orange sun illuminates the peaks saluting the skies. The engine revs in spurts of noise and fumes as I pull my rucksack through the doorway and settle as best I can on a hard metal seat. The bus lurches off down the narrow, steep road that winds away from this small town clinging precariously to the foothills of the Himalayas.

McLeod Ganj is the embodiment of peace, Shangrila itself. Monks and nuns float through town in their long robes of maroon and gold, their faces serene and shining. A tumble of monasteries perch on the ridgelines, and temple domes of gold glint in the sunlight. His Holiness the Dalai Lama lives here and this town seems wrapped in an aura of serene beatitude.

From the bus window, as we leave McLeod Ganj, I see faded prayer flags flutter prayers as old as these hills. *Om Mani Padme Hum, Om*

Mani Padme Hum. The mantra of the Tibetans is in the very ether here; this place is an oasis of calm that calls to seekers searching for what this land garishly promises: gods, Buddha, gurus and that illusive word that rolls from every seeker's tongue – enlightenment. It is all here.

I am leaving behind my first home in India, Rishi Bhawan, an old colonial-style house set in a clearing amidst the forest above McLeod Ganj. Rishi Bhawan had been as tumbled down and neglected as my own mind revealed itself to be. Its door that wouldn't open and the leaking slate roof that dripped in steady trickles when it rained. Around the house were pine forests that leaked a damp earthy fragrance.

I am also leaving Vishwam Gupta, a small man with wide, full lips, who has been my first teacher on this quest for understanding. I had felt so confident packing up my boat in London and saying goodbye to the life I knew, responding to a call impossible to ignore. But sitting every day in a cold damp hall, meditating for hours at a time, threw all that certainty in the air.

The bus lurches downwards, winding around impossibly sharp bends, and the distant snow peak of Triund disappears from view. The jagged rock face, folded in wraps of snow, has been my muse. First light each day offered me a silhouette of its almost perfect triangular peak, the godhead itself, while the furious burst of sunset coloured it crimson against a golden sky. I'd walked up to the ridge below Triund a few days after arriving in McLeod Ganj. The massive rock peak rose before me as clouds swooped in and left a vaporous grey swirling all around. Winter held the landscape in patchy snow, trees etched as ghostly figures in the freezing mists, a lone crow cawing to the silence. The immense silence that surrounded me is what I hope I will find higher still in these mountains.

I'm moving on, to the wilder, emptier valleys. With the recent, warming sun, the spiritual tourists have arrived, earnest seekers of the enlightenment the Buddha proclaimed. From Mandi, another bus will take me higher still, to the Parvati valley, far removed from cafes, bakeries and meditation retreats.

*   *   *

The bus eventually lurches into Mandi's bustling station. I guess the driver is shouting 'everyone off' as the mass of passengers squeeze, with their belongings, out of the door. I do the same, the only westerner in sight. Pilgrims, carrying small bundles of possessions, watch from the sidelines as vendors loudly sell their wares. Sweet corn wallahs hover over embers glowing in a rusty tin, blackened corn lined up for sale. Food stalls are stocked with vats of bus-stand fare, pungent soupy dishes and limp chapattis. Trays of sticky sweets lie behind smeared glass, dotted with trapped flies drunk on sugar. I meet the hollow stare of beggars with their grubby, fingerless hands outstretched: 'Memsahib, memsahib, memsahib' their own particular mantra. As a western woman alone, I am the obvious target. Groups of men scratch in unison as their eyes fix on me. It's hard not to stare back in disbelief – yes, men really do fiddle as they rearrange their genitalia without a flinch. India transgresses many boundaries. This I learned within moments of arriving on the first trip here several years earlier, when the taxi driver of the old Ambassador car, with its torn red leather seats, had kept his goggle eyes more on my friend and me in the back seat than on the road. The mass of men in this male-dominated society requires management tactics. I choose to simply block them out. Often I fail. The onslaught of beggars and people staring, piles of garbage everywhere, shit lining the railway lines, cows mingling in the markets, a scab-ridden skeleton of a dog dragging itself along on two legs, the ogling men – all of it is part of the package.

I am on another metal bus seat, as outside the mountains rise again and snow glistens like icing sugar. Winding up and up, rivers tumbling everywhere. Clouds buffer and swoon in swirls of white against the bluest blue. The visuals are more than I dreamed of as I worked the last shifts, packed up my life for this unknown. I only hope that I can hold on to this sense of adventure as my endless mental chatter gathers its own momentum. What if this isn't right? Maybe it would have been better to stay in McLeod. At least I knew people there. And had a great place to stay. Why be alone? The bus seat is unbearably hard. My lower back aches and if we jolt one more time I may even scream.

Vishwam introduced me to a text written by a Zen Master, the third Zen Patriarch. It begins with the lines: 'The great way is not difficult for those not attached to preferences.' It goes on to say: 'Do not seek for the truth, only cease to cherish opinions.' I think of this now – beauty all around me yet my mind still holding me in its grasp. Self-dissection is as painful to the soul as a knife peeling skin. And just as cruel. The truth is I am having a hard time accepting that I fell to pieces during Vishwam's course. My first ever meditation and yoga course – the very reason to sell my precious boat, quit my life – and I failed. From the moment I sat on the purple round cushion thoughts refused to be subdued. The forty-minute sits became torture. Determined not to move, I clenched my teeth tighter until the aching knees and hips demanded I stretch out my legs. *Failed again!* would come the gleeful voice. I was saved by song as Vishwam taught us chants and there I found some solace. The chanting reminds me of Henry, and the very purpose of this journey: to find out what this life is all about.

On day seven Vishwam led us on a guided inner journey to various stages of our childhood. It was easy to imagine myself as a teenager, coming home one night as a fourteen-year old, so drunk I vomited on the stairs up to my room. At thirteen screaming 'I hate you!' and slamming a door in my mother's face. As an eleven-year-old praying hard before the exam to decide which secondary school I would attend. *Dear God, I promise I will become a Christian if you let me pass this exam.* Begging God for fear of my parents' disappointment if I failed. I did pass of course and kept my part of the bargain too. Twelve years old, at a Christian Union weekend in a draughty manor house in the English countryside, I gave my heart to Jesus. Accepted him as my saviour. Invited God's only begotten son to take my sins away so that I may be saved from the fiery pit of hell. I feel still the bewildering anti-climax as I stood outside in the windy, cool night, scanning the heavens for the fanfare of angels I hoped would accompany such moments. Surely at least the heavenly host would reach down and brush my cheek with a golden wing. Not even a shimmering star.

In Vishwam's meditation I found happy memories of riding a horse along country lanes, the smells of summer all around, my father walking beside me. It was easy to remember myself as an eight-year-old or nine-year-old, riding my bike on the street. Every Saturday evening going 'next door' to elderly Jean and Mary where my sister and I would watch *Starsky and Hutch* on the TV and be served red jelly and sponge fingers with sweet cream in delicate china dishes. I loved those china dishes with floral patterns and glinting gold edges. It was the highlight of the week and a ritual that lasted until I was thirteen when we purchased a TV of our own. Later I wondered if Mary and Jean were indeed two elderly spinsters, or had they been lovers during their life together. I hoped they had.

The bus clambers onwards through the flocks of goats and sheep being herded up the valley now spring is here. The road is steep and narrow and clings to the mountainside, the valley falling steeply below. All along are feasts for the eyes. Old women sit in doorways knitting, toddlers playing at their feet. Men sit around smoking long pipes or playing cards in makeshift chai stalls. Women work in the fields. Massive bundles of hay are carried on heads or tied on backs bent almost double. Wooden swing bridges cross the valley and villages can be glimpsed high above. Yet I take in only half of what is around me.

By the time I reached four years old I could not remember one image of myself. Rather, a blankness and from within the blank erupted a flood of tears. I sat on my purple cushion, unable to hold them back, crying almost uncontrollably. Fortunately the attention went to Claire, another English woman who was so distraught she had left the gompa. Vishwam had not been pleased. 'How can I monitor you all if you leave?' he had declared, and then left on a search, returning some time later with Claire in tow. By then I had pulled myself together, but not completely, it strikes me now, as the same sickening tinge of nausea that I felt just before I broke down has returned to my stomach. The same hint of panic as I set out for another unknown destination. It is as if I have suddenly discovered I have six toes or two noses and have no idea how I never noticed. Now, instead of rejoicing in the magnificence all around I paddle in a muddy pool of emotions, trying to understand why and where the murkiness has come from. *I'm searching for God*, I remind myself. *Yes, climbing higher.* And I am struck by the fact that I still presume God to be seated in heaven, to where these mountains unanimously reach.

*   *   *

As day falls away we reach the end of the road: Manikaran, just visible in the gossamer light. With our arrival I gather myself together. Where is the excitement of new discoveries I've so often felt when travelling? Instead my stomach is tight and my back aches and I will need to find somewhere to stay. Then I can have a hot bath.

A wooden swing bridge is the gateway to the town. The river surges below: the waters of the Parvati. This is her valley, the Goddess Parvati, consort to Shiva himself. The town is cloaked in shadow. A last smudge of sunset sits like a golden crown as I cross the bridge, my pack heavy on my back. The steep valley falls to steaming pools and the icy green river. Ghostly fingers of vapour swirl for a moment, before being whisked away by the rushing winds. I wrap my woollen shawl tight around my shoulders. Temple bells ring out in the chilly air. The bridge is busy with pilgrims and passengers from the bus and the town opens its arms in a fanfare of welcome.

'Didi hello! You need room?'

I look up to see a woman with about ten earrings hooped through each ear, calling from the balcony of a wooden house: 'You need room?' she calls again.

It's simple. A woman is leaning over a railing calling down to me in this land dominated by men. Parvati is a goddess who blesses her people well and as I reach the steps to the doorway the woman is standing there with a smile. 'Come, come.'

Mataji, as older Indian women are called, has a face full of wrinkles. She shows me to a narrow room on the second floor, more like a corridor, with a bed and a pile of thick blankets.

'Khana, khana? Chapatti!'

I smile. 'First washing!' I make the movements but she understands.
'Go, then come here eat!'

'Hot bath where?' I ask in the broken English so easy to adopt.

'This way straight going.' She points with her chin towards the main street.

After bumping all day down winding roads and back up again on a hard rickety bus seat, a soak in hot water is what I crave. A bath! My first in the thirteen weeks I have been travelling. Manikaran is famous for its hot springs. Steam seeps and spills through cracks and gullies. Caught in the light of gas lamps it twirls like a genie finally freed. The smell of sulphur mingles with incense and the stench of open gutters. Even up here in the crisp mountains I find the characteristic smells of India: wood fires, incense, frying spices, kerosene stoves, interspersed with rotting garbage, a pile of cow shit. I follow the street down to where it widens by the river. Steam rises above the dark water and a group of wild-looking holy men, or sadhus, smoke chillums on the steps, their outline murky in the shadows. The sweet aroma of charas wafts with the cold air.

It's dim inside the bathing pools and I wait to let my eyes adjust. Stone, windowless chambers house the women's bath. The dark granite roof is low and it is like a large cave. There is a separate one for the men. The natural hot water springs feed the pool with sulphurous almost boiling water and the pool steams like a witch's cauldron. I find a spot to undress and wrap myself in my lungi. The water is hot and soft like silk. A Sikh woman sits on the side and combs out her long black hair, then soaps herself and rinses with a small container. I'm dizzy from the heat but I stay a moment longer in this sanctuary of women and water. As I soak my weary bones the tightness in my stomach relaxes as I slowly exhale. There is a welcome sense of safety in this enclosed covered space, with no eyes to follow me, no passing comments of *hello yes madam you come here*. And it is a forgotten luxury to soak after weeks of washing with a bucket in the warmth of the midday.

*   *   *

I am Mataji's only guest. I sit on the floor in her bare kitchen as she throws wood on the fire. It is made from earth or clay and has open holes on the top; a fire-blackened pot sits to one side. The flames sneak and snake until the wood is taken. Her chapattis are thick and warm. I scoop up the dhal, hungry from the day. 'How many night stay?' Mataji hovers.

'Only tonight. Tomorrow going up.'

Her face drops and jowls gather around her mouth. 'No, no tomorrow here stay. Rest is good. Later going up.'

I consider for a moment. I like being served food by this motherly woman. Yet I have a momentum in my body that does not want to rest, propelled by some force to an unknown place in the mountains.

Next morning I wake early. There are no curtains across the window and in the pale light the river rushes green. The air is freezing.

'You want charas?' Mataji asks, handing me a tin cup of sweet chai. 'Only hundred rupee tola.' Charas is the legendary Himalayan hash that I've smoked before. It is soft and creamy and smells divine.

'No, thank you.'

'This best, very good charas!' Her smile reveals stained uneven teeth. It's the holy herb of these mountains and a great income for the locals. 'Melana cream' hash comes from this valley and is considered the best in the world.

'Okay, I take a little.' I relent. She breaks it in half and presses it into my hand.

'You stay when coming down.' She flashes me a smile with her broken, blackened teeth.

*   *   *

I follow the river towards the snowfields beyond. Newly planted wheatfields lie in neat brown squares dotted with green. Orchards are full with blossoms of delicate pinks. Purple irises line the pathway and bright turquoise butterflies kiss and flirt. The path crosses a wooden swing bridge, the river a frenzy below. The snowfields are melting high above and the water looks as cold as cold can be. My bag is heavy on my back even though I pride myself in carrying only the bare essentials. When I packed up my life and sold my boat, the belongings I kept fitted into three boxes: favourite clothes, books I could not part with and the antique china plates and bowls I had begun to collect from markets. The rest I gave away. I wonder what I am carrying now that I don't really need. I have my sleeping bag, of course, clothes, a couple of books, my diary – nothing that should feel this heavy. I guess it's my hammock – a double-size Mexican hammock – but I'm not going to give that away. When I stop for the night I will see what I can discard. I climb upwards into this vast wilderness of majestic rocks, over trickling streams where the path is thick with mud and dragonflies with emerald wings dip to the water. Light as air they sail away.

After four or five hours' walking I am offered glimpses of the snow peaks above. After a stretch through a forest fragrant with pine needles, the path opens to a plateau with crops, apple orchards and women working. Men sit on their haunches smoking from a hookah pipe. The smoke hangs above the group, slowly dispersing, and the smell of raw earthy tobacco reaches my nostrils. I have arrived at Pulga – the wildest, highest and most remote place on earth I've ever been. All around me the mountain peaks, like nature's cathedrals, reach for heaven.

The village is a string of wooden houses with thick stone bases, stark against a now grey sky. Kids shout, 'One rupee! One rupee!' The boldest tugs on my sleeve with grubby fingers, so I stop for a moment and smile. I wish I could speak some Hindi, although the dialect here is its own. As a woman alone I am already an oddity, but somehow high up here, in this world overlooked by the abode of the gods, it doesn't matter.

A group of westerners, all dreadlocks and chillums, sit in one of the chai shops. A rough-looking sadhu calls over to me, 'Yes, hello, come sit!' His invitation only inspires me to keep walking. Signs pronounce 'best chai', 'rice plat' in scribbled handwriting. As the houses thin out at the last stone compound a boy leans against the wall.

'Room! You want room?' He seems excited.

'Yes, room.' I take the heavy pack from my back. The sudden lightness in my body causes me to stumble. He pauses a moment then calls out: 'Bapu! Bapu!' An older boy emerges from the courtyard.

'You need room?' says the older boy; his hair is thick and falls over his face like a teen pop star.

'How much?'

'Twenty rupees one night, thirty rupees night time house eating.'

Sounds good to me.

My room looks over the courtyard. Chickens peck in the mud and two cows with soft brown eyes gaze up at me. Their presence is reassuring.

The main house is mud brick, with a slate roof that hangs like an oversized hat. The interior is dim and consists of one large room. I sit on the beaten earth floor as an old woman cooks by the fire. A big black pot bubbles and steams. She crouches on her haunches and kneads flour for the flat breads, or rotis, then slaps them, one by one, on the chapatti plate. She nods to me and briefly smiles; she is missing several teeth. Another woman, with bells jangling around her ankles, herds a group of small children in through the low doorway. The girls have untidy pigtails tied with knots at the end and they all wear trousers and wool jackets. Their feet are bare and dirty and I notice my bare feet are dirty too.

I eat dhal and a couple of rotis, warm and singed, thankful for the lack of chillies. A white-haired, wizened old man comes to sit by the fire and warm his hands. His gold earrings glint in the firelight. From the pocket of his torn woollen jacket he pulls out tobacco in a cloth, carefully filling a hookah with a long nozzle. He lights it with a stick from the fire and blows smoke to the growing dimness.

Apparently forgotten, I seep into my surrounds: this kitchen, the heart of their home. There is no furniture, no sink, no bathroom. I guess this will be the sleeping room too when the daily chores are complete.

Another man arrives with a baby goat. He wraps it in a shawl and leaves it by the fire. The littlest girl goes to it and it licks her hand. After a while I take my leave. The woman at the fire nods to my, 'Dhanyabad, namaste,' and the kids stare with wide eyes. It will take months, years even, for me to realise that unlike the English with their constant infusive 'thank yous', the Indian culture has no place for it – unless someone has saved your life perhaps. The simple namaste, which means 'I welcome and acknowledge the God in you', is enough.

I snuggle in my sleeping bag under the pile of coarse blankets and wonder whether I could invite a stranger into my home without any need to impress. These people have nothing, yet they have a dignity I seem to lack. I saw a poised self-assurance as the women served the meal, the kids ate and left nothing on the plate, and the men took their place. Activities, orchestrated movement that runs as smooth as still water – a sharp contrast to my own turbulence.

Later I wake, the silent black night broken by the muffled moo of the cows. It reminds me of the horns that the monks in the monastery in McLeod Ganj would blow – long, low and commanding. And in the darkness I remember the shame, the embarrassment of sobbing out loud in the meditation course, and how disturbed I was by my upset. The bewildering sadness I felt. Sleep is not eager to return. I fumble for my torch and by the thin light I crumble a little of the charas from Mataji and mix it with tobacoo and roll up a smoke. I open the window of my room and lean out into the freezing night, inhaling deeply the welcome drug.

*　　*　　*

I awake to a dawn of ethereal glory. Pinks flutter across the heavens like angel wings and the mountain crests are tinged with gold. It's as if this valley is suggesting I stay a while, to relax and watch. I ask Bapu if there is anywhere I can stay and make a home.

'One small house field upside. Kalga.' He nods and shakes his head, sending the shock of thick black hair up in the direction of the mountain. He fixes his almost green eyes on me.

'Can I look?'

I follow him out of the village. We cross over two rushing streams and climb steeply up a zigzag path to Kalga. He walks fast and I am out of breath when we reach the top. Kalga is no more than a few houses strewn over a plateau with irregular fields still brown and barren. Parvati shines like a thread of silver far below.

The hut he takes me to stands on the edge of the plateau with views that spill down the valley. It is built of wood and stone, one room on top of an empty stable, with a lingering animal smell. A wide deck, covered by the grey slate roof, wraps around three sides. The doorway is narrow and short and I push the heavy wooden door, ducking to avoid the thick beam. My eyes adjust to the dark and see a square fireplace, a shelf and a cupboard. A pile of firewood and a straw mat lie on the floor and dust spirals in the slanting light. The air is musty.

Outside my eyes blink in the light. I sit and watch as Bapu talks with a group of locals in the fields. I guess they are planting seeds. I light a beedi and know that I am at home. If ever a hut was built for me, it is this one. Bapu comes to stand beside me, smoothing his hair as he speaks. 'You stay, no problem. Three hundred rupees a month.'

'You have some pot for cooking?'

He calls over to the women in the fields and one calls back, her voice loud in the silence. 'Pot no problem,' he tells me.

We walk together down the mountain to Pulga. I buy basic provisions and the grandmother, when I give her rupees for the room and dinner, hands me still-warm rotis wrapped in newspaper. Bapu watches as I carefully tuck them in my very full backpack.

'I carry bag?'

'No, no problem I can do.' Unconcerned, he watches me go.

My bag is more than heavy with the extra kilos of rice, dhal, flour, sugar and chai powder. I keep going, eager to make my home. When I get there, it looks even more perfect now I know it is mine. I throw my rucksack down and swing my legs over the deck. The women in the field watch me and I smile, even though they are too far away to notice.

CHAPTER THREE

A *hut in the hills*

*'The heavens declare God's grandeur and the radiance
from which they arise. Each dawn tells of His beauty;
each night shines with His grace. God's universe is
perfect, awing the mind to stillness.' Psalm 19*

The plateau is a world of its own. To the north three triangular peaks rise in unison, white against a brilliant blue. To the east, a vertical rock mountain, a naked peachy grey. Behind the hut the fields slope up towards the forest. Massive deodar trees, Himalayan pines, line the ridge. Their resin seeps from the bark and spreads a rich heavenly fragrance over the plateau.

My bed is my hammock, strung between the rafters of the balcony. With all this glory I couldn't bear to be shut inside. The first morning I wake before dawn, warm in my sleeping bag. A reddish star hangs low above the mountain peak to the east, as the first sounds drift up the valley. Light emerges liquid and transparent until shapes take on solidity and the day is born. Streaks of cloud in the eastern sky give form to the first idea of sun. Tinged with pink, the pristine white snow peaks provide a perfect canvas for God's palette to play.

The vast surrounds overwhelm me. I feel the utter insignificance of my presence, as I lie cocooned in my hammock strung from the rafters of a small wooden hut that is perched on the edge of a wide plateau several hours' walk from the nearest road. A world far removed from home. Indeed, I have no home. I have sold my boat and I never lived in my parents' present home as they moved from the house I grew up in soon after I left at eighteen, the key to the world firmly in my grasp. I began my new life as a student nurse at The London Hospital, and lived in a room in a nurses' home. It was my first taste of Indian culture, as Whitechapel is a community of Bengali, Pakistani and Indian immigrants. Nearby Brick Lane is home to the best curries, and street markets which jostle with life.

From the nurses' home I joined a group of four others to rent a house, a typical run-down student house with an overgrown yard backing onto a cemetery. All those unsaved souls hanging around. I spraypainted the walls of my room different shades of blue and smoked my first ever joint with Nigel in the downstairs room as orange streetlight stole in through grubby net curtains.

From there I migrated around various council flats considered hard to let. I lived in run-down estates where drug deals took place in the stairwells. I moved from one after waking to loud knocking one afternoon after night shift. I opened the door to see a man who lived down the corridor. He smelt strongly of alcohol and I had slammed the door. He returned with an axe and proceeded to smash-smash until the door splintered and gave way. Fortunately I had already dialled 999 and even though he knocked the phone from my hands, I knew the police were on their way. He held me up against the wall with the axe pressed firmly to my chest and breathed heavily in my face.

The next day my mother happened to be in London and came to visit. Of course I told her about the incident.

'Poor man, he must be so unhappy. Perhaps I should go and visit with him,' had been her response.

'Don't,' I had pleaded.

'Well, I will pray for him anyway.' Her expression was that of slight burden as another suffering soul was added to the list. 'Do you know his name?'

I moved shortly after, this time to a flat that became home for several years: Pott Street, Bethnal Green, with the railway line that ran metres from my room. Every morning I would wake with the first train rumbling and rushing into Liverpool Street.

'All this thinking about homes will not make a fire!' I speak out loud. The sound of my voice surprises me; it's been a couple of days since I spoke to anyone. I swing myself from the hammock and stretch. The air is cold at this pre-sun hour as I collect a handful of kindling from under the house, scrunch up dry leaves and carefully place a couple of small logs. Although the main feature inside this hut is a large fireplace in the middle of the floor, I have made a fireplace outside the hut, just to the side, so I can be with the elements; the surounds are so magnificent I do not want to miss a moment. I am deft with fire but still I take care. When the fire lights with no drama, no rearranging and re-lighting, I can believe that all will be well with the day. I strike a waxy Indian match and it takes three or four matches to find one that produces a flame. The leaves smoulder, slow to take, so I squat low and take a deep breath, then blow the glow to a flame.

The memory of the man with the axe stays with me. I consider my mother's response. It's how it was to have a missionary mother – there were always plenty of others more needy than me. My own response, or lack of it, seems bizarre too. I don't remember feeling anything. I went to work that night, and certainly didn't press charges although the police assured me I could. I had a bruise on my chest that took days to fade. I guess I solved the problem by moving. Looking back now I sense a tightening again in my stomach, a taste of something being amiss. But what? Was it the blank denial that such an event happened? Surely I would have been upset. Scared. The man had lived along the corridor and was often milling about as I returned from work. Surely I would have been scared he would return? I buried it all like an old bone and only now am I digging it up. I stare at the fire, now a hopeful flame. I place the pot carefully on the stones and take a deep breath. A pair of birds, with bright red crests like a monk's head-dress, sing in the trees just beside my house. I banish all thoughts of drunken men with axes; fling them down the valley to merge with other forgotten memories.

Still wrapped in my blanket, I stamp my feet and swing my arms in the chill. Even though rays of the sun stretch over the fire and I can sense the warmth on my cheeks, the air is cold. I wait for the water to boil, a piece of ginger releasing its spice. I take in the day, plastered against a design only the gods can create. If you have never been to these high Himalayas it is hard to describe how compelling the sheer magnitude of this landscape is.

The last words of Christ as he hung on the cross were: 'Verily I say unto you I will be with you in paradise.' Surely this is paradise, but where is he? In the Bible, paradise is beyond the pearly gates, the mythical land where the souls of the saved gather for eternity. And the sinners … well, they burn in hell. This literal interpretation of the Bible and blind belief in heaven and hell was one of the main reasons I turned away from the church in my teens. I began to suspect that the evangelicals had crucified Jesus all over again. As I sit by the fire now, I find a comfort in his words – 'I will be with you in paradise' – and I imagine the Jesus who represents love and healing, with Mary, his wife, by his side.

My father liked to talk about these last words, spoken to the thief that hung by Jesus' side. 'See, this is the glory of Jesus, he spoke these words to everyone. Each and every sinner, no matter what the sin, can seek redemption. Can pray and ask forgiveness and be redeemed in paradise. Remember, Jesus died for our sins.' He would then squint off into the distance as if trying to see God for himself. My father was not a man of many words when it came to his faith. He was a quiet and traditional, yet deeply devout, Christian, the Book of Common Prayer his handbook. He listened to choral music and I too loved the way the voices swooned with a mystical union of sound. My father led a life of order and routine, with his Christian beliefs the pillar of his purpose. My mother, when I was ten, became fully lost to the evangelicals – all fiery hell and damnation. Evangelicals are anything but quiet. The wrath of God was shouted about in no uncertain terms and often our home would be filled with prayer meetings and missionaries returned on furlough, and God, and his rules and commands, was all that mattered.

*   *   *

Water here does not come out of a tap. Across the field is a spring channelled over a smooth curve of timber. Every morning I set out across the empty brown fields to follow the neat grass-lined path to the spring. I fill my 10-litre plastic container and struggle back with my supply for the day. I drink this water and it tastes as pure as the surrounds. Later in the day I return to fill the container again, this time for a wash. Sometimes I heat the water, other days I wash quickly, with a tin and a small bar of soap. A quick wash concealed behind my lungi, almost squealing with the shock of cold, quickly drying and dressing, a skill that takes practice.

The days fall into a natural rhythm of necessity. I collect wood, snapping up the kindling so it is there ready in a heap. In the warm midday sun I sit on the deck and clean the rice and dhal. It always amazes me what I find: small dead insects, stones and dirt, splinters of wood. Then I rinse it, being sparing with the water, and let the dust float to the top. I find little metaphors everywhere. Dust rising, to be tipped away, settling in myself, surprised at the ease with which I adjust to this way of living. Buying a boat, three years ago now, was my way then to step out, to return to a thread of nature even amidst the city. Living alone in my floating home, and when the tide was out my boat sat slightly tilted, on the bank of mud, awaiting the water's return.

When my mind is restless a fog descends. It has the same texture as the foggy blankness that I fell into during the guided meditation experience with Vishwam. If I question, or show any interest in this feeling, it leads to thoughts that are quick to bite, to snarl at my edges. During the guided meditation we were asked to imagine ourselves at five years old, and then at four. I could only remember a time when we stayed with my grandparents in Goring, a village also on the Thames. My father had slept in my bed; maybe he had arrived later than my mother and sister and me and so that was why he climbed into my bed. I remember I wore red pyjamas and I didn't like the feel of his hairs on my skin. I had felt repulsion and now feel badly about this. How terrible to feel repulsed by my own father. What kind of a child was I? I remember that the next day I had cried and cried because I was so sure my mother had bought me the white teddy bear I had seen at the fair. I searched in the cupboards but it was nowhere to be found. This memory floats around me, resurfacing again as I sit on the verandah and pick through the rice. I find it puzzling. But not as puzzling as why I would have felt so much distress trying to remember being little. I can remember plenty of happiness – pony riding, feeding lambs, and the sting of the salt air as I ran across the wide green grass of the Seven Sisters. I remember the chalk cliffs, pebbled beaches and surging dull waters of the sea.

I can almost see the God of the Christians peering down from his throne, pointing his finger at me. 'You down there, just what do you think you are doing?' Rather than succumb to a sense of failure, I walk. Sometimes I walk all day, arriving home for the late afternoon show on the peaks across the valley. I've long discarded shoes, leaving my chappal, the Indian equivalent of thongs, or flip-flops, to gather spiderwebs by the doorway. My feet respond to the touch of the earth by quickly toughening up. This elemental connection is another layer of freedom this valley allows.

*   *   *

I live mostly outside, retreating inside only when the winds blow firm and chilly up from the valley and the pine forest behind whispers and roars, or rain falls in torrents, driving in across the field. The room, with the heavy wooden door shut against the howling winds, is quick to fill with smoky warmth from the fire that I make in the fireplace in the centre of the room. I keep the flame bright. I knead dough of flour and water – warm water is best I discover – and cook flat breads on the chapatti plate. The rain drums relentless rhythms on the slate roof, and thunder shakes the thick stone walls. Lightning illuminates a ghostly white until it falls to black once again.

I wake the next morning from my bed of blankets on the floor to another day of clarity. Blue skies, and raindrops glint and wink and sparkle in the pine trees. As always I sit. Meditation is an art and practise is a key. I cross my legs, fold them as neatly as I can and lay my hands on my lap. I close my eyes and begin the process. I count slowly with the in breath 1-2-3-4-5. Then holding my breath I count for another 5. I let the breath release with a count to 8. The rhythm of in breath and out keeps distracting thoughts at bay, for a while at least. So many opinions! Little discussions with myself – as if suddenly my mind is a stage, full of actors. The lead part is a commentator, critical and sometimes damning. *Can't even sit still for five minutes! Not liking being alone so much huh? You should enrol full time in courses, rather than hiding away up here.* That one breaks the spell. I cannot deny, even to myself the awe and wonder of this landscape.

After morning tea I sit again. Certainly not for an hour like we had to in the course. Sitting for an hour is punishing. I can manage about twenty minutes. To sit in peace with a thin smile upon my lips is proving elusive. I cannot tolerate pain in my body. It distresses me. It is only fifteen months since I had surgery on my back. A disk in my lower spine crumbled to the point of raging sciatica and considerable weakness in my left leg. I tried various alternatives to going under the knife, but finally succumbed to the reality when limping across the Bethnal Green road my leg gave way altogether. I had stumbled and almost fell as the traffic carried on regardless. The immediate result, after ten days in hospital, liberated me. So now, when my back aches I stretch, smell the air and figure out what to do next.

The moon is on her way to fullness. Mandulika is Sanskrit for dusk – 'not day not night' – and this landscape wears it well. Mountains fade to the brush of silver as she claims her hold. I watch the moon grow, trace her path through the night as I wake and stir, the crisp cold expanse bathed in her light. On the night of her completion I walk up to the edge of the forest in the milky light and sit, resting against the silver birch tree. The landscape is illuminated, the moon white and swollen, and only the brightest stars can accompany. Nature spirits work their magic and the grasses sway. In the moonlight my way of meditation is this: in tune with nature. I feel a subtle thread of connection, from the trunk of the silver birch against my back, to the forest and the mountain peaks. With it comes a softening, a quietening inside myself. It is clean and clear, unadorned with dogma.

Now when I sit to practise meditating I bring this feeling in my mind. Instead of counting with my breath I feel the solid earth support me, the caress of air against my cheek. I listen to the birds, the whisper of wind, the occasional voice and jangle of bells as goats are moved up the valley on the path below.

*   *   *

I no longer shop at Pulga but prefer the village of Beshami, on the other side of the valley. It's off the beaten track, with no chai shops or stoned westerners and no Punjabi families on their way up the valley to Khir Ganga, stopping to say, 'Yes, hello. From which country, madam?'

I can see my home as I walk back along the path on the opposite side of the valley. From this distance it is a tiny speck lost in the vast surrounds. I stand on the wooden bridge watching the Parvati rush below. The air is sharp and spray from the river tingles my face, cold and damp. Small birds flit and mossy plants hang in the rock face.

In the market in McLeod Ganj I'd noticed a dark leaf, rather like spinach, for sale in bundles. It grows up here, I discover on one of my walks, so I pick a handful for my dhal later in the day. I also recognise a fern, still young and tightly budded, as something I have seen in the shop at Beshami. The women are planting in the fields close by my hut. They stare at me and gesture with their chins. Seizing the moment to connect, I take the ferns to show them.

'Khana?' I ask as I reach them. They stand and one rubs her back. Another laughs and smiles. 'Khana khana huh! Huh!'

The woman who speaks is called Shakti, I discover as I point to myself. 'Judith, Judith,' I say, then: 'Ab ki nam khya hai?' [What is your name?]

She giggles and pulls her scarf firmly over her head before gathering up the courage to tell me her name. The others stare and talk among themselves as if I am perhaps some unfortunate rarity in a circus. Their cheeks are rosy red and they all are barefoot with ankle chains that jangle as they walk. And they all wear brown blankets pinned over the shoulder, with a patterned border of diamond shapes and reds and blues woven in. This is the local dress and the clack-clack of weaving machines adds to the sounds of the village when I go for supplies. I stare also, with only a few words of language to bridge the gap, as they give curious looks and half giggles. Their untidy hair is pulled back, revealing bright gaudy earrings, several in each ear. Shakti wears nose studs in each nostril the size of a gold coin.

Shakti has a small baby on her back. She unwraps the bundle and passes her over with a few clicking sounds to quieten the little face that has begun to mew like a kitten. A tiny scrap of life, I realise as she unwraps it. I take the baby, who is as light as a feather, and hold her as if she may break. I guess she is a girl.

'Laraki?' I ask.

'Laraki,' she states without a smile.

I snuggle her a little closer, rock her gently as her cries quieten. A sudden bolt of sadness catches my chest as I look at this tiny face before me. I wonder if she is sick. It's frustrating to not be able to talk with these women. To ask how many kids they have, do they like their husbands? Have they always lived here in the shadow of these mountains and what is it like to have daughters when boys are preferred?

I sit on the earth between the planting and the baby lies on my lap staring blankly out to space. The women pick at their teeth with thin sticks. Rotis are pulled from folds of fabric, broken and shared.

'Husband? Husband?' Shakti asks with a gesture I am now used to. Her head nod could be a question or an answer.

No husband, I say.

Shakti translates for the others. Or at least it seems that way. She has many more words than 'no husband'. I sit in the middle of a field with women who I know are speaking of me, yet I have no clue what they are saying. All eyes are on me with a mix of curiosity, disdain and pity. I silently chew the piece of chapatti handed my way. It is pointless to offer more. How can I explain I am travelling alone – with no husband, nor any want of one? For a brief moment I want to be understood. But really how can I expect this group of local women to understand anything of me?

I hand the baby back to Shakti and she rewraps the shawl and swings the tiny girl up onto her back once more. The little head is lost in the blankets. The women spread out again, resume their work, and the dull thud thud thud sounds out over the empty brown fields as the earth is broken up before the seeds are planted. I return to my fire and cooking. I add the ferns but they cook for too long and turn to slime.

*   *   *

Another cycle of the moon graces the heavens. The new moon, known in India as a Shiva moon, hangs like a smile above the valley to the west. I watch her grow, night by empty night, alone in this world of silver white. The power of the moon, celebrated when witches and lore was all we knew, is obvious in the magic all around me.

Perhaps it is this magic, her swell of the feminine, that brings a longing for company. It comes like a sudden rush of cold air from the north. Vishwam, the meditation teacher in McLeod Ganj, told me of Sabine, a French woman he knows who lives here in this valley. 'You can be good friend to each other,' he had said.

Shakti now comes to the hut if she sees me sitting outside or on the deck. It is a curious friendship, based on a few sprinkled words and different nods of the head, but a connection, a sense of ease, is there. Perhaps we both silently ask the same questions, a life so different we can only guess. The blankness of not knowing, a page eagerly wishing for words. I do not feel it with any of the other women whose voices are harsh and stares more blatant.

Shakti points to the plateau across the river when I ask if she knows Sabine. 'Sabine!' Her enthusiasm is an omen. 'Same you, same you!' So close, I had no idea! Why didn't I find her before, when I first arrived even? Five weeks I have been up in this valley and I have been having a courtship with myself – no distraction, no agenda, just a simple slowing down.

Now as I knead dough, add raisins and gur – chunks of brown palm sugar – a little cinnamon and bake buns after dinner is cooked, I am eager for this meeting with another woman, a possible kindred soul. The fire burns late into the evening, for warmth and light; the flames, my evening entertainment, dance for me alone. And as I sit and watch the swaying sashaying tongues I wonder again what I am doing. What has brought me to this place where I am right now? A twenty-six-year-old English woman sitting by a fire, up in the Himalaya, in a valley named after the consort of a God named Shiva. Searching for God in a land proliferated with gods yet still I cannot find. Maybe God, and the peace and presence I had felt that night when Henry died, are not one and the same. And how is sitting here cooking buns on a fire, tucked away from the world, aiding my search? I have no answer. It suddenly feels as if all I have done is run away from a perfectly good life.

*   *   *

After a steep climb through trees I find myself in front of her house. It's bigger than mine, with two rooms and a wide deck running around three sides. A woman sits on the deck and stands when she sees me, suspicious, without a smile. Catching my breath for a moment I am startled at the sight of a western woman and unsure now if this is what I want.

'Hi, I'm looking for Sabine.' It is too late to turn around.

'Yeah, who's asking?' Her accent is thick, and her tone does not suggest welcome.

'I'm Judith, a friend of Vishwam from Dharamsala. He sends greetings.' I hope it is enough. Her face softens.

'Better come up, here round the back.' She holds out her hand as I step up onto the deck. Her hand is rough and I can feel a callus. 'Don't get so many visitors up here. Here ... sit here.'

A baggy cardigan hangs to her knees over a pair of red leggings. Her hair is cropped short revealing her pale cheeks. Her eyes are large and brown and have little red lines in the whites, dark circles beneath adding to her appearance of tiredness. I wonder if she is maybe unwell.

I notice now her body too is thin and am glad I brought the buns. She looks hungry.

'Sit, sit here,' she tells me, moving a blanket folded like a pillow to the mat near the fire pit, but I sit on the edge of the deck and lean back against the wooden post. A small flame flickers in the fire pit that is set into the deck. Steam erupts from a pot. Herbs, I guess, the pungent aroma of goodness. I can see out across the side valley, to the roof of my own hut. Any hint of the Parvati is hidden behind the trees. All this time we were living so close! Sabine's home is secluded, held by an arm of shrubby trees that drip a canopy of branches to the emerald grass.

'I live across the valley in the hut just across there,' I say. 'I hear you stay a long time here. It is so beautiful. I love it.' So many words!

Sabine stares at me a moment then sits and folds her legs into each other as easily as Vishwam did. She leans over and takes the pot from the flame. 'I heard another western woman was there. Locals tell me. Most people just head up the valley. Take a bath in the hot springs – Khir Ganga. You been?'

'Yeah, a couple of times. Went the other day. Great to have a hot bath.'

Khir Ganga, the legend tells, is where Parvati appeared to Shiva when he was spending years in meditation here in her valley. He was hungry so she appeared to him and from her ample breast she fed him khir – milky sweet rice. Now hot water bubbles from the rocks and a couple of baths have been built. I walk up there on days I need to roam, leaving early for the whole day excursion. When I went a few days ago, the last stretch of the path was still covered in ice and my bare, leathery feet hardly noticed the cold. The springs are in a meadow of lush psychedelic greens with the valley sides reaching steeply up. Wild flowers and rich meadows, boulders and pine trees. Smoke rose from a hut where a group of local men wearing brown wool jackets and the topi hats, cooked rice and dhal, brewing chai for a couple of sadhus, a handful of hippies and a Punjabi family who had walked up from Manikaran. I gathered from listening to the westerners' conversation that they sometimes stay for days. I never invite connection when I am at the springs, I simply observe, happy to appear mysterious even, but usually they are all so stoned they don't notice. I soaked in the warm almost scalding water, gazing out at the rock face of the valley under a cloudless blue sky.

'You like a tea? I was just going to drink.'

'Sure. Here, I made some sweet bread.' I unwrap the buns relieved I added the raisins and the extra gur. She mixes a spoon of thick honey in the tea, a witch's brew of sticks and leaves. It tastes as pungent as it smells and reminds me of a brew I used to make when I was living on my boat.

'This mountain tea. Good for body,' she tells me, dipping the bread after breaking it into smaller pieces.

'You find these herbs here?'

'Sure, many plants grow here; these mountains full with herbs. This is dried mix from Manikaran but here places growing. Have to know where to look.' She has a way of looking straight into my eyes as if expecting an answer not from my lips.

It is the first conversation I've had in weeks where I haven't had to work to make myself understood, or had to limit myself to one or two words to keep it simple. Just as I relax and settle in my position, a baby cries from somewhere inside. Before I can exclaim my surprise, Sabine is up. A breath escapes with a rush, as if I have been held inside and can finally let myself out.

'Ah, Mila!' she coos and is back, trailing a shawl, with the baby on her breast.

'You have a baby!'

Tiredness etches more lines across her face. 'Yeah, this is Mila, my petite cookoo.' The baby has a shock of dark hair. As she searches for the nipple, she hears my voice and turns to find the sound. Her eyes stare for a moment then turn back to her mother's breast.

She suckles as Sabine arranges herself back beside me. Once her nipple is firmly in the baby's mouth she tells me she gave birth up here in this house in early November when snow had fallen early, with only her son, Luan, to help. Apparently Luan is eight years old. 'This other part that the baby is attached to, what its name?'

'Maybe the placenta?'

'Yeah, this thing, not coming out and Luan he puts his hand up inside, pulls it out. After, much bleeding. He goes down mountain to Manikaran and one French woman there. She come here and stay and help. I am very lucky. Much blood coming after birth.'

'Wow.' *Oh my God*, I want to say. *Is your son okay? Isn't it a bit inappropriate to have your kid stick his hand up you and pull out a placenta?*

Mila looks at me with wide baby eyes as she sucks from Sabine's breast that hangs like a small scrunched-up sack. It looks so intimate, a baby at the breast.

'Did you stay the winter up here?' I ask, not sure how to follow this conversation now.

'No, no. Too hard with baby and such weakness. Took long time to recover from birth. Still too much power lost. I need to be strong to live the winter here. Snow very deep for many weeks and keeping wood for the fire is much work. Winter time living in Manikaran.' She gazes down at Mila but it feels as if she is someplace far away. A pair of long-tailed magpies squawk and fuss in the walnut tree, then abruptly fly away. Her face seems to sag a little more and she fiddles with Mila's hair, then continues drinking her tea.

What did I imagine? An uncomplicated woman living alone yet eager for company? It's not what I have found, except perhaps the bit about being eager for company. It suits me. I can leave my own dilemmas far away and step into the role I know and love: caring.

Sabine sighs and passes me Mila, who arches her back and cries as she is handed over. Sabine makes no move to take her back so I stand and jiggle about and she quietens, grabbing a fistful of my hair and kicking her chubby legs. There is no sign of Luan and I ask Sabine about him.

'He is in Goa. Coming soon.' Goa is way south and must be hot and steamy. Even here, up high, the sun is warm. She takes Mila again who finishes with the breast and pushes it aside. Sabine pulls down her shirt and gives the baby half a bun then sits her on the deck with a piece in each hand.

She passes me a joint already rolled that was resting in a bowl made from a polished coconut shell. The charas here is soft and crumbly with a sweet taste. I light it and smoke trails off across the clearing. Mila plays on the floor with a plastic doll and a piece of wood.

'Good life, no?' Sabine settles herself against the post, swinging her legs off the deck. The tops of the trees are lit as if by an angel dipping golden wings. The sky is navy blue high above.

'When did you first come to India?' I ask.

'Twenty years before.'

Twenty years ago I was six.

'I came with my father. We drove overland with a bunch of other hippies. My dad was a hippie,' she adds, as if necessary. 'And you?'

'I came for a few months four years before and now I have been here four, nearly five months.'

'Ahh! Good luck to find the Parvati. Energy here is full of Shakti. It's woman place. Parvati flows from the arms of her lover: Shiva himself.' She sucks on the last of the joint and blows the smoke slowly from her nose.

The magpies are back. The walnut tree is their home and their fluttering courtship makes me smile. Their tails are long and the male, when courting his lady, spreads it like a fan.

'So for twenty years you live in India?'

'No, no! Mon dieu!' She picks up Mila and clucks to her in French. 'Most of last ten years I live here, Goa and this valley. Luan was born in Goa, by the sea. It was stormy and crazy. Maybe why he is wild, too much wild.'

'How do you know Vishwam? I thought he said he met you in Nepal.'

'Yes, in a monastery. Kopan it is called. We both were doing sort of a retreat. Luan was four. The nuns loved him. I needed that retreat. Too much low mood after Luan born. Tibetan teaching is much of compassion. And karma, everything karma. Better to be happy then. Ha, not always so easy!'

'I just did a meditation course with Vishwam,' I add.

'With Vishwam? He is teacher now?' Her smile widens and she again holds me with her eyes. 'Yeah, he liked to meditate, could sit very still.' She laughs. Surprisingly, it irritates me like a buzzing fly.

'I think he has been a teacher for a few years now,' I tell her, suddenly defensive of my new meditation teacher.

Sabine is not interested. 'Mila I named after Milarepa. You heard of him? A great Tibetan yogi.'

I have, but I say nothing. Sabine too seems bored with the conversation. I let the charas take hold – the sudden rearrangement, the stepping sideways from myself and the way the greens and blue above amplify in colour and nothing really is worth worrying about. Mila starts to fret and Sabine takes her and walks a little in the clearing, the red of her sweater adding another dimension to the vista.

Afternoon light stretches shadows as I collect enough kindling to remake the fire, and place several logs over the growing flame, confident it will take.

'Merci, thanks, for fixing up the fire. I was just thinking time for tea. No, what is the English way? Ah yes, tea time.'

'I can make, if you like. Must be busy enough with having a baby and all.'

'No no, I do. Sit.' In a moment she has a pot of water on the fire and a flame licking its edges. She throws in another handful of herbs from a cloth bag by the fire. While it brews she disappears for a while inside then returns with food for Mila.

'Rice and apple. I warm a little with milk. Slowly slowly no more milk from me.'

She warms it on the flame then sits with Mila between her legs spooning it in her little mouth. Mila clucks and coos in between mouthfuls and I smile at her and realise again how surprised I am to see this scene – a mother alone with a baby – all the way up here. When she finishes eating I take her and walk slowly up and down with her till she wrestles herself free, reaching for the doll to chew on.

The air is cooling as the sun slides low, its shadow traced on the peak just visible across the valley. I want my vast display for the sunset show.

'Sabine, I must go. Not much light left for walking.'

'Sometime you come and stay if you like. It is fun.'

I sit a moment longer. Sabine is silent. I swing Mila in my arms again then pass her to her mother. She grabs her breast and begins to suck.

*   *   *

Sunset does not disappoint. The last splash of pink is as vibrant as the flames from the fire as I feed it more wood. Sabine is loud in my thoughts. We passed a fine day with ease yet her one comment, her flippant dismissal of Vishwam, has stuck like glue. Do I really care what anyone thinks? Surely it is my experience that matters. The map of my own interior is not as familiar as I may have thought. I am only a beginner in this land of the Buddha, gods and goddesses. I want the peace, the sense of vast presence I tasted when Henry died. If sitting with a meditation teacher brings some understanding, that's good enough.

Tonight I can't be bothered to cook. I feed the fire instead and let the flames dance in front of me. In the quiet of dark, a blackened night betrothed with stars, I want to escape from it all. *Yeah*, I mock, *climb higher in the mountains and see what you find.* Maybe wilder valleys, completely uninhabited, with no one at all to disturb me.

CHAPTER FOUR

Parvati

*'Oh Goddess Parvati, share with me your powerful
yet gentle strength so that I might devote myself to
bringing more beauty and soul into my life.'*
A mantra to the Goddess Parvati

A man sits on Sabine's deck. He wears striped green and blue shorts and a t-shirt with a cartoon picture of a dog playing the drums. He smiles and nods his welcome as I hesitate. 'Bonjour! Bonjour! Come on up.' He offers his hand as I step onto the deck. 'Bernard,' he says, oozing a French accent, and smiles again.

'Judith,' I say and thankfully it is enough as he returns his gaze to the trees.

I wait for Sabine. She comes after a while, across the clearing, carrying the baby and a bundle of something. I take Mila who smiles and coos. I coo back and she grabs at my hair.

'You meet Bernard?'

'Yeah, sure.'

'He just came from Goa, Luan is here too.' She smiles but it looks like an effort. I lift Mila high above my head. Her hair is beginning to curl, and with her dark eyes and long eyelashes, she is very pretty. I have no idea who the father is. Maybe Bernard. He rolls a long thick joint and smokes it as we sit, his legs reaching low over the deck.

'He is in a world of his own.' Sabine leans across and half whispers in my ear. Sadness sweeps across her face, a sadness I have seen in her eyes before. 'Too much drug trips in Goa.'

'Acid?' I ask.

'No ... ketamine.'

Bernard wanders off to lie under the walnut tree, blowing smoke up into the thick leafy branches. I've never heard of ketamine.

'Ketamine,' she declares as if it is a brand name breakfast cereal. 'It's used for animals before operation, what this called?'

'Anaesthetic maybe?'

'Yes, yes! This. It is for horses mainly. People take and have big trip. No good. He took too much.'

Her son has travelled halfway through India with this man. 'Where is Luan?' Suddenly, I'm concerned.

'Down in the village. He runs wild up here, never helping me much. Always so much to do with kids.'

Mila is fussing and Sabine is irritated. Dark shadows circle her eyes and I wonder if she has been crying.

'Come, let's take that laundry to the river; I'll help you.' Clothes are scattered across the steps. I bundle them in a lungi. 'Come, Mila, let's go play in the water!'

Sabine takes a moment to agree. Then we walk across the clearing past Bernard who offers a languid smile, then through the forest until the path brings us to the river that churns and slides through rocks smoothed from the endless caress, down to the Parvati below.

I scrub nappies against a stone, sitting next to Mila whose feet dangle in the crystal clear water. Sabrina pounds clothes against a rock as if she is willing them to tear into shreds.

'You're giving that shirt a hard time!'

She doesn't respond. Mila fusses and splashes with her feet, so I take her and walk slowly up the river, stepping from rock to rock. The coolness is delicious. Sprays of moisture hang for a moment in a rainbow. Birds chatter in the pine trees, gnarled roots offer tiny sandy coves where the water laps and little stones lie like treasure.

Mila grows heavy in my arms and I cradle her against me. Her eyes flicker then close again. I have never felt connected to a baby before. I can feel the pull of love and protection circle us like a guardian angel. I walk back carefully, following the river down to where Sabine still pounds clothes. She stops when she sees me, wipes her hands through her hair.

'See, this is what we want it to be, sleeping baby and birds singing in the trees.' She sits beside me, covering Mila, who sleeps in my arms, with a thin cloth against the midges. 'It's good to have company and woman around.' She holds my arm and tears prick my eyes at the sudden tenderness.

'For me too, Sabine.'

She spreads her shawl and I lay Mila in the shade. Oblivious to it all, sleep claims, completely consumes. 'Now Luan is back, I worry for him. He is so rude, so wild, running off half the day. I don't know, maybe he better in France and going school. This life up here no good for him.'

'He only just came back, no? Give him time to settle. Is Bernard any help?'

'Help!' She spits the words: 'Bernard help?'

I let it rest and doze in the mossy grass as the clothes dry in the sun. Mila wakes first, hungry. Sabine pulls her to her breast, already leaking milk. It drips in a thin trickle from her nipple. She has chapattis tucked in her bag; she breaks one in half and feeds Mila.

I chew mine slowly then cup water from the river in my hands and drink. The cold and freshness is exhilarating. Walking back she shows me where mint grows in wild abundance. As we say goodbye she kisses me on the lips. I wipe my lips as I walk down the path. The kiss felt intrusive.

*   *   *

The very breath of Parvati is filling me up. In the late afternoon clouds emerge from the peaks opposite, taking their place as actors in the sunset show. Behind my hut is a rock, and there I sit, listening to the birds in their evening activities while the air is heavy with the scent of jasmine. Evening light falls slowly all around. The clouds take the stage, overflowing with pinks and gold. Twilight, as day gives way to dark, lasts only a moment, night always eager for her domain. On moonless nights the sky is beyond glory, blazing lights in a mandala of wisdom I can only dream of.

A sadhu lives across the fields. I have seen him a couple of times as I walk up from the bridge taking the pathway home. He nods as I pass. His lungi is a vivid red and sometimes in the afternoon I see him carry his pot over to the stream, a red splash against the greens. I ask Sabine about him when I next visit.

'This baba lives here many years, speaks good English. He is back? I think he went on a pilgrimage.'

Suddenly she is calling: 'Luan, Luan!' followed by a stream of French. Her face tightens to a scowl. A boy appears through the trees, a thin kid with a mass of black hair, quite long. He looks older than eight and eyes me with interest.

'Hi. Je suis Judith, je reste la.' I point to my place across the valley.

He surprises me with perfect English but Sabine hooks into him again, and he faces her with fire blazing from his eyes. I have no idea what she is saying but her tone is ugly. Bernard appears from inside. 'Hey, hey! Les enfants, shanti, shanti, shanti! Mon dieu, Mila dormi!' He sees me and raises his eyes. 'Oh la! Sabine too much angry!'

I know very little about kids and parenting but Sabine doesn't let up and I don't like it. I don't want to stay.

*   *   *

I see the sadhu again, on my way back from a long walk through the forest. In my arms is a bundle of ferns so I cannot fold my hands together as I like to do. 'Namaste,' I say as I pass. He nods without stopping.

Some days later he comes across the fields early, with a bag in his hands. I offer him a cup of chai I have just brewed.

'No, no, thank you,' he replies, and touches his hand to his chest. 'I was taking the honey fresh from the bees. They are generous and I thought you may like to try.' He offers me a container.

'Thank you.' I open it up and it still has honeycomb, waxy and golden like fine amber. Later I take the container washed and clean back to him. He is sitting in the sun with a chillum mix in a small coconut bowl by his side. 'Thank you for the honey. It is very good.'

'Accha. We use as medicine here for many things. Also you can eat.'

Unsure whether to stay or go, he answers the dilemma.

'You may sit.' He smiles and I climb up the wooden steps to his deck. He has a thin chiselled face, a long white wizard's beard and hair knotted on his head. His body is taut, strong and youthful; only his wrinkles and white hair suggest age. Draped round his neck are two strings of beads and another is wrapped around his wrist. A silver ring sits on each long finger.

'You stay here long time now. Good place, huh?' There is something of the eccentric professor in his pronunciation of English.

'I like it. The mountains are beautiful and I love the way the river sings, like a prayer in constant motion.'

He smiles and his face lights up. 'Ha! It is a good place. Good meditation place. Good energy place.' He continues to mix the tobacco through his fingers, crumbling in bits of charas for the chillum.

The source of the Parvati high in the mountains beyond, he tells me, is over a pass through meadows where the shepherds take their flocks for the summer months. He walked up to visit the glacier source of the river. 'Silence, oh very great silence. One cave is there, sweet water and a little firewood. Night time is very cold! Parvati herself gives shakti, inner fire, then cold is no problem. Coffee? You like coffee?' He pulls out a silver espresso machine from a tin trunk to his side.

'A German man gave me.' He chuckles like a wind chime then unfolds himself from sitting and squats on his haunches to prepare the coffee. He unscrews the pot, pours water from a lota, a stainless steel container, by his side and after rummaging in a newspaper package, tips ground coffee into the machine. He screws it up again and places it on his fire. The familiar aroma of coffee wafts with the scent of wood smoke. It is a strong brew sweetened with a generous spoonful of honey. The bitter-sweet taste curls around my tongue. It is the first coffee I have drunk since leaving England months ago. From his deck I can see the glinting waters of the Parvati as the valley opens up in a classic V shape, falling far below.

'Can you tell me something of Shiva?' I've never had a conversation with a sadhu; it seems the best thing to ask. He still squats, sipping his coffee even though it is scalding hot.

'Shiva is everywhere; if you have an interest I am sure you will come to know.' He nods as if he already knows. After he finishes his coffee and throws the dregs off the balcony, he sits in full lotus position, his feet tucked on his lap. He looks completely comfortable and I wonder if he sits like this most of the day.

'Meditation good for knowing Shiva. You meditate and keep your question firm in your mind. Pray to Shiva and he will hear.' His eyes twinkle and I find myself smiling wide. I cross my legs too, but I can't quite achieve the full lotus.

*   *   *

I spend more time with the Parvati, perched on one of the many boulders guiding her journey, listening to her music as she cascades and tumbles. I bask in the sun's hot rays under endless blue heavens. Completely unseen from pathways above I freely plunge in wrapped in my lungi. Between the boulders are pools holding stiller waters, icy and tempting. I spend hours by her, singing softly and finding her name, 'Parvati Ma', delighting my lips. Maybe this is the way to Shiva: through his lover Parvati.

It's been days now since I have visited Sabine. Usually I go every few days. The other day when I returned from a long walk up the valley I found a batch of her cookies wrapped in a cloth by my door. Is it since the kiss on the lips that I am reluctant to visit, or is it the harsh way she can be with Luan that leaves me wishing she were different? A mother who cooed and calmed, not cursed and screamed. And I feel guilty for not visiting Mila. There is something going on between Mila and me.

She sees me and is all smiles, throwing out her arms, and I can't resist. I think of being a mother myself with a baby, a daughter of course, but somehow I can't imagine myself parenting older children or teenagers – what a thought. Mila is a baby looking for any love she can get.

On the night of the third full moon I feel restless. This restlessness lodges in my being. It is early July and monsoon is on its way. I'm reminded of the saying: 'If you want to make God laugh, tell him your plans'. The idea I had even before I left London – to travel to Ladakh – has lost its hold. This had always been my plan – to visit the remote plateau where Tibetan culture and Ladakhi culture still survives. But now I find no pleasure in the thought of travel to another unknown destination. I want to return to Dharamsala. These ten weeks in the high mountains have filled me with fresh clear air, pristine nature and the greatest gift of all: solitude. Also I have only one month left of my visa and I know I can extend it in Dharamsala. I walk up to visit Sabine and tell her of my plan. I've missed her, I realise, as I sip her mix of herbs and take a pull from her joint.

'Maybe also in Kulu you can extend,' she says. 'Monsoon in McLeod Ganj is very full on. Rain, rain, rain. More so than here. I already did one monsoon in very rainy place. Everything gets mould and smells. Better stay here. You can come stay here some days even. Better to do monsoon in the mountains higher up. Or Ladakh! Ladakh has less monsoon.'

I smile. No, it's clear: McLeod offers me something more. This time in the wild has filled me up. It's time to refocus, fall into the Buddha once more.

'I just feel to return there. And Vishwam is doing another yoga course.' I smile, and Sabine does too. It doesn't matter too much for me who sits on the cushion up front, even if he does sit a whole lot stiller than us mere beginners. It's about the words, the teaching of the Buddha. It is about showing up on the cushion myself, stamping my direction clearly on the empty page of my life.

'I'll tell him I met you.' Mila squirms in my arms and I take the cue. As we say goodbye Sabine again kisses me fully on the lips.

'I'm sure I'll be back, Sabine. These mountains have imprinted on me my soul. Besides, I want to see how Mila grows.' I fold her and Mila again in my arms and hold them tight. I have the sense Sabine could stay right here, held in my arms, forever. And in this embrace I sense my own completion of living wild – yes, hiding away up here, as magnificent as it is. I want more; I want to resume my search, take my place again in a hall of students eager for what I too seek. Easy to gaze out at mountain scenery, walk for hours in rich fragrant forests, smoke the local charas until my mind subdues. But it never does. And this is what leads me on, returns me to the only teacher I know: Vishwam Gupta and the saintly surrounds of McLeod Ganj.

*   *   *

I give my leftover supplies of rice and dhal to Shakti. The crops are flourishing, standing tall to sway in the breezes. The women come less often now the work is done, just once in a while to pick grass that they take in bundles on their backs down to the village.

'You going?' She stands from where she has been bending to gather a small yellow flowered grass and rubs her back.

'Yes, going.'

'Come back?'

'I hope so.' Yes, I hope so. With more experience in meditating I will return for another retreat. Maybe next time I will stay for the winter, have a real sense of solitude while the snow piles up around me.

The pathway is ablaze with summer. Butterflies dance, and the Parvati sings to me all the way down. Wild irises open their white petals to reveal delicate mauves and intricate secrets. Outside the small hastily set up chai stalls, marigolds bob their orange heads in rusted tins. The goats and sheep are on the move, flocks of them crowding and bleating and blocking the path while shepherds whistle and shout 'hup' to keep them moving to the higher pastures for the wetter summer months.

After the quiet mountains, Manikaran seems to buzz with life. I take the same room in Mataji's house. She remembers me, although I am sure I look a little more rugged with a good few knots in my long hair. 'Didi! Didi! Yes, stay room!' she says with a burst of toothy smiles, then slaps me hard on the back.

At the hot baths the other women, all Sikh, wear saris wrapped around their ample bodies, not even a hint of nakedness. The partial light and steam suggests an ancient, erotic artwork. Women tip their long, thick, black sheets of hair over their heads, and with slender hands wring the water out. Legs and feet are scrubbed, soap lathers in foamy bubbles.

It is ten weeks since I bathed in this same pool. I feel a wild sense of power from the weeks of walking barefoot over earth paths trod by locals who know only that world. My body feels tighter, more trim, and this claiming of power allows me to feel that strength within myself. I have conquered, overcome, the weakness displayed last time in the course with Vishwam. I will return there, to sit again on a meditation cushion with my head held high. I say a prayer of gratitude as I soak in the thick, steamy water and give thanks to whatever gods are listening. 'Kahan se aiya tum?' A plump Punjabi woman is asking where I come from. For a moment I am not sure what to answer. 'London,' I reply and it is enough for her. She smiles and carries on washing. I close my eyes again. London is a million miles away.

*　　*　　*

I emerge to evening sunlight high on the valley walls. Manikaran is already well in shadow. Bells ring out from the main temple and I follow their call up the smooth rock steps. A bell hangs over the temple entrance and more steps lead down to the surging river where a group of women wash pots. The temple is white and the domed roof a faded gold. The bell rings again and I cover my head and go on in.

A smooth oblong stone, known as a lingam, is mounted on a circular marble stand, decorated with a ring of yellow flowers. A candle burns with a hesitant flame and smoke curls from incense in a bowl of sand. Pilgrims stand before the lingam and the priest places a red dot on each bowed forehead. I watch for a while then sit on the steps facing to the river below. The Parvati pours green and silver waters. Sadhus sit by a steaming pool. Potatoes simmer in half-submerged saucepans and an old man dangles a muslin bag of rice to cook in the hot sulphurous water. Steam curls in the cold air, vanishing in moments. Nearby is another group of sadhus, near naked figures with matted hair, squatting easily on their haunches as if they could stay like that all night. They pass around a chillum, coughing then spitting with accuracy while waiting for their potatoes to cook in an almost boiling river.

Mataji is at the door when I return. Her beady eyes sparkle like a bird. She brings me food: potatoes and the same bitter green leaf, thick chapattis and a bowl of dhal. I eat and, fully satisfied, climb into the bed. I'm asleep in an instant.

*   *   *

I leave very early the next morning from the bus stand across the bridge. I whisper goodbye to the river, hardly visible in the dark, but I can hear her rushing by and pray to return again to her valley. As the bus fumes choke the pristine air I wonder why I am leaving. Maybe, I reason, if I didn't need to extend my visa I would remain. Suddenly I think of what I am leaving behind. My own secluded home, a landscape and a routine that satisfies. Perhaps the sadhu could have taught me more of meditation. Then I remember Henry and his Buddhist teachings that inspired me. In McLeod Ganj Buddhists are all around. I settle in to the bus seat, ready to wind back down the valley and then up again to McLeod Ganj.

CHAPTER FIVE

———～Ⅲ～◇◇◇◇◇～Ⅲ———

Monsoon rain

*'Do not dwell in the past, do not dream of the future,
concentrate the mind on the present moment.' The Buddha*

Vishwam Gupta swells like the monsoon clouds threatening rain. 'Very pleased you are here, Judith. It is going to be a very good group, many excellent students!' He smiles with his wide lips tight together as he welcomes me to the group. We sit before him, eleven spiritual tourists, in the same dusty gompa, the same maroon cushions. Vishwam sits with his cream shawl flung loosely over the shoulders, legs neatly folded on his lap.

'Try to observe yourself sitting on the cushion. Take a little distance. Remember the breath, your breath, here as a constant friend to keep you in a Buddha-like state of equanimity,' he murmurs, then closes his eyes and sits as still as a statue. It is the first day of a three-week long intensive.

After weeks of living in the wilds and to my own intimate rhythm, I throw myself into the routine and the structured days. It's like being back at school after long summer holidays, bending my limbs during early morning yoga and stretching my concentration as I sit in meditation. I curse the difficulty of this simple request: to sit quietly for an hour.

I begin the hour full of enthusiasm, following the in breath, the furry feeling in the nostril with the out breath. My brow is almost furrowed with the concentration. Yet within moments I am with Sabine and her troubled relationship with Luan. What if I had told her that I could see resentment in his eyes that made me sad? Or that the shadows in her eyes made me wonder why she was hiding up in the hills with her young family. And what about me? Why was I hiding up in the hills, happy to care for another whose troubles seem more obvious than my own?

We learn of the four Noble Truths of the Buddha as he sat in his state of enlightenment. I find myself dwelling on the first Noble Truth. That in life there is suffering. Right here in India, of course, it is everywhere to see: horribly deformed beggars, children with bloated bellies, mangy dogs dragging injured legs. I remember the young men I have nursed, the carnage of AIDS written all over their bodies. Swollen legs oozing sores, brain lesions, pneumonia that left bodies feverish and gasping for breath, thin chests wracked with coughing. Yes, I can easily agree with the truth of suffering. Simon and his mother who just could not accept her son was gay. Addicts who tried so hard to go 'cold turkey'. Stephan, the flamboyant and exotic nineteen-year-old with an abscess in his eye from injecting into the only vein he could find. The stories he told me of working as a rent boy in New York. I wonder now if I showed him my sadness for such a young life wasted. He had died about a year later. Had I cared enough? Did I show him, and the countless others, that I too would grieve for their passing?

It's a gradual slide to the niggling distress gnawing its way from somewhere inside me to face the internal deformity, a hidden, secret place, where something is greatly amiss. Sitting on that cushion, I scrutinise my life, the stable happy family I grew up in. All through my teenage years I was so glad my family was 'normal' because my parents were not getting a divorce. It must be something about me: a gross shortcoming, a failure, my façade only a show, and cracked at that.

When I first left home I discovered my ability to drink. Indeed, my first proper relationship suffered badly because I passed out from alcohol on more than one occasion. I had casual lovers – late night couplings then searching for clothing in the pre-dawn darkness so I could slip away unseen. Giving myself away, not even for a gold coin. I only just passed my nursing training, as I had taken so many days off. Sitting in this cold hall, listening to the distant drums and horns of Tibetan ceremonies, my life looks dismal. I scrutinise my past for evidence of my worthiness as a human and find nothing more than a sham really – running a busy ward, night shifts covering for the whole medical unit. I calmed down when I bought my boat. Still, I had lovers and left a string of broken hearts. I spent holidays alone in Greece or Turkey where I had short romances or one-night stands, swigging down the ouzo, out of my depth. Faking, then faking some more. The jury within does not take long to reach a verdict: guilty of failure as a decent human being.

I sit in the early hours. Fresh from sleep my attention is sharp. I have my old room again at Rishi Bhawan with a mattress on the floor and a fireplace in the corner. I listen to the sounds of the night falling away to dawn, the noisy raucous call of a crow piercing the silence. These early hours offer a glimpse of peace, a resting in myself, as the thoughts that chatter like an unwelcome radio have yet to wake.

*   *   *

The days pass as quickly as the rains take hold. It rains often in torrents, easing to a trickle, leaving the sun to stretch her rays. Wispy fingers of mist envelop our clearing and bring a sudden silence before they creep away. Silver slithers, reluctant to leave, float like ghosts against the forest of liquid greens, a collage of abstract form.

As we sit in the hall the rain pounds on the roof. I lose myself to the rhythmic roll of the sound, concentrating on my breath, counting slowly, 1-2-3-4, as I inhale the cool damp air.

Vishwam coos and smiles; he seems to find himself irresistible, sitting like a statue, his cream shawl thrown neatly over his shoulders.

As much as his pomp and posture irritate, I know his words hold a key for me.

He tells us that Buddhism offers a philosophy for happiness. A way to understand the mind and to see that it is our thought patterns, our conditioning, our habitual way of responding to life that limits our potential for abiding peace. I listen to his words but often they float away like the mists.

Each day the torturous process of sitting continues. Henry had told me of waking at 3 am to sit in the freezing dark of the monastery, as he had coughed and hacked up more bubbling froth from his suffering lungs. It had always sounded so harsh and unnecessary – those long hours of meditation – yet now, sitting here surrounded by monasteries of my own, the urgency is real.

'Ah, so much suffering of the minds from the western worlds!' Vishwam is guiding us again on a meditation to experience ourselves throughout the various phases of our lives. I decide to sit this one out. I will keep my eyes closed and just simply meditate but I will not follow his instructions. The thought of it is already upsetting and I want to stand and walk out.

I've always believed my childhood was much like everyone else's but it's obvious now that my parents were more intensely religious than the average Christian household. As a pre-teen sitting next to my mother in church, I remember barely daring to breathe, as the slightest movement would bring her steely stare. Sitting on my hands, the wooden pew so uncomfortable, wishing I hadn't squeezed into my new drainpipe tight jeans. The preacher: Brian Hewlett. I can see him so clearly as if he were before me again, ranting and raving for hours about the certainty of hell for those who don't believe. His fists pounded the air, as he stood in the pulpit, elevated from the mere congregation. 'Only the saved will enter the kingdom of heaven.' I heard his words as I fidgeted on a meditation cushion in the gompa, the monsoon rain pummelling the tin roof. 'Only those of us who repent, who fall to our knees and beseech God for forgiveness. Every time we stray, like lambs away from the flock, the devil is there, dressed as the wolf. The devil stalks your soul. We must be strong, with the word of God our armour, strong to beat the devil wanting to tempt us from Him. Sinners there are plenty. We are all sinners until we repent. That is why I say to you now, if there is anyone amongst us who is not saved, now is the time. Give up the ways of heathen pleasures, worldly temptations put here by the devil himself.' On and on he would speak, shouting almost, and sometimes I imagined him frothing at the mouth.

I used to wait for the hymns, when the congregation came alive, singing our hearts out as if this was the only time our own voice would be heard. *I know my redeemer liveth, it is well it is well with my soul.* An older lady banged away on the piano with her Sunday-best hat barely staying on her head.

As a small child I was scared of the devil. I would check behind the door, look under the bed and make sure he wasn't hiding, ready to pounce. And again, here in the Tibetan domain of McLeod Ganj, I find a deep-rooted fear that I have fallen from the arms of God: a patriarchal God who decides our fate of heaven or hell. How many times had I been told that the worst sin of all is to turn away from God and worship false idols? I question now if it was nothing short of madness. The split in the mind as the sinner and seeker face their shadows. The intricate web again. The spaces in between suddenly seem vast, and I fear I may have fallen through, a long time ago.

Vishwam soothes with creamy words. He stands even, unfurls from his vigil. 'Ah so much pain to be born and grow up. This is when suffering takes its root, as parents cannot support the inherent Buddha nature of a small child. Samsara clutches us all to her own breast.' He stands before me and smiles. I squirm and hope he can't see my confusion. That I am really doing fine.

*   *   *

When we finish the morning session he invites me to his room.

'We can speak some more in private,' he tells me.

And I go. I'm eager for an arm to lean on. He is reading and the first afternoon we simply pass the time together. I have a letter from my friend Val, who also lived on a boat at the moorings. Sometimes when

I came home from a day shift we would drink tea from her fine china cups, her in her denim overalls and with short red hair, me in my track pants and t-shirt, still smelling of sweat from the bike ride home. She was a delicate, sensitive woman, clearly troubled by her grandfather who had sexually abused her when she was a child. She had often spoken to me about it. I had thought she was quite obsessed by it and at times I felt unsure about what to say. Her letter continues with her difficulties: the panic attacks and the new counsellor she is seeing.

Vishwam is firm in his reply. He seems disappointed that I ask for his response, when the advice is so simple. 'Remember the teaching, Judith, remember the dharma. It is all karma, Judith. Nothing happens without a reason. This is her karma. She has to bear it. Who knows what she was involved with in a previous life?' Her letter remains unanswered.

By the third afternoon I accept his invitation to come later, after the evening session. He tells me to sit on the bed beside him and I do. Then he reaches over and holds my hand. 'Judith, you have such a wonderful grasp of the dharma,' he enthuses. 'It is so exciting to have students like yourself in my class.' I look up at him, his wide lips held in the slight smile, his short tidy hair and well manicured hands. It is obvious what is going to happen and I decide there and then to let it. What was I thinking anyway? I came to his room after dark, when I live a good walk away from the town itself. Was I going to walk back alone with my torch after a quick chat? No, of course not. I have been a willing participant and this numbing realisation sends a blush across my cheeks.

I sleep with Vishwam even though I am not remotely attracted to him. His penis is so small yet he hovers over me exclaiming how perfectly it fits inside me. I can barely feel a thing. But there is nothing like being the chosen one to lift spirits that have slumped. Momentarily at least.

*   *   *

And still the rain comes. It's been two weeks now of endless downpours that ease to drizzle, only to lash again. The roof in my room leaks a steady drip. Rishi Bhawan in the wet is not nearly as charming as it was in spring. Rivulets gush from the forest and the grass is a swamp, dancing with a thousand raindrops. Mould replaces the musty dank.

Every day I take a comb to my long curly hair; the tangles are beginning to resemble dreads. My Cornish ancestors have given me spiral curls and it's been the main feature, you could say, of how I look. Men have been attracted to me for as long as I can remember. When I was little I never liked being told I was cute; I hated wearing frilly dresses and wanted to wear shorts like a boy. But by the time I was a pre-teen, the older teenagers at the church youth club returned my vaguely flirtatious advances and from about thirteen I had a steady string of boyfriends. Innocent, of course, although it caused grave upset for my parents. My father collected me from the school disco one evening, having seen a boy's arm around me. Later that night he'd lain beside me on my bed and told me clearly no boy should touch me. *Only I can*, his hands seemed to say as they rested on my thigh. Or did the words actually come from his lips? My mother's concerns were more about her faith. 'Darling, please do not even consider having a boyfriend who is not of our Christian fold. The Devil will tempt you. Choose from the church and remain within the flock.'

Alone in India, eyes follow me almost everywhere I go. The local mountain folk are mellow, used to the western influx, and by nature indifferent. Living alone up in the Parvati I had felt completely safe. It's the Indian tourists in McLeod Ganj who bug me. 'Yes hello! Madam, which is your good country?' 'Madam, hello, we want speaking.' My irritation is growing. Not least because after several nights of submitting to Vishwam and his pathetic penis, I discover he is also sleeping with another student. Alternate nights. Jennifer, the one who has confessed she is taking lithium but wants to stop now she has found the dharma. She reminds me of those who 'found Christ', perfect candidates for the weekend healings, where my mother, among others, would speak in tongues for the Holy Spirit to heal troubled souls.

I muster the courage to end the affair. To my vague questioning as to why he didn't tell me he was also having sex with someone else he declares: 'Do you know what a great gift it is to share the teacher's bed? You will be wiping away years of karma just by lying beside me.'

At least he still has Jennifer.

*   *   *

I'm not sure whether it is the vulnerability of being often alone or a growing resistance within me towards anything to do with men, but I decide to shave my head. I hope to be androgynous. I convince myself I am doing it because I am serious about my quest, that I am letting go of attachment to my image. I will finally prove to myself I am doing right.

After yoga finishes, on the last morning of the course, I visit the barber. The barbershop is next to a vegetable seller on one side and a restaurant, the Lhasa Café, on the other. Now the monsoon is here the offerings on the vegetable stall are limited, with only potatoes and onions, a few tired bundles of leafy greens, a wicker basket of carrots and a pile of tomatoes. As I stand in the slimy street a cow wanders so close I need to move out of its way. Across the road is the Tibetan temple, the bells continually ringing. A line of Tibetans turn the golden wheels inscribed with *Om Mani Padme Hum*. Each time the wheel is turned the prayer is released to the ether. Old women, with bright pieces of turquoise in each ear and their hair tied in thin plaits, walk slowly; others turn malas in fingers and touch their heads to each wheel.

The streets of McLeod are slippery with mud and the drain that runs down the side of the narrow road overflows with black water. To reach the barber's shop I must walk across a slimy stone spanning the open drain like a bridge.

The barber finishes polishing his scissors and turns on a radio to release a blast of distorted Hindi film music. He is a small man, like most of these mountain people, and has a fine head of grey hair. Two red vinyl chairs sit before mirrors. On a shelf are half empty bottles of oils and potions, a comb and another pair of scissors. In the corner is a photo of Shiva surrounded by flashing lights. Stubs of incense burn.

I seize the moment. 'Ji! I need hair cut!'

The barber turns and nods. 'You sit down.'

He points with his chin to the empty chair. The seat is hard and slippery. I look at myself in the mirror. Maybe he could just have a good go at getting all the tangles out. A group of nuns walk past, their robes bright in the sudden burst of sunlight. Their black heads shine like velvet. An Israeli woman I have met before sees me and smiles. She steps over the drain and stands in the doorway. She has an exotic beauty and short curly hair.

'Getting your hair cut?' she asks.

'I am going to shave it off.'

'No! Don't do it! You will regret.' Her accent adds to her passion. 'We have to shave for the army. It is horrible! And you have such beautiful hair.' Her response could be an omen, a warning, but just this thought is enough to banish my doubt. What does she know?

'I want a change.' I have convinced myself at last. Thankfully the Israeli woman doesn't hang around.

I opt for a number one buzz cut, not complete shiny baldness. The barber seems unconcerned that he is shaving a western woman's hair off and I guess I am not the first. He smells of beedi smoke and hair oil. I watch my sun-bleached hair fall on the floor and hear the buzz of the clipper close to my head. I can feel the coldness and can hardly bear to watch in the mirror. The pile of hair grows at my feet.

'Finish, madam.'

A complete stranger looks back. My face is so different I am shocked. Part of me loves it; my eyes look suddenly very large and it suits me. Then doubt jumps in and I feel naked and exposed. Startled, I stare at this face in the mirror. Who am I then, if who I think I am changes the moment my hair is removed?

'How much?' I ask.

'Madam, it is eight rupees.'

Walking back up to Rishi Bhawan it starts to rain. The feel of the rain on my head is like the sweetest kiss from the heavens. I run my fingers over and over the stubble.

I sit in class and Vishwam is delighted. 'Ah, very great. A true step in following your path for the dharma!' He runs his hand over my exposed head and a tinge of nausea stings my stomach. Have I yet again done something to please the teacher but not myself? At least sex can be erased with no trace. *I wanted this, I want to be free from my identity*, I remind myself. *It is change, a new beginning*. I have kept my hair, carried it back with me in a plastic bag.

*   *   *

Now the course has ended, I want to move. The ongoing dampness covers everything in my room at Rishi Bhawan with thin creamy mould.

'You fix the roof and I will stay,' I tell the chokidar.

'No money for roof fixing. This big money. After rain finish you come back.'

'Tikhai ji,' [Okay then] I say in my newly practised Hindi.

I find another home in the village of Dharamkot. Dharamkot is a handful of white-washed houses sprinkled up the valley, traditional mountain-style houses with wide overhanging verandahs and mudbrick walls. I have two rooms above a family living downstairs. It is one of the only two-storey houses in the village and the upstairs has been added on for the purpose of renting to a tourist like me. The small room at the front has a wall of windows with a vista of the village spread in clusters up the valley. I can also see the hills opposite and the beginning of the path up to Triund. The sky is vast and offers a perfect vision of cloud forms as I settle into my new abode.

I have three weeks left on my visa and I have no interest at all in returning to England. I want to go to Varanasi, the holy city flanked by the River Ganga, and to a retreat in Bodhgaya, where the Buddha attained his enlightenment. I also want to come back here, to McLeod Ganj. It feels so familiar. I am more and more sure that a place I used to dream of often as a child, in vivid detail, is this hillside and forest, with the thick deep greens of the pines. Always in the dream I would be running down through the trees as the pine needles let their perfume free.

Soon, though, I will go to Thailand to renew my visa for India and check out some monasteries I've heard about. I've shaved my head, after all. Monastic life is calling.

*   *   *

On the ridge above my new home is Tushita, a retreat centre full of silent souls apparently deeply at peace. I join the Tushita library and eagerly peruse the shelves. I notice that it is not the teachings of Buddhism that attract me but books on the Hindu deities. The more I experience Buddhism the more I miss the notion of God. The inherent emptiness of all phenomena leaves me slightly bewildered. I want the pageantry and possibly I want the all powerful, all loving 'other' to focus my yearning on. My born-again-Christian household gave me plenty of scope to reject the notion of God but I want to discover what 'God' really is. What is the presence that unfurled around me the day that Henry died? What is the Atman, the god within, that I read about? I want to know for myself, unfettered by parental expectation or the fear of falling into the lap of Satan.

One early morning when the mists still linger, a woman who I have seen in the Tushita library sips a chai at the local chai shop close to my new home. I notice her like one does a spiralling leaf caught in a web of sunlight. She is tall, even as she sits on the edge of a bench, eating a cinnamon roll.

'I love this, that I can eat a good cake here in these mountains with also a good chai.' She smiles and licks the sugar from her fingers. She speaks with a European accent and I guess she is Dutch. I too order a cinnamon roll with my usual chai.

We walk together along the track through the forest to Tushita. It is drizzling; fine mists touch my cheeks. The damp chill tingles over my scalp; my naked head receives the rain.

'You staying in Tushita?' I ask as she opens her umbrella.

'Yeah. Come under too, if you want.' She holds the umbrella out, a deep pink beacon against the dank green of the trees.

'I like the feel of rain. I just cut my hair off.'

She turns to look at me. 'Do you wish to be a nun?'

Her face is round, almost heart shaped; her thick chestnut hair tumbles down her back, combed and shining. 'Maybe.' And we laugh.

The rains are loosening. Cloud forms hang like a painting, then climb the valley, merging as one. Winds crescendo through the forest. I meet her again the next day. 'So good the rain is resting a moment!' I say, eager for conversation. I feel I am meeting an old friend and tell her so.

'Yes, I feel this too!' Her smile is so warm. Her name is Helene and she is Dutch.

'I'm Judith. I stay just down there.' I point to where an old woman sits in the sun knitting.

'Come for breakfast if you like,' I say. 'Tomorrow or the next day.'

She does the very next day. 'Ah, this is more fun! Monastery life is difficult for me, always silence!'

'I'm leaving soon,' I tell her. 'Going to Thailand to renew my visa. India still holds many answers for me.' Or perhaps questions, I realise.

'Me too! I am going to Japan to find work and I want to see the beaches of Thailand before I go to a city. When do you go?'

'Soon. I have only two weeks visa. I will take a train to Calcutta then buy a ticket from there. The train journey is almost three days!'

'Let's go together. It's so much better to travel with someone. Let's travel all the way to Bangkok together.' Simple as that plans are made. How expansive and rare this freedom is.

*   *   *

The rain eases to misty magical days. The greys fade to let the sun shine in bright bursts once again. Windows are flung open, blankets and bedding left out to air, faces upturned to welcome in the warmth.

Making the most of these last days I walk and explore. At the far edge of the village I notice the white dome of a temple surrounded by a rock walled garden. A flag flutters briefly, a bright orange splash. A low whitewashed building nestles into the hillside, partly hidden by the forest. The garden is well kept even after the monsoon. Red and pink dahlias peep over the wall. I can see someone tying up a crop of sweet corn. He looks like a sadhu in an orange shirt and as he moves up the path into the house I notice he wears a lungi.

The wooden gate is easy to open and I follow the steps up through the garden; the red dahlias strain in the light to meet me. The flag lies idle now against the white dome of the temple. A black lingam sits on the usual stone base, with a carved snake curled around the base. There are smudges of black from the gooey incense, a single oil lamp and a red hibiscus flower.

A thin trail of smoke seeps from the slate roof. I hear a little cough as I walk up the rest of the slate steps. I am confused by how confident I am walking through this garden with no invitation. I hesitate a moment at the doorway then peer into a dim room, almost bare but for a fire pit and the sadhu sitting cross-legged against the wall.

'Namaste,' I say, my palms together as I step into the room.

'Namaste,' he mutters in response. He stares a moment more then says, 'Behtou, behtou.' [Sit.]

'I was taking a walk and saw the temple.' I would say more to explain but he already is nodding. 'Tikhai tikhai.' He dismisses my explanation and motions for me to sit near the fireplace. A white cat jumps up to the window ledge, catching the light with his shadow. The Babaji nods again as his gaze falls back to the fire. He has black shoulder-length hair, oiled and combed, and his skin is darker than the locals'.

I settle myself to sit cross-legged, surprised by my boldness, the spontaneous way I am following my interest. I am sitting on an earthen floor by a small glowing fire with a sadhu who looks like he is moulded into his surrounds. How easy it would have been to hesitate and how glad I am that I did not.

I have the sense that he does little else but meditate by his fire. No words are spoken and I find a natural quiet in my own mind. Perhaps this is what an ashram is: a place to sit and meditate. After some time he yawns then coughs. The spell is broken. I sit for a moment more then offer a 'namaste' again. He folds his hands together and says: 'Hari Om.' The sadhu up in the Parvati used to mutter 'Hari Om, Hari Om', a mantra to invoke the sacred. The Hindu equivalent of 'Glory to God'.

As I stand up a nagging self-consciousness sweeps in like a sudden downpour from clear skies. I am uninvited here. This is uncharted water and I do not want to capsize. I step outside. A rainbow hangs across the valley, precise and vivid, a perfect arc in the late afternoon light.

*   *   *

Helene and I book our train tickets. We will leave in two days' time and I want to visit the Babaji once again. I push open the gate and walk up through the garden, and my stomach ties a little knot. I pause again at the temple and touch my hand to the stone base of the lingam, as I know now to do to receive a blessing, to pay respects, to remember the fact of God, whatever that may be. A stub of black incense still burns and the sweet smoke fills the small shrine.

He squats on his haunches by the fire, eating from a bowl. He glances up at me without a pause. I decide to simply sit, keeping my gaze fixed on the fire that smoulders and the few glowing embers. I hope to be invisible. Yet still I steal a glance and see him intent on his task, scooping up the rice in his fingers, mixing in pickles. When he finishes he washes his fingers into the plate, pouring water from a cup. He sits back and belches loudly, still with his hand over the plate. He wears a woollen waistcoat and a lungi that looks old and worn. After a moment he takes his plate over to the tap by the doorway, rinses it well, then disappears outside and I hear him talking to the cat that answers in little miaows.

I am surprised by how at ease I feel. Silence here is as definite as a shaft of sunlight. This ashram offers the Hindu gods I've been reading of, a temple in the garden, a fire that is tended for more than warmth and cooking. A sadhu who wears the mystery I want. I hear him cough just outside then he comes back in and I notice how wide and capable his feet are, how strong his calves look. He sits again at his place between the fire and the opposite wall; a brightly coloured picture of Shiva with a lingam before him hangs just above where he sits.

'Babaji, your temple is for Shiva?'

He looks at me with his deep black eyes. 'Temple lingam hey, Shiva hey.'

'Can you tell me something of Shiva?'

'You inside mind quiet, mind clean, you Shiva knowing.'

He returns his eyes to the fire. 'Shiva lingam no end, no start. This Shiva.'

He then mumbles something I can't quite hear but offers nothing more.

I study the pictures on the walls: Shiva with long flowing jutta, dreadlocks, strong, with his trident clasped in one of his hands. In the other he holds a drum. He looks like a man-god, with his almond eyes and beatific smile. Babaji watches me just for a moment and as I notice his glance I feel it again: that sense of recognition. I want to say, 'So here you are! Here is where I find you!' But of course I don't.

'God very kind,' he tells me. 'This form of Shiva looking our eyes are happy and hearts happy. Happy mind easy for God thinking. Shiva, God, same, same. Ashram place only for God looking. Tikhai?'

'Tikhai, Babaji.'

He rummages in a cloth bag by his side and pulls out a piece of charas and places it on the rim of his fire pit near a glowing ember from the fire, empties a cigarette into his hand, then crumbles the now soft charas into the mixture and rubs it well with his thumb.

'Shiva prasad,' he says and smiles. His face lights up like a child. 'You little smoking?'

'Sure, Babaji.' It's been some weeks, since I was with Sabine up in the Parvati.

He fills the chillum, muttering, 'Om,' in a low rumble. Each task is precise. Smoke plumes as he lights the end with a burning stick he pulls from the fire. Red sparks fly into the air. He passes it to me and I take a small pull with a sublime sense of ritual. The smoke is hot in my throat and the rush is immediate. I decline more and he nods. When it is finished he empties the chillum, knocking it gently on the palm of his hand, and throws the ash by the woodpile.

I lose myself to the orange flame that gently licks as sculptured embers glow. Sadhus seem to be men of few words. Birdsong comes in symphonies from the garden. The quiet is easy to fall into – like a warm bed at the end of a busy day. He rocks slightly as he sits then tidies the fire again, manoeuvring the coals to allow a small flame. In the corner of the fire pit stands a trident like the one Shiva holds in the picture. On each prong is half a lemon and a red cloth is tied around the shaft.

'Babaji, I go soon to Calcutta.' I startle myself. My words sound loud.

'Accha!' He looks at me then nods. 'Calcutta Kali place. Bengali people Mother worship, Kali Ma.'

He says 'Kali' with a smile, as if even with this invocation she is appearing to him.

I watch him place a pan on the fire, pour water from the blackened kettle, reach for a jar from the shelves to his side and throw a handful of tea powder in the steaming water and I realise all of a sudden that I am leaving. This knowing had been abstract and now as it cements before me I feel grief, a wrenching away from the known. The village around is my home: the early morning sounds of the family below me, the smells that seep up from the kitchen, and the women themselves, with their thick oiled hair and woollen scarfs, anklets that jangle and an elegance in whatever task they perform. Watching them work all day I sometimes feel lazy, unworthy of all this time to do as I please, to read a book or stroll up to the chai shop, to take long walks in the forest and see the monkeys scatter pine needles as they swing above. Or walk down the hill to McLeod Ganj for supplies, another waxy candle, or bread from the German bakery. I might stop at one of the many cafes owned by Tibetans and order momos, steamed vegetable dumplings, while at the tables around me other travellers tell stories and laugh loudly or sit alone, also contemplating as they eat. I realise I no longer feel as if I am travelling, but that I have arrived somewhere that invites me to stay.

Babaji passes me a tin cup of chai. He lights a beedi and throws me the packet. I want more of this too, sitting by a fire with a sadhu who has not even asked me my name, to drink chai and smoke beedis and talk more of the gods. Instead I will be leaving, sitting on a hard metal bus seat as we wind our way downwards to the plains.

'You when going?' Babaji asks.

'Two days' time. With the night train from Pathankot. Long journey to Calcutta.'

'Ahh long, two three days only.'

I uncross my legs and clear my throat.

'Going?' he asks. I nod and he rests on his haunches for a moment before disappearing out the doorway. I can hear another door open, then shut, and in a minute he is back. He hands me a postcard of Shiva sitting on a leopard skin.

'You Shiva taking.'

'Thank you, Babaji.'

'Tikhai, you take. Good journey, safe journey.' I take the postcard as if it is treasure. He walks outside with me and the afternoon is further on her way to evening than I realised.

CHAPTER SIX

Calcutta

*'We cannot all do great things, but we can do
small things with great love.' Mother Teresa*

Helene's hand is cool in mine as we wait for the bus. It's a four-hour journey on a hard tin seat to Pathankot train station. The wrench in my heart is perfect: leaving the known, striding out once more. The last sunlight touches all with gold, a simple finale of liquid pink, thin streaks of purple against translucent heavens.

The night air at Pathankot is heavy with stale heat and a thin moon lies low in the west. A train's loud horn resounds above the general commotion, and huffs and puffs of smoke announce its arrival. The platform is chaos, a mass scramble to find the right carriage. Porters balance trunks on their heads, bags under their arms, thin legs bent under the weight. A mass of people pushes forward as beggar kids dart between legs to surround us. A wave of claustrophobia laps at me. The quiet of the mountains is suddenly eons away and my breath tightens in my chest. I steel myself to the task before me. I am so glad to have a travelling companion and give a quick prayer of thanks to a god I am sure is here. Helene stays close as I lead us through the scrum.

Men in military uniforms walk in twos or threes, guns slung over a shoulder. 'Bhaisaab, we need help,' I say as I hold out our tickets. A group crowds around and frowns. Suddenly a face lightens. 'This way, madam. Please you come.' He is charming, with his polished boots and black moustache. He weaves through the crowd and finds our carriage. Rusty brown with bars on the murky windows and already crammed with people. Finally we are seated on bunks in the women's compartment, six berths segregated from the rest of the carriage by a door that locks. What a delight! We have the top two berths and arrange our sleeping bags for the long ride to Calcutta.

The constant rhythmic sound of the train as it rushes through the night, bursts of activity as it pulls into a station, permeate my sleep. Light finally stains the sky and the flow of scenes through the window becomes our entertainment. When the other women in our compartment are awake the bunks are rearranged, and Helene and I sit by the window as India, uncensored and hidden but for our passing interest, displays herself. Smoke curls as women stir pots on brick fireplaces outside a small hut with a low thatched roof. A small boy herds his white goats; girls and women with pots of water balanced on their heads lead a cow or carry a baby on the hip. Men clean their teeth at a pump. Others squat on the edge of fields, with a water pot to one side.

Every village has a small temple or a mosque and distorted sounds crackle from loudspeakers. And everywhere, green after the monsoon. Herons and storks fish by stretches of dirty looking water; naked children run, waving as we pass. Bright coloured saris splash turquoise and purple against the green of rice paddies and bronzed red earth.

'Indian women are so beautiful,' Helene says as she watches a mother bathe a small child by a well. The train has slowed and instead of fleeting images we watch as the child is dried with her sari. 'They must be the most beautiful of all races.' She does not hide her attraction to the female form. It is true anyway, the graceful way a sari hangs over a shoulder, a waist revealed in effortless elegance.

The train flies along at a steady pace, slowing on the edge of towns. Pulling into a station brings excitement, the air full of shouts.

'Mungphali! Mungphali!' shout the peanut wallahs with their baskets balanced over a shoulder. Twists of newspaper full of warm peanuts sprinkled with salt are two rupees. 'Chai! Chai! Chai!' cries the chai wallah, carrying a big kettle of hot sweet chai and a basket of little clay cups. Chai is one rupee and we drink one at every station. We try a samosa but it is so full of chillies we can't finish it.

I watch the endless parade of life through the open window of the train, and the air rushing past brings the smells of the small fire burning by the railway track, of the buffalo as they wallow in the filthy swamp beside the track; and the sounds of the loudspeaker and the distorted music blaring from a temple, the shrill call of a mother to her small child. This rich and immense expression of life pulls me only to the present and I notice how much more available to it all I am now after months in this country. No time for daydreams, of what may or may not be found in Thailand, or what my life will look like in some future time. There is too much going on right now, this poignant unfolding as a population and their lives are everywhere to be seen. No wonder the Buddha came from this land.

The two toilets at the end of each carriage are merely a hole in the floor. They stink, and bits of other people's shit line the hole. The water tap looks like a health hazard. We just do what we have to do. Helene pulls out antibacterial hand wipes.

The women in our carriage are bemused by us. They are two motherly types who chatter non-stop, every now and again smiling and nodding at us, tilting their chins as all Indians do. They have endless parcels of food wrapped in newspaper – chapattis, bananas, small samosas, even potatoes. The wide, dark eyes of the two Muslim women peer from their burkas. With thin wrists with long fingered hands, ankles with delicate chains, and elegant shoes, they exude a mysterious coyness and sit very still. Since meeting the Babaji I want to speak some Hindi but I only know a few words, not enough to even have a small conversation. Helene is reading a book of Buddhist teachings and I want to say to her, *Put it down. Just look out the window; it is all you need.*

The train slows as we inch our way through the edges of a sprawling city. *Lucknow* is written on a big sign as we heave into an elaborately decorated ironwork building teeming with life. The two Muslim women quietly leave the carriage and I watch them out the window as they follow two men. They walk single file and are quickly swallowed by the crowds. The train stops here for more than half an hour and we get off to find food on the platform. A puri wallah throws circles of dough in a vat of hissing oil. Helene looks as if she'd rather be somewhere else than on this platform with men everywhere, people all around, smells and sights that shock, and scaly dogs and beggar kids rushing towards us.

'Not much choice,' I tell Helene, as I order two plates of puri and soupy vegetable served in a leaf plate. She looks at it unconvinced. 'Dip the puri in the soup,' I suggest. 'They are quite good.' I hope neither of us gets sick from this very basic station fare. The station is a universe of its own. An old woman in a filthy sari picks her way through the pile of discarded leaf plates. 'Le le!' the puri vendor calls and throws her a couple of puris that she wordlessly tucks into a fold.

Standing there on the crowded platform, I have an unusual feeling and almost want to break the journey here. I have to reason with myself to stay on the train. I could pull my backpack off the train and stay a couple of days then meet up with Helene again in Calcutta. As absurd as the idea is, I have to convince myself not to do it. I decide I cannot leave Helene. She is out of her depth here on this crowded, chaotic platform. Anyway, we are travelling together now, to Thailand and a holiday in the sun. Suddenly the idea of a holiday is unnecessary, indulgent, after all that India has revealed.

'I have no idea why, but Lucknow may have something of interest for me,' I tell Helene as I dip the greasy puri into the spicy, soupy subze – grateful to her for the hand wipes yet again.

'More like we are the interest!' Helene has little tolerance for the stares and looks from men. Eyes are on us from everywhere. I sit squashed close to her on the dirty wooden bench and glance around. Sitting on a suitcase nearby is a neatly dressed man, his hair oiled and combed, his eyes fixed on us. The packs of men-boys who walk arm-in-arm and openly leer are the worst. 'Hello, madam, which country?'

They stare at our breasts as they speak. On the train ride from Bombay, months ago now, I had woken from half sleep to find a man sitting on my bunk. I had kicked out at him and shouted and he slunk away but not before grabbing my breast. It had hurt.

'I know. The last train ride I took, a man grabbed my breast really hard. It was awful.'

'Judith, that's assault! Were you okay?' She pushes the leaf plate that by now is leaking the soupy, spicy vegetables all over her hands to the end of the bench, and turns to lean closer to me. The concern and outrage in her eyes disarm me and my own passive acceptance.

'Well, no I wasn't.' As I speak, I feel the knot of anger twisting in my gut.

'It's assault and the man should have been challenged at least!'

Challenged by whom? Me?

'Try not to focus on it. Don't let it overwhelm you. Isn't this what we have been learning about, a way of not reacting?' I want to convince us both.

'I just hate being stared at! It's like being surrounded by wolves.' Helene wraps her long cardigan more tightly around her. She has an air, I am noticing now, an innocence maybe, or is it a vulnerability that suggests easy prey. I am wearing an Indian shirt to my knees and loose trousers. A shawl covers my shoulders. And I have a short fuzz of hair instead of my long curly locks. I cannot pretend that I do not miss my hair. I can feel exposed and shameful almost. But I have proved a point. An aspect of my femininity has gone.

I don't know what to say. I can hear that it's getting to her. I can shut it out, keep my eyes downward. As I stare at the dirty station floor I have that sense again, just like I did when I filed away the man who smashed down my flat door. It seems I am very good at just blanking things out, hassle from men included. That grey feeling of gloom creeps up again on me. I hear myself sigh and feel the familiar tension in my stomach. The mass of life all around us on the station platform pulls me from my thoughts, demands my presence. There is so much more to India than the unwelcome attention from men – endless possibilities. I watch the puri wallah. His face is soft and shadowy, lined with age, his hands deft and agile as they manipulate the dough to puff and grow to crisp golden puris. He reminds me of Babaji suddenly, and the way he too was so deft with fire and brewing chai. What a privilege, it strikes me now, to have met such a man. Inspired by his quiet and simple being, the ashram with all its charm, I long already for my return to this country where sadhus meditate by fires and temples house the gods, and life carries on regardless.

I squeeze Helene's hand and we smile at each other. I notice again her hazel brown eyes and for a moment we could be anywhere in the world, just her and me. Then it's gone, snatched away by a beggar. 'Paisa, paisa,' he groans. The coins rattle as they fall into his empty tin.

Back on the train I take my *Lonely Planet* and check Lucknow. I read of botanical gardens and a couple of buildings from the Raj. It has a large Muslim population and the old city is full of mosques; it also boasts a zoo that is open every day.

*   *   *

Howrah railway station is India's largest. We wind our way through throngs of people to the taxi area. Beggars descend on us, their deformities in full view. Stumps instead of hands reach for my shirt.

'Chello, chello!' [Go, go!] I hear myself scream, all the Buddhist compassion gone in an instant. They follow with low moans and finally we push ahead through the crowds, intent on finding a taxi. A host of taxi and rickshaw drivers spot us. 'This way, madam, please come.' 'Cheap and good hotel.' 'Madam! You sitting here down.'

'Yes hello, taxi!' The driver is opening the door and we fall in, eager to shut out all this madness.

'Youth hostel, youth hostel,' says Helene. We've heard it is an okay place to stay. We crawl through traffic-jammed roads. Trams career along the tracks in the middle, buses and taxis weave around mopeds and bicycles. Two people sit in a rickshaw pulled by a man running through the traffic, his lungi tied around his waist like a mini skirt. Eight months I have been in India, and it feels like my first day.

The youth hostel gives us a bed and we wordlessly recover from the momentous journey before visiting the Thai embassy to apply for a visa.

We walk past market stalls with row after row of exquisite cloth; fruit barrows with sellers shouting their prices – bananas, pineapple, watermelon, pomegranates cut to reveal juicy pearls of the brightest red. And then a few metres away is startling pain and poverty. We are easy targets for outstretched hands wrapped in filthy bandages, or stumps with open sores, flies swarming. People with missing or useless legs push themselves along on boards with little wheels, calloused hands held up. Lepers hobble after us, clinging to our sleeves, pus oozing from open wounds, until we walk even faster. I try to avoid looking, but it is impossible to remain unmoved.

On a crowded street lined with plastic lean-to huts, a man is laid out on the pavement. He is naked save for a dirty cloth around his groin. His limbs, thin as sticks, are twisted up at impossible angles. His head is slightly shaking, turned to one side. Flies swarm around his eyes and half-open mouth. A worthless amount of rupee coins barely cover the bottom of the rusty tin next to his shoulder. I add a one-hundred rupee note. Helene can hardly look. She quickens her pace and I notice how yellow his eyes are and that his hands are shaking. I want to cry at the utter helplessness beneath the hot sun that beats down all day. And the life that carries on regardless.

Beggars are everywhere in India. Giving a few rupees here and there is part of the deal. In McLeod Ganj beggars sit outside the temple holding up a tin with a smile. Others wander in the main square – the old woman with the thick walking stick, or the thin dark-skinned woman, with a line of barefoot dirty kids in tow. Here they are more persistent, almost aggressive.

The child beggars really get to me. I cannot find a place to store it all in my mind, but after a couple of days I adapt to the madness enough to simply cope.

'You could work at the hospice for a while here,' Helene suggests. 'You could be so useful, especially as you seem to like so much about India. You really seem to fit in.'

'It's true. I could come back and inquire about the Mother Teresa charity here.' It is a real possibility. In the past I considered applying for Medecins Sans Frontieres, or Oxfam. I will be back; I have a return ticket safely tucked in my money belt.

A thin, wiry man pulls two fat school children along on his handcart, spitting what looks like a line of blood to the road.

'Surely that man needs to see a doctor! How can anyone let him do that!' Helene is as affected as I am. Not only are there confronting scenes of poverty, but men turn and stare wherever we go, their eyes at our breasts, hands fiddling in their pockets. Helene gives rupees to every beggar, which adds to the chaos. As soon as a coin exchanges hands other beggars swarm, all intent on receiving a share. This morning as we left the hostel, I changed fifty rupees into coins so I could oblige with ease. Helene is repulsed and concerned at the same time and her face expresses it all.

'Wait, wait, please wait!' she pleads to the woman with the scrawny baby who thrusts it almost in her arms. 'Memsahib, memsahib, paisa dedo, paisa paisa,' the call almost a moan. Finally everyone had a coin and there were smiles from some but the mother still followed, grabbing Helene's shirt.

'Why don't they just take the coin and go?' Helene is completely out of her depth. 'Chello, didi,' I say, taking charge as the woman gathers up the scrap of life in her dirty sari.

'They are teachers for us. We also want more, are not satisfied with what we are given.' She isn't convinced and neither am I. It sounds like something Vishwam would have said.

As chaotic and confronting as Calcutta is, I feel much more in awe of India now than when newly arrived, eight months ago. I still see all the poverty and filth and desperation, but my attention finds other details now. Little shrines set in unexpected places dot the streets. Most are for Kali with her many arms and necklace of skulls. Babaji said it was the city of Kali and she is everywhere, riding on a tiger with her fierce face and her tongue hanging out. Other temples have Krishna playing his flute. Some have a Shiva lingam and they all have bells, incense, and a flickering lamp. At one, a priest sits giving blessings. I receive a red dot between the eyebrows and a handful of sweet prasad. Helene is amazed that I eat it, sure that I will get sick. 'Judith! You can just pretend!'

I laugh. 'It's food from the gods!'

Early the next morning we fly east, to the land of the dawn.

CHAPTER SEVEN

The promise of paradise

'Dharma is the religion. People nowadays, however, have become attached to and view the Buddha as a god – instead of seeing him as a human being who attained enlightenment and had great compassion for others. They are not aware that Buddha teaches that anyone can follow his path and find the way out of suffering by and for themselves.' Ajahn Buddhadasa

Bangkok is the city of vice. Older western men walk arm-in-arm with young Thai women, their faces thick with make-up, short tight skirts barely covering their thighs. In the many video bars women serve, their faces stretched in big smiles. It's a startling contrast to the sea of men in India.

We take the night train and then a ferry over clear blue seas to the islands we dreamed of. Koh Phangan is a party island and a place to hang out. An outrigger canoe takes us on to the tiny village of Than Sadet, a small sandy cove with red rock cliffs. Helene's relief and joy to be back in nature mirrors my own. Sunglasses on, hair trailing, her easy smiling self has returned. A river merges with the sea and coconut palms fringe the white sand beach.

We find our place up on the cliff, a neat wooden bungalow with a deck wide enough to string my hammock. It holds us both as we gaze out over the cliff to the emerald blue water that stretches to a languid cloudless sky. Along the beach three restaurants serve coconut soup, fragrant curries and plenty of rice. The local people are as relaxed as the scenes, the boys with long hair and an eye for western women. Fishermen mend nets, painted boats bob in the bay, their reds and greens reflected in the water. It's an Impressionist's dream. Women with curved knives clean hollow-eyed fish in wicker baskets. Dogs hang around, hopeful for the discarded heads.

At the far end of the beach, a brown shallow river spills to the sea. A wooden bridge leads to steps carved in the rocks up and over a rocky knoll to the cove below. Westerners have claimed this beach – a small indent of sand lined with palms – and naked bodies lie bronzed and confident.

I feel exposed. I have only the inch of stubble sticking up from my head in this world of cool travellers. No Buddhist seekers here. I miss my mane to shake and hide behind.

'Image is an interesting thing. Don't worry about it; you just look like a woman wanting to be a boy!' Helene is joking but the words sit and stay. She is back in her element and I notice that she is taking the lead now. The ground beneath my own feet is sinking like the sand.

'Judith, I don't know how you looked before but I like your hair short. Anyway, really there is nothing you can do now but wait until it grows.' She fixes her hazel eyes on me and her slightly moist lips glisten.

I am not feeling very heterosexual on this beach in Thailand with bronzed bodies sunning themselves. It is the curve of a hip that catches my eye or the way sunlight falls on bare smooth skin, skimpy bikini pants covering not very much. Several times in London I met gay women at a party or bar and realised they were coming on to me. I felt curious but that was all. Except one night when a kiss goodbye lingered and tongues met, her lips so soft and welcoming, yet I had held myself back, leaving an awkward moment until the static settled.

Here on the beach Helene and I sleep in the same bungalow, swing together in the hammock as stars beckon to the beyond. I like the way her arm hangs loose across my breast, the feel of silky smooth skin as our legs entwine. I notice how my hand wants to run slowly, very slowly up her thigh, trace the downy hairs up to her belly button. The way her nipples stand like pinkish buttons as she shakes the water from her hair after an early morning swim when the air is still cool. The mound of fur peeking between long brown legs, like a secret wanting to be shared. On the sun-kissed beach of Thailand I want to say yes.

When the tide is out, rocks are left exposed, dressed in lime-green lichen that swirls around in the shallow water like mermaids' hair. The jungle is alive with cicadas that ring and hum throughout the day, silent for a moment then again calling in unison, shrill vibrations reaching near hysteria, only to all fall silent again.

One afternoon, as the beach falls into shadows and the sun throws sparkles in the water, Helene rubs my back casually as we talk. I feel her fingers caress and stroke and without moving I ask: 'Helene, are you seducing me?'

She doesn't answer at first, but her fingers slide lower, stroking until the burning is almost unbearable and I want to kiss her. But there are others around us, also enjoying the light, the shady cool and the lapping waves that leave trails of moisture on the dry sand.

'Maybe,' she whispers, close to my mouth.

We walk home arm-in-arm, stopping for a beer at our favourite cafe.

'I like you with short hair, you know.'

'Yeah?' I drink my beer with my eyes on her lips.

'I would like to see you in jeans and a white t-shirt. No bra.'

She leans forward and rests the cold glass on my forearm. Suddenly she is bold and dangerous almost, and a warm blush reddens my cheeks. Halfway up the path to our hut she pulls me to her, there on the rough-cut steps. Her mouth tastes of beer and the lingering aroma of coconut. I find my lips hungry, parched. Her own moist kisses intensify as her tongue searches. And all of a sudden I pull back, as if an alarm has suddenly rung from inside me. Awkward, embarrassed, I can use the excuse I decide on – not wanting to kiss on a path where locals might see us.

'Hey,' she whispers. 'You taste so good.'

I'm crumbling with shame. What have I done? Led her on and now I cannot. She pulls me up the path, oblivious to my internal disarray.

'Slowly slowly,' I mumble then start to sing. 'Slow down the pace for me, little woman … you're jamming it too fast for me.'

She's laughing now. She climbs into the hammock and watches me. I fumble for the small head of weed I was given yesterday and roll it up with the bits of broken cigarettes I always seem to have somewhere in my pack.

Helene does not smoke. 'You mind?' I ask.

'No, go ahead.' She has pulled back. I can feel it.

I watch her in the hammock, a long leg thrown out. As I inhale I feel a rush of relief. It's okay, it's okay. Why not explore? It's not the first time I've been attracted to a woman. Go for it. The moon is almost full and already risen. I watch her light fall on the swaying ocean. The weed is strong. I take another pull then stub it out.

And then I am there in the hammock too. She pulls my mouth to her and I run my fingers inside her shirt to her nipples – firm tight buds – and the feel of them stirs my own. And now she has one in her mouth and I moan, but all the while I am screaming to myself and I sense a panic rising, an overwhelming shame streaming from my pores.

'I can't do it,' I tell her, simple as that. Her hand is stroking me and I clamp my legs firmly together.

'I'm sorry. I thought we were on.' She runs her fingers through her hair, creating some order where she can.

'I'm sorry, Helene.' I struggle from the hammock and half fall onto the deck. I want to cry. *No! No!* I scream even louder to myself.

'Are you okay? What's happening? Hey, it's no big deal. Come on. Come back here. You look really upset.'

'Sorry, I don't know what happened. Maybe shaving the head has made me a nun after all. And sex doesn't belong to this. I don't know.' And I wonder then if I should tell her. That for some bizarre and strange reason I think I may have been abused when I was very young. But even thinking I would say such a thing pushes me further into my confused and clearly twisted self.

The night is perfect – full of possibilities for lovers to write poetry and seal the words of each other's secrets. Instead we hold hands and watch the moon reflect on the ocean. 'I'm sorry,' I say to Helene, 'really I am.' I see her smile in the half light and soon after we head inside to escape the mosquitoes that start to swarm. Our brief eroticism allows us to sleep entwined, with the sounds of muffled murmurs as the ocean surges against the cliffs below.

Our days have been numbered from the start. Helene has a ticket to Japan to find some modelling work. I am sure it will be easy, her round face full of beauty and lips so kissable. I do kiss them. Kissing, I have declared, is fine.

'I didn't meet anyone like you before.' Helene scrunches up her face and I have to laugh. 'You're kind of complex, you know.'

Her sweetness and ease with my erratic and bizarre sexual behaviour only highlights my own strangeness. Yet we still plan and daydream. 'Let's meet here in March and stay the monsoon; the beach will be ours!'

'No, no, come with me to the Parvati, where her ice cold waters paint pictures of love flowing from massive mountains ...'

Helene leaves a few days later from the little town with the harbour. I watch the ferry till it is a blot on the horizon.

*   *   *

Koh Phangan has a small monastery in the hills, offering a ten-day vipassana retreat. Vipassana (clarity of insight) is a traditional Buddhist meditation practice and this wat, as monasteries are called here, is run by an Australian couple. It's geared for the novice meditator. Beginners just like me. Accommodation is simple: a grass mat on the floor, a mosquito net to cover. I am lucky I have a room to myself. The gods are kind.

This is my first silent retreat ever and it's a profound change to go from days of idle languor to a regimen of bells. Sixty participants sit, walk, work and eat, and of course meditate – all in silence. The wake-up bell rings in long echoing tones at 4.30 am, for a 5 am meditation. At 7 there's an hour of yoga, with breakfast at 8. After that, we each have a job to do. Mine is to clean up after breakfast, part of a team to wash the big pans and pots and wipe the tables. For the rest of the day, broken by lunch and a rest time, there is alternate walking meditation and sitting meditation. In the evening we listen to a dharma talk. I never knew time could drag so.

The meditation hall has a large golden Buddha statue and a gold painted design around the cornice. The sides are open; the teacher sits out the front. Some meditations are silent; others have instructions on vipassana. The instruction is mostly to follow the breath, trying to bring awareness to the sensation as the breath enters the nostril. 'The whole idea is to develop awareness and equanimity towards sensations, thoughts and feelings experienced by the body-mind phenomena,' the teacher intones. Her name is Rosemary. Her voice is just a little too sweet and she sits straight-backed, neat, tidy and serene.

I am finding this all an effort. More than an effort – it is painful. With Vishwam we sang and discussed things, and every day had half a day's break. Just me, myself, I – from daybreak to night ... I am not great company. My legs ache after fifteen minutes of sitting. It seems that my lower back, where I had surgery, is not coping with sitting cross-legged for an hour. I become anxious that it won't hold out and I will somehow break apart the disk that was fused. What have I done now! Fucked up my body as well as my mind. It takes a lot of willpower not to stand up and walk out but I don't think I could handle my own opinions if I did.

I relive the moments with Helene. I had surprised myself with how turned on I felt – possibly, I believe, more than I ever have with a man. *Yeah but you couldn't look at her, could you?* The voice snakes its way into my thoughts, and the coldness slices my memories in two. It's true too. *And what a scene you turned it into. You don't deserve friends like Helene let alone a lover like her.* I had found it profoundly embarrassing to see her eager passion, her celebration of her body and the pleasure it gave her. After our initial night of confusion I had found a compromise. We kissed, caressed and I explored her and her hidden creases, her tight bud of pleasure, until she exploded in my arms. Reflecting on her patience now makes me want to cry again. Imagine if she was a man! He could have got angry, insisted it was now his to take. I probably would have agreed. And the night, our last together, she had self pleasured. That's what she called it. 'Come on, give yourself a treat if you won't let me.' No, I told her, I never did it. Never felt a need. 'Well, what am I supposed to do?' she said. 'You've gotten me all turned on, honey. Kissing is fine, sweetheart, but … hey, don't you know what you are missing?'

I had nothing to say. But as I sit here with a mosquito whining in my ear and my legs screaming to stretch themselves out, I realise that all I have done is just pretend. And I remember the first time I let a boy explore me, there in Sandford Park lying on the grass after dark, and how it was to feel absolutely nothing once his hand crept lower than my waist. As if I was numb. And then, ever since, I became more and more skilled, until I almost fooled myself. Yet Helene with her deep guttural chorus, her body contracting in spasms of pleasure, has never been my experience. 'Why don't you want to kiss me in the daylight?' she had asked. 'I just prefer darkness,' I had replied, trying to sound mysterious. I don't think I was convincing. So often, sex with men has been while alcohol filled my veins. My nakedness with Helene left me self-critical, all too aware of the soft, plump flesh on my thighs. Her legs, the long brown sinew with soft yellow hairs all the way down to her toes, loved my caress. Her flat belly, her height, and long cascade of hair: perfection. When she questioned me about my withholding, why I was reluctant, I had put it down to it being my first time, my tentative exploring. Yet I felt my own fruit ripen, sensed the possibility of what a bud can flower to.

Certainly more than with the last man I was with. Vishwam! How could I have done that! I squirm as I remember his suggested 'We may practise the special Tantra reserved for more promising students of the dharma'. Self-flagellation again and the whip is sharp. At least from the mental variety the gashes cannot be seen. Or can they?

Walking meditation seems so pointless. Walking up and down, up and down, then up and down again, on a small area of pathway, with the other participants just metres away. I experiment with walking very slowly, step by little step, watching the ground, amazed at the activity of ants and bugs living underfoot. Mostly I am confronted by negativity. *This is so pointless! What am I doing walking slowly up and down this grassy path!* The memory looms of the first course with Vishwam and the way I fell apart. I wonder in a panic if I'm doing the right thing after all. Perhaps it is all a mistake and meditation is just not for me.

Lunch is red rice, vegetables and salad – clean food. And of course I eat more than I need and the case against me builds inside. *Why are you taking more sticky rice? Well, it's delicious. Yes, but restraint is what is needed. This is a monastery, can't you get anything right?* I am pinned down inside myself, at my own mercy. For a brief moment I understand insanity.

The smooth flow of Steve's voice settles me again on the cushion. 'Vipassana is the modality chosen by the Buddha himself as the way to gain mastery over the negative aspects of mind: greed, anger, lust and jealousy. It is the personal purification of the mind. Choiceless observation of things as they are.'

My first personal interview with a teacher is with Steve. Jagged with exposure I sit before this man I barely know and as soon as he introduces himself and smiles, his clear eyes meeting mine, I'm filled with shame. I prefer to cry silent tears than to share how hard I am finding it, how self-berating I am. I do not know myself any more.

At the end of the ten days he shakes my hand. 'Be kind with yourself, be kind.'

Rosemary offers her own support. 'Take care of yourself, Judith, take care.'

I used to be the one giving such advice to others, supporting them in times of need, confident and sure of my role. I slink out of the monastery alone.

Released from the days of silent order I reclaim a sense of myself. I climb into the hammock, full of thoughts of Helene. Apart from my awkward sexual aspect we had fun. She was a good friend, easy company. I feel her absence. The scenes are flat, varnished with haze. It's an ache I just can't put my finger on, niggling and disturbing my peace. It visits with the tide, comes in waves, only to depart again, leaving the sands smooth and empty. Swinging in the hammock is not the best remedy. The head of weed is quickly consumed. I didn't leave my life in London to idle away my time, swinging in hammocks on lazy beaches. I came because I am on a quest, and until I can savour and visit that peace I know is there, somewhere, I'm not going to rest.

* * *

Wat Suan Mokkh is in the south of Thailand, an established monastery under the guidance of the Thai master Ajahn Buddhadasa. I arrive to find that the revered elderly teacher is very sick and unlikely to live. He is confined to his room under constant care and obviously not giving any audiences.

I had hoped that meeting an enlightened Buddhist master would dispel the darkness but it is not to be. I am given a room in the women's quarters, a besser-block cell with a small window, a bed, and a set of shelves. In the shared bathrooms, a trough of water stands in the centre and, Thai-style, we wash by scooping water from the trough with a bright plastic jug.

A loose daily program is set and we are expected to attend but nothing is obligatory. I find it easy to break the day with regular sits in the dharma hall. The monastery is set among expansive, forested grounds, cared for and nurtured. In the tradition of forest monasteries, nature is an integral part of the teachings. Butterflies as large as plates slide between the greens, dragonflies hum and frangipani trees drop heavenly scented flowers. Wild orchids flower on long stems and statues of the Buddha sit serene in a lily pond, the purple and blue lilies rising from the still water. The other westerners keep to themselves, and apart from an occasional brief, easy conversation, I am happy to be alone. It is easier, I realise. At night I shut the door to my besser-block cell and congratulate myself for managing another day of meditation.

The silent retreat begins the following week. My determination amazes me. Yet what else to do?

* * *

Across the main road and along a red earth path is the newly built retreat centre. I see banana trees for the first time ever. I have eaten bananas all my life and never known how they grew. The deep red velvet flower that hangs beneath the bunch I find exquisite. I walk behind two monks, their ochre robes in harmony with the earth. They carry an orange umbrella to shield them from the sun, and their shadow falls behind in a pool of coffee brown.

This retreat is easier. Perseverance has paid off. I try really hard to meditate, sitting as still as I can, concentrating on the technique being taught. I'm beginning to recognise the evening dharma talks, but I guess I need to hear this teaching over and over. I make it my practice to remain with my head bowed to the floor, avoiding eye contact with any of the other participants. *Ah well done, another day when you kept your eyes to yourself.* No sneaking smiles, or contact at all. I also gird myself at meal times. No, I won't be the one who is going up for seconds. Rather, I begin to moderate, each day taking less.

Every morning we have yoga and I love it. I am very flexible and have a natural ability for the postures. Since learning a routine with Vishwam I have kept up my own practice and do at least the sun salutation every day. Days pass by, I am suspended in this haven, and then it's over. I return to my cell across the road, back in the luscious surrounds of the original monastery. It seems to suit me here and I find a sense of wellbeing that I want to hang on to.

A woman joins me one morning as I put wet clothes on the line behind the kitchen. She has a few towels to hang. As she stands in the sunlight, her thick red brown hair shines. It's tied in a messy ponytail and strands have broken free and frizzle out at the sides, glinting almost gold. Ingrid is a gypsy and has the face of a fortune-teller, with wrinkles around her eyes and mouth, and small rolls of skin hanging like jowls. She wears an armoury of silver bangles; little shells and colourful beads dangle from tiny chains and anklets jingle as she walks. I wonder if she takes them off for the retreat time.

'Hi. You came before the last retreat. I saw you but you looked like you were hiding from the world and didn't want company.' She is smiling, watching me as I hang my shirt. 'My name is Ingrid, this is my home now.' She stretches out her hand and I shake it with pronounced formality. The breeze is picking up and billows a lungi between us. She parts it like a curtain and smiles again.

Ingrid loves her food, taking piles of sweet potato for lunch. It is very good, cooked with lime leaves and coconut milk. The kitchen nuns fuss over her and treat her like a child. She plays with them too and I notice she can speak some of the language. I imagine she is someone for whom laughter is a must. Later in the afternoon she joins me as I sit in the warm afternoon sun and tells me she is in love with the American monk who gave the discourse at night in the retreat.

'He is in love with me too, you know.' Her German accent somehow adds to the drama. 'We are waiting till the right moment to leave together. Now he has met me he wants to be rid of his robes. I have to be happy to just be here and see him every ten days for these retreats, full of silence, but my heart is full of yearning.' She gazes up at the hibiscus bush, dripping with red flowers. 'He writes me so beautiful love poetry.' Her voice trails to a hushed whisper. She is sure very soon he will be 'throwing down the robe'.

I have seen him, the tall American monk, with a thin face and pinched nose. His very blue eyes are made bigger by the thick round glasses that add to his regal air. I liked the way he spoke; he made the stories relevant for us and he was funny too. He had such a passion for the teachings, for the understandings he'd apparently taken all these years to master.

The other woman in the monastery with us is Kelly, a young bright Canadian, in her twenties and fresh out of college. A dedicated yoga practitioner, we meet in a covered pavilion every morning and practise, with the sweet perfume of frangipani flowers, their season almost over, wafting from the waxy yellow flowers that drop like a snowstorm from the trees outside. I pick the freshly fallen flowers for the altar in my room. I bring flowers each day for the pictures I have: one of Shiva that Babaji gave me, a couple of Tibetan deities, Green Tara, the goddess of compassion, and a simple picture of the Buddha himself.

Lost in this world of mostly women, my days simple and routine, removed from the world, I find the constant self-criticism ease. I realise one morning, while I'm walking back from the morning sit, that not one of my friends or family, anywhere, actually knows where I am. I smile and laugh out loud. And a moment later I decide to write to my parents. I wonder what they would think of the Buddhist teachings. I imagine my father would be inquisitive, might even enter into discussion, but it would not deter him from his strict Christian commitment. He'd think that to worship anything other than God in heaven, the God of the Old Testament, was a sin. No wonder when, as a teenager, I started to date boys, my mother pleaded with me to only date Christians. It would be challenging to have your daughter step out of the fold. My mother is less involved now with the Evangelicals. I am not sure why and must ask her when I am next visiting. I wonder when that will be. A few years ago she travelled in Thailand herself – took off, for a month on her own to visit with missionary friends living in Bankok.

They both would enjoy the nature here. I remember how much we loved being outside when I was a child, walking as much as possible. Mum took us badger watching and we'd build a hide so that at sunset we could sit in it, quiet as possible, and watch for badgers. We never saw one but we did see rabbits and pheasants and, one time, a fox. My mother was happy in nature, relaxed. I realise how difficult it must have been for her to be so tied to the house. I never really appreciated all that she did as a mother. Recently she has bought a sailing dingy. It is her love to sail in the river while my dad walks or sits in a deck chair marking exam papers. And as I see my father so clearly in my mind, I am swamped with bewilderment. I do not understand why I could have been so distressed, so confused, and I can only believe there is something desperately wrong with me. *How unworthy you are*, I hear myself say, yet the voice is not my own.

* * *

After two weeks the quiet is interrupted by another influx of westerners queuing up to register for the next retreat. On the day before the retreat begins I walk alone to the retreat complex, stepping outside the gates for the first time in eighteen days.

Wendy, the Australian woman recently ordained as a nun, asks if I can lead the yoga in the morning. I am surprised. *Me? You're asking me! If you actually knew me you surely wouldn't ask!* I smile serenely and casually agree, as if every time I stay in a monastery I am asked to lead yoga. Wendy is tough. It was Wendy who would check the rooms for anyone slacking during the last retreat and I had a feeling she enjoyed the task after I heard her dressing down another participant who had opted out of one of the meditations.

I teach what I learned with Vishwam. I wake each morning early, keen for the program. I add a relaxation at the end, a technique I learned while working with the dying. This is more like it! Having a role gives me confidence, a place to sit down within myself, a place to belong.

The dharma talks begin to inspire me. Every teacher brings a different slant, or maybe my mind is more receptive. Life *is* full of suffering, a constant grasping for happiness outside oneself. The constant measuring of experience – judging it right or wrong, good or bad, this or that. It's a stream of chatter from the crowd of commentators, a merry-go-round of emotion and thought. No wonder it took the Buddha a long time to attain enlightenment.

The retreat over, I move back to my room in the monastery. I am not ready to go anywhere. The monastery is busier; ten others also stay for further meditation practice. I hear a Swiss man mention Lucknow. My ears prick up and I move closer as he's speaking about a teacher he met there. I have a strong feeling that I will visit the teacher he is talking about and I find the courage to ask him the teacher's name.

'Poonjaji. He's a teacher of Advaita.'

I have no idea what Advaita is, but I want to go and see.

I spend my last week in this sanctuary fasting on papaya. I find it easy and enjoy the light-headed feeling. I notice the chatter in my mind is also a little quieter. 'Hah!' I joke to myself, 'maybe I can starve them out!'

Ingrid is still waiting. 'This is the last time I give my heart to a man! Why is it he keeps me hanging like a puppet on a string?'

Of course I cannot answer her but our goodbye is sweet. She hugs me tight. Her round mound of flesh feels warm and motherly.

'Goodbye, Judita. Come back again when India gets to your stomach!'

CHAPTER EIGHT

The Bodhi tree and the Buddha

'Peace is all around us – in the world and in nature – and within us – in our bodies and our spirits. Once we learn to touch this peace, we will be healed and transformed. It is not a matter of faith; it is a matter of practice.' Tich Nhat Hahn

Even as the plane touches down in Calcutta I can smell India. I roam as I wish, through dark alleys, crowded markets, along pavements awash with life. I eat in the many dhabas, open to the street; watch a shirtless cook wipe his hands on his dhoti, his chest sprinkled with sweat. The dhal and chapatti are always good and I drink the water wherever I eat and my stomach does just fine. I have had enough of buying bottles of Bisleri. I move through the crowds, my eyes averted and sure of my path. As soon as something interests me I pause, and within a second I am prey. 'Hello, madam! Yes you looking.' 'This best price. For you special price.' 'Madam! Madam! One rupee, one rupee.' The thin hand pulls my bag. 'One rupee.' 'Madam, you wanting hashish, best hashish.' 'Madam, rickshaw! Good price!'

Every street has a steady line of the homeless. A man sleeps on a pile of rubbish, and flies swarm. Kids shit then wash with water from a rusty can. Metres away women scrub blackened pots in a trickle of water while others collect cow shit from the road to dry in the sun. One moment enticing aromas from spices fill my nostrils, then a putrid smell of rotten flesh: a dead pig bloated and black in the gutter.

I laugh as I realise the wisdom of non-attachment to experiences, but already a beggar is locked on my heels. He is missing most of his nose and his skin is grossly pockmarked from leprosy. I dodge and weave to rid myself of his low, persistent, 'Madam, madam, madam, very hungry, hungry, madam.' I stop so suddenly he almost bumps right into me.

'Bhai, das rupee.' I put a ten-rupee note into the tin hanging from the stump of his hand. He is old and filthy. He doesn't exactly smile but his milky eyes twinkle a little as he gives the usual nod of the head. 'Who are you? What's your story?' I want to call to his retreating back, but he's gone in an instant, swallowed by this city.

A choked sun merges with the haze and is finally lost with the smog on the horizon. The bells take up the call. Arti, evening worship: a throng of worshippers, bells ring in rhythmic disorder as the street vendors and traffic carry on regardless. Loudspeakers crackle. The pujari hands out prasad, dots red on the bowed heads before him.

I stare at the image of Kali, her body black, a garland of orange and yellow marigolds and a red silk cloth wrapped around her shoulders. I pray to her to guide me through her land. Prayer is obvious when the gods are all around. My route is clear: Bodhgaya, where the Buddha sat under the Bodhi tree, 2500 years ago, for the cosmos to reveal its eternal truth.

*   *   *

Lamas sit on raised platforms. Ample bodies swathed in maroon, yellow hats with pointed flaps, like magicians conjuring spells as they chant from texts. Their rumbling recitation of prayer is as ancient as the mountains from where they have come. Beneath the sweeping limbs of the Bodhi tree a thousand candles burn. Monks sit in long lines, an undulation of maroon, as day after day pujas are held at this most auspicious site. The chai shops are full of westerners discussing the latest retreats and teachers. Tibetans come here for the winter too, setting up stalls to sell their jewellery and shawls, woollen hats and jackets. Buddhists from all over the world come as each Buddhist country has its own temple here to honour the life of the Buddha, Siddhartha.

Over a hundred westerners sit the retreat held every year in the Thai temple, led by an Englishman who was once a monk, Christopher Titmuss. My allotted space is in a two-bed kuti (hut), rather than the dormitories or line of mattresses along the outside verandah. Good start, I tell myself, the gods are kind once more. Surely a sign from above that I am on the right path. My roommate is Carla, an older Dutch woman, overweight and bustling with anxiety about the minimal conditions. Her voice is loud in the quiet of the temple grounds.

It is still an effort to sit for forty-five minutes. When the bell rings it is a relief. I look forward to sunset, perched on a flat roof where I can watch the smoke from charcoal burners rise to the sky.

On alternate days there is a small group sharing. 'I am finding it much easier than when I sat the first retreat in a monastery on Koh Phangan,' I say. 'I find I am tired a lot. It is still not easy to sit comfortably for more than twenty minutes or so. Is it really okay to just change my position?' As I talk my mind is saying: *Oh for God's sake, who cares. Just shut up!*

Sharda, the teacher, doesn't answer my question. 'What are the feelings when your body is uncomfortable? What are you feeling when you are tired?' Sharda is as I would expect a meditation teacher to be: calm and centred. She holds eye contact until I have to look away.

'I am feeling fine!' is my quick response. Sharda holds a space of silence for some moments then moves on to the next person. A neat and tidy German man asks about the perceived observer of thought and the depth of his question brings me another layer of shame. All the while the invitation is here. I let it pass like an unopened gift. Why am I not being honest? Here is the opportunity to share what is really going on.

*   *   *

Carla is annoying me. She snores loudly at night and at rest time or early morning she talks to me with whispered questions of no significance. 'You know if I can get toothpaste? I am forgetting to bring.'

I attempt to tolerate her, and convince myself to try harder, but she becomes a source of intense dislike till I can't stand the sight of her, fussing about, offering titbits. 'These beds are so uncomfortable!' she says as she stretches and groans. 'Is it time for the exercise now? Oh yes it is, look it's already 6 am.' I have become an extension of her inner dialogue.

Wow, look at you getting so worked up! You're really furious now, hey? my mind mocks as I try to practise loving kindness. What is it about retreats! I have a personality change the moment I sit on a round maroon cushion. I have returned to India full of excitement, sure of my path, and yet here I am again all scrunched up inside as soon as the gong for silence sounds loud and clear.

It isn't just Carla who is disturbing me. When I find moments of peace in my meditations I am all of a sudden swamped with a black sense of doom. Images of myself as a child come with devastating confusion. Why was he in bed next me? Why do I remember that I wore red pyjamas and how unwelcome his skin felt against mine? One night I stumble from sleep with the sense I am choking. I want to spit and scream and as I wake fully I find it hard to hold on to my sobs.

This evening, the dharma talk is on love. Christopher opens. 'Who has been experiencing love? Love in any form we understand. Would anyone like to share with us?'

Hands go up. Three people, one after another, give poetic renditions of feeling so much love for the roses and such, the perfection of nature and overflowing love for all the others on this retreat. The last person to share recites from Rumi: 'I am here, this moment, inside the beauty, the gift God has given, our love: I turn my face to you and into eternity: we have been in love that long.'

A hushed silence falls through the room. Christopher asks if anyone wants to share feelings of non-love and I am horrified to find my hand in the air. The only hand waving, like a red flag of danger.

'Yes! Please do share with us your feeling of non-love.' He smiles then looks away.

Squirming on the cushion, my voice shrinks to nothing. 'I have been feeling really irritated.' Have I done this?

'Yes? At what?' He turns to me.

'At someone on this retreat.' I shrink further and fear I'll collapse in a heap.

'How do you feel towards yourself while this irritation is being experienced?'

I know there are words inside somewhere. 'I try to do better.' Oh my God! My face burns. If ever that hole could appear and swallow me up it is now.

'How do you feel about yourself when this anger is there?'

'I am not angry!' The words almost singe as they fly.

'Okay, then when this irritation is there?' His voice is smooth.

'I am trying to not be irritated – and it isn't all the time.' I am caught. There is no back-pedalling now. The crack has been publicly exposed and I have no idea how to repair it.

Christopher is unrelenting. 'So when this irritation is happening – and if you don't mind I would suggest it is happening probably more often than not or you would not be sharing it here – you are expecting yourself to be beyond this feeling, or thinking that if you sit longer and squeeze your eyes tighter shut, the feeling may go away?'

My face is burning hot. My voice is small. 'I also feel irritated with myself.'

'Why are you not kind with yourself while this annoyance is happening?'

The ripples recede and the answer comes, reflected in the quiet.

'Because I don't love myself.' The words hit me like a bullet in the heart. *I hate myself, I hate myself, I hate myself.* If I had a dagger I would stab my own heart. When the evening talks finally wind up I slink as fast I can from the hall, back to my kuti, not daring to queue up for the evening hot drink.

It is a joke to think I can attend a retreat, meditate even. Voices in my head tell me I am no good, a worthless human being. A crowd follows me around, catching me unaware. Kicking me when I am already down.

I make an appointment with Sharda and just doing this is a relief. I need help. I have no idea how other people are doing. It looks like everyone else is cruising, loving the silence, themselves and all of it – everyone but me. The meeting is in her room. She has a small kuti and we sit facing each other on cushions on the floor. Sharda is a small woman with a genuinely sweet face. Her eyes sparkle and she wears an emerald blue scarf that reminds me of the ocean. On a shelf is a photo of an elderly man with a big smile. His eyes seem to hold mine.

'Who is this photo of?' I've barely sat down on the cushion before her.

'This is Poonjaji, my teacher.'

Goose bumps rise all over me. 'Is he the teacher in Lucknow?'

'Yes, he lives there now and gives satsang.'

I want to know about this man, Poonjaji. 'I have heard of him before. This is the first time I've seen his photo.' My eyes can hardly leave the image. 'I want to go to Lucknow. I want to meet Poonjaji.' It has been my plan since hearing about this teacher back in Thailand. Now it seems almost urgent. In fact all the fuss of these last days seems a bit insignificant. Maybe Sharda can just tell me a bit more about Poonjaji and I can go.

'Great,' says Sharda, 'you can travel with me!'

I anchor myself in my breath. Meditation teachers have it right: the breath is a harbour from the storm.

'Now how are you doing with this retreat? Your exchange with Christopher the other evening was very touching. Thank you for your honesty.'

I pause a moment and consider. Do I really want to expose myself to this woman, this neat and ordered and very kind woman sitting before me? I can barely cope with myself any more and I am not sure I want to open up the can of worms. I lift my eyes from the rug between us and look at her steady gaze. I'm surprised to realise she is genuinely interested. I take a breath and the sigh that escapes surprises me again.

'Look, I can't stand the woman I am sharing a kuti with. At first I was so glad to have a kuti and not be on the verandah with everyone

94

else but she keeps talking to me, stupid things, and she is driving me nuts. I am trying my best to not react and remain calm but I feel like a real failure.'

'What is she saying?'

'Oh stupid things like, "What time is it?" Then she answers for herself. Or yesterday she couldn't find her toothpaste. The other day she wanted me to get her some tea before it ran out and she wanted a shower first, or something. I don't know, she is just bugging me and she snores and I find myself really bothered by her.'

'You could have come and said something to me or one of the helpers. It is not fair that she is not respecting the silence.'

Her response takes me by surprise.

She goes on. 'It is intrusive when another invades your space. And she has been. Do not give yourself such a hard time for being so upset by it. Your feelings are as valid as hers. You have the right to set a boundary here.'

It had never occurred to me. A well of water weeps down my cheeks into my hands as I try desperately to cover my despair.

Sharda soothes with sounds and a gentle hand on my thigh. Tissues and cushions, I have heard, go hand in hand. Her sense of care unlocks the valve.

'I feel as if I am two different people. It started when I sat a retreat in McLeod Ganj last April. It wasn't a silent retreat but towards the end I started falling apart. We had to focus on ourselves at various ages. I felt so much pain in me. I don't know why. I couldn't see any image of myself. All I could feel was incredible sadness.'

'Mmm,' Sharda soothes again, reaching out her hand and resting it on mine. 'That sounds very difficult. Did you have good guidance from the teacher?'

I think about that for a moment. 'No I didn't.' Then I crumble again as I am filled with shame when remembering Vishwam. 'Well actually I didn't really talk to him about it.' I'm certainly not going to reveal that I had sex with him a few times. I cast my eyes down to the floor, wishing in a way I had never come. But then I look again at the photo of Poonjaji and at least I know my direction after the retreat is over. Maybe I can just leave early. Accept this time it didn't work out. Keep the memories of the monastery in Thailand instead.

'Sounds like you have had a bit on your mind. Thank you for coming and sharing it with me.' Sharda looks at me with such kindness it is disarming. The hut seems too small and I want to escape. I shuffle on my cushion but she isn't picking up the cues.

'Do you know why you felt so upset? Was there a reason that you felt such pain?'

'No, no nothing that I can think of. I had a relatively happy family, all normal as most families are. They were strict Christians and very religious. When I did a silent retreat in Thailand it happened again. I just felt like a mess emotionally and it is not how I am used to being. I feel confused about myself.'

Tell her, a small voice whispers, *tell her about what you remember.* The voice startles me. And I think to the other night when I woke almost in a panic. And how the memories of my father lying on my bed confuse and unsettle me. I feel a sweat build up in spite of the winter cool. I stare at her, my mind completely blank.

'This can happen. It is often not until we stop our usual routine and take ourself out of our comfort zone that the pains and traumas of childhood show up. We take great care to cover up our hurts because this is what we learned to do as a child. All I can say is to be very easy with yourself and practise as much loving kindness towards yourself as you can.'

Her gentleness is like a delicate perfume.

'You can come and see me every day if you need. It is why we are here. Let me tell you again that what you are experiencing is not uncommon. It takes a lot of courage to come and sit on a cushion, respond to bells and wake-up calls and remain silent with your thoughts for ten days. It's great you are here.' She leans forward towards me, rests her hand on my thigh. Her touch startles me again. I feel so completely and utterly unworthy and fall a little further into my inferno of shameful confusion.

*   *   *

Lucknow is an elegant city full of cream-coloured buildings left over from the days of the Raj. I book into the Chowdhury Lodge, a guesthouse that serves 'bed tea', or very sweet chai in a white cup with saucer and teaspoon, every morning at 6 am.

HWL Poonjaji is a robust man already in his eighties. He is known to most here as Papaji. Five days a week he comes to a house with a large hall to hold satsang. Satsang means 'meeting in truth'. Every morning, several hundred westerners line up in the cool air, waiting for the gates to open. A lot of the westerners are sannyasins from Pune, and the ashram of the now-dead Rajneesh, or Osho as he is known. I will stay two weeks, and already have a train ticket booked for Sikkim. I want to check out the monasteries there. Monasteries, I have decided, are where I should be.

There is a tangible presence in the room when Papaji sits with us all. He teaches Advaita, a non-dual philosophy. Self-inquiry is important, he says. He suggests we inquire: 'To whom does this thought arise?'

The day before I leave for Sikkim Papaji holds a small satsang for those of us who have been on the Bodhgaya retreat. The energy in the room is thick with silence. I feel a strong urge to be close so I move to sit by his feet. I have no choice. I look up at him and after a moment he glances down at me with twinkling eyes that seem so full of love.

'Yes?' he says with a playfulness that makes me smile. I stare into his eyes that are at once filled with light and bore into my own.

I ask: 'Papaji, who is looking at who?'

He laughs, with his light infectious giggle. 'This is a very good question!' His eyes dance and sparkle and a sense of peace and wellbeing overcomes me. I stay at his feet until the satsang ends. He smiles again at me as he stands to leave.

The next day at the railway station I find my train has been cancelled. I am not disappointed and book another ticket for a week later. In any case, it will still be cold in Sikkim.

I continue to sit at the back of the satsang house watching the scenes and listening to Papaji give his talk at the beginning of satsang. It is my favourite time. He talks of knowing your true self, that enlightenment is possible, here and now.

The following week I pack my bag again. Waiting on the platform at the bustling, chaotic railway station I remember sitting on the bench with Helene six months ago. I haven't heard from her for a while. Japan had not been as much fun as she had hoped and she had returned to Amsterdam and her lover and life. I remember too how strongly I felt pulled to Lucknow and how I had wanted to even leave the journey there and then. A sudden rush of feeling overcomes me as I remember too sitting before Papaji last week and the way he looked deep into me.

When the train pulls in I find that the carriage with my berth isn't part of the train. The station officer is unhelpful. 'Madam. This carriage not available.'

'But I have a ticket!'

'Sorry, madam. Not available. Train full already.' His face is expressionless, his head nodding slightly.

It doesn't take long to realise that maybe it is just not the time to be going anywhere. I surrender to Lucknow, the pollution, and westerners full of songs and questions. Five days each week I take a tempo, belching thick black smoke, to the suburb where satsang is held. There are several of us from the Bodhgaya retreat still here and we have formed a little group. After satsang we eat a thali, eleven rupees for a plate of rice, a bowl of dhal, and then six other tiny stainless steel bowls of different curry. Lucknow is a vibrant city, the full deal of northern India with chai shops selling the best samosa, markets with stalls of colourful vegetables, milk shops selling thick curd in clay pots, chunks of paneer and of course sweets. I mingle in the laneways of Nahri bazaar, squeeze past the large cow chewing garbage, then retreat back to the hotel when the crowds, the traffic, the stares and noise become too overwhelming. In the evening I stand by the small Hanuman temple across the road and watch as the pujari waves a lamp of flame and chants, ringing his bell with eyes half closed. All around, the chaos continues but I believe that in these simple acts the essence of India is held.

Satsang continues to give a sense of peace, even if it is only for the few hours in the morning. Initially, in the first weeks of my stay here, whenever I met with Sharda, the meditation teacher from Bodhgaya, my cheeks would redden and an immediate sense of shame crept over me in remembering our interview and why I needed to see her. She has left Lucknow now and it is a relief not to encounter her any more, to be reminded of that distress.

Papaji has a magnetism that is irresistible. I find my eyes watching him, an easy quiet in my mind as he speaks. His words fall on me like nectar.

The Guru is one who shows Light
And gives Peace to the devotees
Even without them asking for it.

This is how it is to be here in Lucknow. I dutifully show up at satsang house, but dutiful to myself, because every morning I awaken to a simple joy that I can again sit and bathe in his presence. I have found a shelter from the storm, yet every day I am reminded of the first Noble Truth of the Buddha – that in life there is suffering. Like a persistent rash that won't go away, I dwell on my failure, waiting for someone to say *Hey, aren't you the one who admitted to not liking yourself? Wow, how does that feel?* I stare at myself in the small mirror in my sparse hotel room, wishing again I had not sacrificed my hair. Yet when I sit in satsang and tune in to my breath, turn my attention to my self, a sense of wellbeing settles within me.

An older couple I met on the retreat in Bodhgaya also stay at Chowdhury Lodge. They have taken me under their wing. I am grateful they are here, holding my hand and keeping me connected. I know that if I become too solitary my inner world can be like a swamp, with unknown shapes lurking in the black water.

The other seekers I meet are not here for a holiday either. Most have a meditation practice and often at sunset the flat rooftop is dotted with people sitting quietly, watching the sunset. At dawn they do yoga, or chi gung. Lucknow is not a place to come to unless you plan to sit in satsang with Papaji.

The Presence of the Guru is Satsang. Only Satsang will take you out of suffering
Because it shows you the silence that you have always been.
Satsang is abiding as your self, not as 'I am so and so'.

Satsang means a place of seclusion, of Quietness. It is a place within your Heart.

Come to this Satsang naked.

By early March the mountains call. It is hot now in Lucknow and the time has been profound. I feel a sense of peace and wellbeing, stronger in myself. As if the hard work of meditation retreats and dedication to satsang is paying dividends. Sikkim suddenly seems unnecessary, another place to window shop in this spiritual marketplace. It is clear that I will go back to McLeod Ganj and this time my berth is here, the carriage attached to the train, and I am on my way.

---ᴡᴡᴏᴄᴇᴛᴏᴏᴛᴇᴏᴏᴡᴡ---

The orange flag

'In spring, hundreds of flowers; in
autumn, a harvest moon;
In summer, a refreshing breeze; in
winter snow will accompany you.
If useless things do not hang in your mind,
Any season is a good season for you.' Zen poem

Spring brings tight bronze buds on naked limbs. Delicate greens unfurl against the cold silver sky. The chill tingles in my bones. Rishi Bhawan is still empty from the long forlorn winter months. I feel a small rush of joy as I stand before this dilapidated house. Triund, the ridge below the mountain peak, still wears a blanket of snow, the peak itself a mottled white and grey.

I take the small room at the back of the house. It has a separate kitchen with a cold slate floor and opens to a sheltered patio where I can warm myself in the morning sun. In the market, I buy bread from the German bakery and apricot jam, rice, dhal, spinach and tomatoes from the vegetable wallah. I also buy candles and another picture of Tara, the Tibetan goddess of compassion.

There is a pile of wood by my door when I return so I light a fire in the fireplace to chase away the damp. I set up my small altar and place Tara's picture on the windowsill. I put the picture of Shiva next to the one of Papaji. As the damp air chills and mists float down through the trees I shut my door to the day.

*   *   *

He has remained in the attic of my mind but now steps clearly into my thoughts. I smile as I cross the wooden bridge. The stream is full with snowmelt, and the gate creaks as it opens. The garden beds are bare and I pause at the temple, fold my palms to the lingam. A smudge of incense still burns and the same sense of belonging allows somewhere inside me to relax. My soul knows this imprint.

Smoke curls from the roof just as it did six months before. 'Namaste!' I call and poke my head around the doorway. Babaji sits by the fire. He looks up as I enter. His face remains curt, then in a moment he speaks. 'Ho, ho! Namaste!'

I realise how much I have wanted this welcome, his recognition. 'Behtou, behtou!' [Sit, sit!] he tells me, gesturing with his hand.

The fire is neat, a small glow of flame under the pot. The tridents have fresh marigolds strung around them and the silvery ash is smooth. Babaji wears thick socks and a cream blanket around his shoulders. His beard seems longer and his hair is tied in a neat knot as if recently oiled.

'When you come?'

'Last week, Babaji.'

'Accha.' He is silent again and I am quick to fill the space.

'What are you cooking, Babaji?' The smell is like the forest, dank and fecund.

'This medicine. Leaf boiling boiling, tea coming. Good for body when cold time.'

'Winter time must be very cold. You have much snow?'

'Winter time is winter time.' He holds my gaze. 'Everything resting, much time for looking God, inside.' He places his hand over his heart. 'Much snow coming. Beautiful looking.'

'You learning some English, Babaji?'

He laughs his light laugh, flashing white teeth. 'One Israeli boy stay, speaking some Hindi. Me little English learning.'

I lean back against the whitewashed wall and tuck my legs beside me. The burlap sack curtain at the doorway lets the wind seep in and I pull my shawl tight.

Babaji takes a small pot from the shelf and throws in a handful of tea from a jar. He unwraps a cloth bundle and empties cardamom pods and cinnamon sticks into his hand. He breaks the tight pods open, crushes the black seeds between his fingers then tips the lot into the pot. Then pours water from the fire-blackened kettle and rests the pot on the fire.

'Chai piou?' [Tea drink?]

He pours milk from the kamandal by his side and watches the liquid rise as it boils then pours the chai into two stainless steel cups.

The chai is sweet and creamy and the cardamom is rich. Babaji slurps noisily and lights a beedi. He passes the packet to me and I take one. These little rolled up bits of tobacco leaf are hard to keep alight and after relighting it a couple of times I give up.

Babaji laughs. 'This Indian smoke. Sometimes smoking, sometimes no smoking.'

I let my unease vanish with the smoke. This is too good to be distracted by my inner chatter. It is six months since I sat on this earth floor. There have been so many images, experiences and emotions – stories grand and dismal. Yet here I am, in surroundings unchanged. Even the cat sits in her place on the window ledge. I'm invited in too – to sit within myself in that place of rest. To notice the chill as the breeze moves through, to hear the layer of sound as nature sings her song, a profound quiet that fits like a glove.

I rinse my cup then sit for a while longer. Time has no hold. No idle chit-chat, just sitting. Babaji sits with his eyes mostly on the fire. Every now and again he looks up.

'Tikhai, sub tikhai?' [Everything okay?]

'Sub tikhai,' I repeat. [All good.]

I have no idea how long we sit but the cat awakens and stretches before disappearing out through the sack door.

'Your country going?' he asks.

'No, I went to Thailand to make new visa for India.'

'Accha, Calcutta going?'

'Calcutta very big city! I saw many Kali shrines.'

'Kali place. You go Ramakrishna temple?'

'No. No I didn't.'

'Ah, very strong place. Ramakrishna number one Indian saint.' He nods and falls again to silence. I don't want to overstay my welcome for this first visit and decide to take my leave.

As I stand and arrange my shawl he looks up. 'Going?'

'Yes, Babaji, going.'

'Tikhai.'

'Namaste, Babaji.'

He nods briefly. 'You come sometime, eating time, afternoon time.' My first official invitation – and as I walk back through the forest I wonder why I left so soon.

The very next afternoon, late, I visit again. A cold rain falls and stings my warm cheeks. I hurry up the path through the garden.

'You no umbrella taking?' He tuts as I arrive with wet hair and my shawl too damp to wear. He fetches another. It smells of him: incense and wood smoke. The room is cosy with the burlap sack down and the fire burning free.

'Tikhai?'

'Tikhai, Babaji, tikhai.' I settle cross-legged. Babaji sits as he always does, smoking a beedi, glancing at me. A pot sits to the side of the fire and the aroma of cumin seeps unseen.

'You eating?'

'Thank you, Babaji.'

From the storeroom he fetches a bowl of flour then squats again. He pours water from his kettle, kneading the mixture with hands that are big and strong. He breaks the dough into little balls, places a chapatti plate on the fire and rolls them out on the wooden board, thick perfect circles. He puts one on the now hot plate and rakes glowing embers from the fire for the half cooked chapatti to rest against. After a moment the chapatti puffs and browns. His hands dance as they work. He is intent on his task until a pile of wrapped chapattis sit on the lid of the pot by the fire. He replaces the kettle, tidies the fire, takes the flour bowl to the tap and disappears outside.

Watching his routine soothes me. It is like watching an artist who has perfected their craft; the simplicity of his actions reassures me that all is in order. All is well. Ritual gives definition to the sacred. I hear the temple bell ring. Babaji returns with a stick of incense, sits again then waves it around the fire, murmuring, 'Om, Om, Om,' with his hand on his heart. Every action is precise. He breaks a piece of chapatti, spreads it with ghee and places it in the fire, then carefully throws a handful of sugar into the flames with a few more 'Oms'. The sugar flashes blue in the fire. With his palms together and eyes closed he prays, softly, as if the gods are near enough to hear. 'Hari Om,' he finishes.

If there is such a place as heaven, this will do it for me. Sitting by a dhuni – a sacred fire – with a sadhu about to serve me food, food offered to the gods first. I savour each mouthful – kidgeree, rice and dhal cooked together with cumin, turmeric and ginger. A spoonful of ghee on top melts to a pool and thick chapattis scoop the food into my mouth. Sitting here by his fire, I feel something of what I am searching for.

Babaji eats quickly.

'Chapatti more? Rice more?' he asks.

'Bas, Babaji, bas.' I finish up and take my plate to the tap. With a scoop of ash I clean the plate and lean it against the wall to drain. I take my place again as he puts the black kettle back on the flame.

'You like this sitting is better,' he tells me as I cross my legs. He sits on his heels, with his legs folded beneath him, his back straight as a rod. He nods as I do the same. 'This way sitting better for food stomach going.'

I smile. 'Babaji, you much English learning.'

'Accha?' He looks at the fire then adds: 'All for time pass. This doing, that doing, all for time pass.' His eyes again fall to the flicker of flame. After a moment he adds, 'Only for God looking. God looking, then no problem.'

Silence again settles all around. The kettle boiled, he again piles the fire with wood and the flames surge and sway in the cold breeze that comes through the small opening of window.

Day is losing its light to a moonless evening. 'Night soon coming,' I say. Time to go before dark descends. 'Thank you, Babaji, namaste.'

'Hari Om, Hari Om. Sometime you coming, no problem.'

I climb back up the path through the deodar pines, the wind cold and the night descending. It suits me, I note, this climate, and the freshness of the air and the smell of fires from the village below drifting in the trees. I reach Rishi Bhawan and unlock my door. A moment of fear rises in my throat as I realise my vulnerability at staying here alone. No doubt the other rooms will fill fast once the days warm. I pee outside on the grass and then shut the door. I make the fire, and sit watching the flames before turning in early for sleep.

*   *   *

As the days warm, the white-capped mountains shine in the sunlight. Long-tailed magpies court in the fig tree; butterflies dance and the wild clematis vine bursts into purple. Nature seems held in a spell of love. Once again I take to the hills and walk the path to Triund and back again in a day.

Sometimes I feel like I am carrying a wounded child on my shoulder, one who whispers in my ear, 'I'm hurting; take care of me.' I do not know how to respond and dump her on the ground but she trails after me, calling in the mist. I have decided to leave my emotional disturbances well behind. *I'm stronger than this*, I tell myself, and prove it in so many ways.

The moon traces her light longer into the night. I am careful to leave several days between visits. I do not want to presume my welcome. I can sense when the day is right. I find myself thinking of him and a little tug on my sleeve sees me planning my day for an afternoon visit.

I notice the lightness in my step as I walk down the pathway through the deodar trees.

Babaji squats on the verandah in the afternoon sun, a pile of leaves by his feet. He is sorting them and throws the stalks away into the garden. He greets me with a mumble, intent on his task. When the pile is just leaves – twigs and stalks gone – he bundles them into a cloth bag, tying it tight.

'Mountain place going, upside. This leaf good for breathing purpose. Sub tikhai? Judith, tikhai?' He looks at me then, waiting for my answer.

'Good, good,' I say, realising how seldom he uses my name. He pronounces it as 'Judit' and it reminds me of when I often have been known as Judi.

He settles himself on his haunches, bare feet splayed wide. His feet are calloused, his skin a rich dark brown, almost black.

'Babaji, you staying up the mountain?' He looks wilder than usual, his hair shaggy, and his feet are caked in dirt.

'Yes, yes, one cave place, sometimes liking going. Quiet time. Morning time today ashram coming. Now sun coming, western people coming and ashram busy hoijayaga.'

He lights a beedi, pulls his shawl around his shoulders, and sits back against the wall, a coconut bowl, a cushion and a book by the side.

'Tea drinking?'

I know by now it isn't so much a question. As I retie my scarf, I notice the holes and make a note to buy another. I have been startled to see my reflection recently: I am looking a little feral. My hair is thick and tufty again, seven months after shaving my head, and it's best covered with the scarf. It's still a surprise to see myself with short hair. I really liked my long curls. I stretch and Babaji brings the flowery brew of herbs. I let it cool and take a deep breath.

'Babaji, why do you have a Shiva temple?'

'This ashram place. Every ashram temple having.'

'Yes, but why a Shiva temple?'

'Mountain place is Shiva place. Himalaya.'

He pulls on his beard and finishes his tea, throwing the dregs in the garden. Looking at me he speaks in a flow of Hindi.

'Sab Bhagwan, sab Bhagwan. Mandir meh phir appka maan souchna hai Bhagwan kelier … sab karma yoga hamara zindagi sab Bhagwan kelier …'

'Babaji, some words I understood. You said: "Everything is God, everywhere is God's temple".'

'You Hindi learning is better.' He looks at me unblinking. 'This temple for God to rest. You looking temple, you mind thinking God. You cleaning temple then mind clean coming. This life, sadhu life, only for karma yoga, serving, plant potato. Garden work: then planting for God. No "me" doing this, doing that. Only for time pass. Bas. Only for time pass. All is God. My life – only for God. Tat Tvam Asi.' These last words – *Tat Tvam Asi* – he speaks slowly, carefully. He places his hand over his heart, as he tends to do, and mutters a few 'Oms'. 'Tat Tvam Asi – you know meaning?'

I remain silent.

'You are "That". This all you need,' he says.

The sun casts long shadows, withdraws its warmth. The air chills. 'You eating, tikhai?'

'Sure, Babaji.'

'Mountain subze eating, body strong feeling coming.'

I follow him to the dhuni room. He knocks embers from the glowing log, arranges small sticks and in a moment a flame springs up. The pot in place, he adds spices and oil, stirs, then throws in a handful of dhal and replaces the lid. From the storeroom he brings earthy potatoes. He washes them at the tap and chops them into small pieces.

'These potatoes from your garden?'

'Ha. Garden growing.'

He throws them in the pot.

'You eating food from own garden place then medicine food eating. Food eating from here there then body sick. Garden place full energy stay inside. No truck riding, other place coming. This no good. This world place too much problem. People no care where eating food. Here, there, this, that. No. Me eating garden food. Sattvic food. Body happy.'

His gaze falls to the fire and he is quiet. This shared silence is a new experience. Similar to sitting in satsang in Lucknow, but more personal, intimate almost. Relating is usually based on talk, connecting through words, filling in the spaces. This connection is all about silence, the long gaps between words. Of course I never had a friendship with a sadhu before and I suspect that all sadhus like to wear silence as Babaji does. He disappears inside himself, motionless and serene. Accepting the invitation, I revert to techniques I learned on retreat. I try to be fully present to this. I relish this time of simple sitting. Breathing in, breathing out; the quiet reward.

Babaji never speaks while eating. I keep my gaze on the flame. It is my anchor. The chapattis are thick and I guess made of cornflour or 'makhi atta'. The meal is a slop of dhal with greens and potatoes.

Dark already plays shadowy games as I wash the plates using ash from the fire. I scrub at the blackened pot with a piece of coconut husk. It takes a lot of scrubbing to get the fire-black off. I sit again and drink hot water, his custom after eating.

'You torch taking?'

'No, Babaji.'

Reaching into his box he passes me his torch.

'Chandra ma, some light giving also.'

The moon is halfway to fullness, silver in the clear night sky.

'Namaste, Babaji, thank you.'

'Tikhai, tikhai.' He almost waves me away with his hand.

The batteries fade and die not far up the path. Patchy moonlight falls in pools. I stumble in the darkness, and concentrate on finding my night eyes, letting my gaze be soft and sure. I know if I walk with complete presence and intuition I will find my way.

* * *

The day after full moon sees me almost skipping down through the forest. The first rhododendron bushes are beginning to flower, adding a promise of red to the greens.

No smoke curls from the roof, the sack cloth hangs listless at the door. I pull it back anyway and there is Babaji lying on blankets on the floor, wrapped in a shawl. I stare, unsure, afraid even. 'Babaji! Babaji,' I call.

He opens his eyes. 'Ah, Judit. Come. Mushkil hoijayaga.'

'What happened? Are you sick?' I have to hold myself back; the impulse is to rush to his side, hold his hand even.

'Accident coming.'

He pulls the blankets back to reveal his shin wrapped in bloodstained cloth.

'Wood chopping, wood flying and here inside going.'

His leg is swollen, red and inflamed. 'Too much pain. No walking.'

'Can I take this cloth off?'

He leans back on his makeshift bed. 'Never before this,' he says. He had been chopping wood when the accident happened. The milkman heard his call and helped him get comfortable. 'Some opium eating and pain away going.'

I peel the wad of cloth off gently. A piece of wood about an inch thick has embedded itself in the bone, like an arrow. The shinbone is exposed. I wish I had antiseptic, a sterile gauze and bandage.

'This bowl fireside place. You see? This leaf medicine inside.' He groans as he sits himself up.

'Babaji, first this cleaning. This wood piece is still in bone. It has to come out.'

The wood chip is splintered. Enough is still outside to get a good grip. 'Babaji, how much opium did you eat? I have to take this wood out. I have antiseptic ointment at Rishi Bhawan. Let me get and I will come right back.'

'No, no, this leaf doing!' he insists. 'This leaf me giving.'

'Babaji, this wood piece will make a bad infection. It needs to come out.'

'This leaf medicine putting and wood chello. You helping, tikhai.'

It is pointless to argue. I pass him the bowl and he scrunches cloths in a wad over the wound. I tie it tightly as a bandage. At least the leaves will stop anything sticking. He straightens his leg, wincing as he moves.

'Babaji, you have to let me take that wood piece out!'

'Out taking more problem coming.'

The opium may have worked for the pain but I wonder if it is clouding his reason. It's clear he will not agree.

'Babaji, shall I make you tea?'

'You fire doing?'

'Of course!'

I rekindle the fire with little sticks from the pile, grateful that the flames catch hold in an instant. I stare at his leg. Infection is a possibility and if a bone becomes infected it can be nasty and very painful. I wish he had let me clean it at least. I hope the leaves work as a poultice and can draw the wood out. If it hasn't dislodged by tomorrow I will insist.

'Babaji, tomorrow this wood still inside, you let me take out, or try at least.'

He leans back on the cushion and his eyes have a far away gaze.

'You chai making, tikhai.'

I take the spices from the tin and brew a pungent chai, adding extra sugar to his. He may be in shock from the wound. But his eyes are closed and he looks serene, half asleep almost. Then I remember he has eaten opium and the medicine is doing its work. I set the chai quietly by his side. He winces again as he props himself up on his elbow.

'Can I get a pillow for your back?'

He doesn't seem to understand and slurps at the tea in noisy sips. 'Bahut meeta. Accha, hai!' [Very sweet, good.]

He falls back into a stupor. I smooth the ash around the flame then take a couple of bigger logs and place them carefully over the embers. I want to build the fire up, to warm this room for the evening. The fire is sacred to sadhus. For those that wander from place to place, the dhuni becomes their temple. To blow on the flame would be unclean.

I break the small sticks into tiny pieces and it works; a flame takes hold, greedy to burn. Babaji stirs again after what seems like a long while. He needs to pee and tells me to fetch a bucket from the shower place. I bring it to him, unsure of how to help, but then just take myself outside.

'Babaji, in England I am a nurse.' I want to make him feel comfortable. Or maybe I want to make myself at ease. I take the bucket to empty.

'Nurse very good. Mind happy coming,' is all he says, unconcerned with my task. He rubs his foot a while, kneading it with his fingers. He is muttering under his breath and settles himself slowly back against the cushion.

I sit by the fire, keeping the flame low. I love to do just this: to have a fire to tend and watch. It is another day where the clouds hang low, folding us in their damp. A thin suggestion of light falls through the little window. I step outside and stretch. A bird calls in the forest, over and over, and the trees are dark smudges in a collage of greys.

Babaji props himself up as I come back in. It is so cosy now, with the fire burning low, a smoky scent of pine, of juniper, a haze hanging in the dim light. He waves away my offer of help.

'Beedi smoke?' He throws me the packet.

He speaks mostly in Hindi. 'This body bahut mushkil hoijayaga, opium accha lagta maan kush, hai.' [This body big problem coming, opium good feeling, mind happy.]

He's so funny I have to smile. His peculiar mix of Hindi and English, the lilting way he speaks, lying under his blanket complaining a little.

'Babaji, you hungry? I can fix something for you.' He has obviously not eaten all day. Day is rapidly merging with night and thoughts of returning home pull me to action.

'No. Sleeping now is good.'

'I'll come back in the morning.'

'Thank you, thank you.'

*   *   *

Before the sun is up and over the mountain I am there. He is sweating, even in the cold of early morning, and in a lot of pain.

'Wound accha?' It is swollen and oozing yellowy pus. The piece of wood, at least a couple of inches long, has been pushed out and I show it him, relieved I will not have to insist on taking it out myself.

'Tikhai out coming, now leg good coming.'

'Very good, Babaji. The leaf has done its job.'

The bone is still exposed. He has used neem leaves – well known for healing properties – and ginger root. I put a wad of it over the wound and bandage it up, then roll up a blanket and elevate his leg.

'It is good for the blood flow,' I tell him. It is obviously painful; his leg is hot and the swelling reaches his foot. 'Babaji, maybe more opium eating?' It is the only painkiller he has but still I smile at my boldness.

'Opium accha hey. This box you passing.' He points at a wooden box. It is heavy as I pass it over. He rummages around, and finds a piece of opium wrapped in plastic; it's gooey and black. 'Doud garam banau chinni kesaat.' [Warm the milk and add sugar.] He breaks me off a piece.

'Eat, eat,' he says. 'Garam doud ki sat, phir pet accha hai.' [Explaining that drinking warm milk protects the stomach.]

Me eating? I say to myself. Not sure. Oh why not, I could do with a little reality escape. Rishi Bhawan now has other travellers staying. Others who like me create a home in the dilapidated place that still has enough charm, but only just. The company is welcome, passing chats, at times sitting under the fig tree where someone has a drum or a didgeridoo. It is then that the insecurity snakes up, the fragile split within myself, a paranoia almost that my deformity will be noticed. Yet I am not sure what exactly that deformity is. I wear this eggshell persona all too easily, but it's as if it is lurking in the shadows, waiting for a chance to take the stage.

I break what he has given me in half. 'Little for me, Babaji.'

'You little eating, me little piece eating.'

I eat my piece and the taste is intense. The milk is warm, sweet and creamy.

'You no eating this before?'

'No, Babaji.'

Though I had. Years ago on my first trip in India, on a train ride in the south, my friend and I were given some by another passenger, 'to make the journey pass more quickly'. I can't say it did. Time took on its own meaning as sounds and sensations poured themselves into a different mould altogether.

The morning slows and the sweetness lingers. A light drizzle sets in, just enough to make music on the slate roof. The cat curls up on Babaji's blankets. The opium has brought a delicious dreaminess and a sense of all being well. Babaji speaks now and again: 'This body problem. Atman inside, no problem.' Atman is the Sanskrit word for the soul.

I rest against the whitewashed wall. My body feels heavy and light at the same time. The fire trickles orange into the grey. Shadows define their form and dance.

Hours later I stroll down to the village for beedis and sugar. The forest is alive with precise patterns. I notice the mossy banks and the way the greens shine with an ethereal light. Indents and smooth arches in the roots of the deodars come alive, the world of gnomes and elves not confined to storybooks after all.

When I return, the milkman's wife is sitting in the doorway smoking a beedi, talking rapidly to Babaji. He is peeling a root with a knife, breaking it into little pieces that she then pounds in the grinder. When she passes the powder back, he tips it into his hand and drinks it down with a glass of warm water from the kettle.

'This local medicine,' he tells me when she has gone. I didn't exist at all when she was here. I slid effortlessly into the shadows, unsure of my role with a local at his side.

I want to re-dress his wound but he says no. We drink a chai and I notice the bundle of chapattis the woman has brought. 'Babaji, you want to eat something?'

'Opium eating, no hungry feeling coming.' I agree.

'You some temple work do? Two days no cleaning.'

In the stillness of dusk and with a late bird calling up above, I take the broom and sweep the floor, the steps. I fill the little clay oil lamp and renew the wick. I dust the lingam with my sleeve and replace the flower with a white dahlia, balancing it on the flat lip of the yoni where the snake curls. I shake out the red cloth, ring the bell and, as I light the incense, I quietly sing, 'Om Namah Shivaya.' I survey my work. Greatly satisfied, I return to Babaji.

It is cosy in the room and I put another log on the fire, piling the embers to a glowing cauldron of orange.

'Chapatti warm, tikhai. This storeroom one jam finding,' he instructs. 'Little eating tikhai.'

The chapattis I find are thinner than Babaji's.

'Thick chapatti, pukka sadhu roti. This household chapatti,' he explains. The dog appears right on cue and I throw him a chapatti. I spread some plum jam on ours, and we eat a couple each.

Babaji needs to pee but he can hardly stand. He leans on me and hobbles to the doorway. I bring the pot and walk down the path a little to give him privacy. Rain falls again and the day is gone. I tidy his pile of blankets, remake the makeshift bed and help him settle.

'You night time here sleeping is good.'

I'm not even surprised. 'Sure, Babaji.'

'You this room sleeping, blanket inside.' He gestures with a nod of his head to the door off the dhuni room.

The door sticks a little as I open it. A light bulb hangs from a wire. The yellowy light reveals a low bed with a mattress, shelves made from a plank of wood balanced between bricks, three half burnt candles and a box of matches. On the wall is a picture of Shiva, standing tall and fine with long dreads and snakes wrapped around his neck. I open the window a crack to let in air.

I return to the fire to cover the coals with ash. Babaji has told me that his fire never goes out. I step outside, pee around the back of the ashram and say goodnight to the darkness. Babaji is nearly asleep. I pull the sack cloth down over the door and head to my room, curling myself up under the coarse blankets that smell of smoke and mustiness. I sleep soundly all night and wake early to Babaji coughing. Then spitting, coughing, clearing his throat. It is cold, and dawn is barely a suggestion.

It's too early to start the day so after stepping quietly outside I return to the room and sit. I wrap the blankets around my shoulders and settle to my vigil. Sounds within the silence, the stillness of the ashram all unfolding. The clang of a milk bucket as the family behind the ashram milk their cow, words exchanged, and someone calls in the dawn. Babaji coughs again. I get up, stretch, and begin the day.

Babaji falls back on his pillow with closed eyes. He seems to be chanting under his breath and takes no notice of me. The quiet is welcome and I stay with the breath, counting to four with the in-breath, then to four with the out-breath, then another four before breathing in again.

Babaji stretches, yawns loudly and utters a few 'Oms'.

'You chai banau … tikhai?'

'Tikhai, Babaji.'

'Leg too much hurt. This no good. Much problem leg, no good coming.'

I cannot start my day without tea and it seems he is the same. After chai is sipped and finished I check his leg and it looks no worse. I clean it and make another neem leaf poultice. The swelling has gone down. It is still an angry red around the wound and pus has built up again over night.

'Babaji, I think you won't lose your leg. It's going to get better.'

For a moment he looks alarmed then laughs when he sees my smile. 'You accha, aadmi. Accha hai.'

I'm glad he thinks I'm a good person. His words give a small flutter in my heart. I add extra spices, split the tight green cardamom pods to extract the black seeds, and let them simmer in the boiling milk to take full advantage of their flavour. He sips and slurps in silence. I wash the cups, sit again by the fire, then worry that I am presuming the position too readily and move to sit against the wall in my favoured spot.

'You my room going and book taking. Hindi learning book. This book you looking and here bring.'

The door is not locked but it's bolted and hard to open. The room has a feel of quiet, a place where activity is kept focused and exact. Along the back wall is a low altar, a plank of wood resting on bricks. A small Shiva lingam sits in the middle of pictures of Shiva. A bundle of incense lies on the altar, matches, a coconut bowl and an opened packet of beedis. His bed is a mattress on the floor with a blanket folded. On a rope strung by the window hang a couple of orange lungis and a shirt. A pile of herbs dry on newspaper, and leaves, bundled, are drying upside down. On another shelf sits a row of books. I find his Hindi learning book and another on Shiva by Swami Shivananda. I dust them and carry them like they are treasure.

Settled on the verandah I start to read. *Shiva is a magnificent god, abiding as the supreme being of Sat Chit Ananda: truth, consciousness, bliss.* The words satisfy me like cool water on a hot day. Satiated, I put the book to one side. The orange temple flag waves like a wand of colour. The rose bush in an old rusty tin has three buds ready to bloom. Small birds dart and flit and a dog barks nearby. A man and a boy pass on the path to the village. The deodar forest stands silent. I consider Babaji and a sadhu's way of life. A life of restraint and discipline, a life lived for God. When he speaks of the mind, his mind, it is as if it is somehow separate from him. 'Mind be mind. Me inside Atman,' he says. 'No me doing this, me thinking this. All for God, bas. My job only for "Om Namah Shivaya".' It is as if he roots himself firmly in the earth of God's garden, and all around him life buds and flowers, and changes with the seasons.

It's a couple of days since I ate a proper meal. And now that Babaji's leg is healing, he could use nutrition. I stand, stretch and head to the fire.

'Babaji, shall I cook some food for you?'

'Me no eating. You something cook and eating.'

I don't dare attempt to make chapattis, although I often do, but cook kidgeree – rice and dahl together. The spices I can find but I have to explore the storeroom for rice and lentils. The cupboards are old and need a good clean.

'You something cook, me little eat. Fire cooking no problem?'

'I always cook with fire, if I can,' I say. 'Sometimes I live with only a fire and, anyway, to look at the flames is my favourite thing.' I notice I feel proud to say this, eager to share something of myself. He watches me and says nothing.

With the kidgeree cooked and left to relax after all that boiling, I tidy the fire and smooth the ash. 'Shall I offer the food?' I am unsure of what to do next.

'Doing is tikhai, not doing is tikhai,' he says. I will take any opportunity to partake in his ceremony. I light a stick of incense and serve a small spoonful of rice into a katori, a stainless steel bowl. 'Om, Om,' I murmur as I offer the food first to the flame of fire that has cooked it.

Babaji has tiny beads of sweat pricking his forehead. I pour water for him to wash his hands. 'Me torra torra eating.' I serve him just a little but he hardly eats a thing. 'This outside put, kutta eating,' he says when finished and winces as he leans to pass the bowl.

I put the scraps out for the dog. I wash the plates and tidy up, return the room to order and calm. I am not someone who needs order but it pleases me now to pay attention to detail. I put more wood on the fire, wrap a shawl around my legs, straighten my back and take my seat within myself.

I stay for the next two days. Each day I attend to the temple at dawn and dusk, ringing the bell a little longer each time. Each day I tend to his leg. Babaji teaches me the Gayatri mantra. 'Gayatri mantra powerful mantra. Morning time, when sun coming, this mantra saying.'

With his permission, I write on the inside back cover of the Hindi learning book as he pronounces each word: 'Om Bhubhuvah swaha – tat savitur varenyum – bargo devasya dimihi – dhio yonaha prachodiat.'

We repeat each word together, slowly. 'What is the meaning, Babaji?'

'This mantra meaning you book looking.'

On the third morning it is already light when I awake. Dawn breaks into birdsong; yellow light appears in the east. Babaji sits in his place at the dhuni. His leg is outstretched beside him.

'Namaste, namaste!'

'Baba! Your leg is better!'

I squat down by the fire, pleased to see him up.

'Aah, slowly, slowly, good coming. One stick taking and going, no problem.'

The wound is definitely better, the infection clearly under control. If the sun is warm later, he can uncover it and let the air and sunlight help the healing. As I sweep the temple, I know my stay has come to an end and I fall from the heights these days have given me, free fall back to earth.

Babaji is trying to pull himself up, balancing with his stick. He steadies himself before hobbling to the doorway. He shooes away any offer of help and gingerly manoeuvres down the step then hobbles along the path. I watch him limp and curse. He can hardly bear any weight. He washes at the tap, combs his hair and beard, and places the dot of sandal paste between his eyebrows. I will stay for breakfast then head home.

He puts the kettle back on the flame, squeezes a lemon into a couple of cups then pours hot water, mixing in a spoonful of sugar. 'Today no eating. Opium eating then body resting is good.'

My role is over.

'Roti lau,' [Bread take] he commands. He has warmed one on the fire and spread a generous dollop of ghee. He passes it to me. 'Eat! Eat!'

I chew the roti and sip the lemon water. I eat slowly. Not even chai this morning.

'Okay. Babaji, me chello!'

'Tikhai. Dhanyabadji. Hari Om.' He smiles up at me, leg outstretched, stick to one side. I gather my things from the room and pull back the blankets: my departure as sudden as my arrival.

Walking back up the path through the deodars I feel like I am re-emerging from another world: a sanctuary of silence where I had a purpose in my day and company that thrills. There is a mysterious aura to Babaji. A sense of all being well that calms me. There is a beauty and grace in all he does – even with a hurt leg – that pleases me. He wears that same mantle of peace I had sensed in Henry. Yet with Babaji, it is like a coat he has worn forever.

Rishi Bhawan is quiet, the morning still young. I throw open the creaky window to let in the pine-fresh air. I sweep and tidy, and heat a pan of water for a warm bucket bath. A group of black and silver languor monkeys pass by in the trees. The mountains are visible; patchy snow still hugs the prominent triangular peak but Triund is bare.

I light incense and sit by my makeshift altar: the photo of Shiva and of Papaji, a few stones and crystals around the Buddha statue I bought in Bodhgaya. It seems to me that Shiva is a way to attain what Papaji is talking about: that God is within and all there truly is, is consciousness. I take the photo of Papaji and hold it. On the back are his words: 'The Devotee, the true devotee, IS the heart of the divine.'

And, from the Ashtavakra Gita, a small book of scripture: 'I am without beginning, middle or end. I am never bound. By nature I am pure and perfect. This is my firm conviction.'

I know meditation is a vital key. I pick jasmine from the creeper in the fig tree. The buds are still closed, awaiting the sun. I place them around the photos, then sit and pray to know God.

* * *

A creamy scar on his leg is the reminder of days spent wrapped in his world. One afternoon a man and a woman sit on the verandah. Newly arrived from America, here to sample some of what I too am searching for.

'Yes, this is our first time to India. We are here to walk in the mountains and hopefully learn yoga.' They are newly married and take the room next to Babaji's.

Babaji is quiet with more company, often declaring, 'Me no English,' when asked a question. He tends to the fire or just sits still. Silently watching over the evening meal, he stirs the bubbling pot and rolls the chapattis. It is early May and tourist season. I miss the spacious availability of Babaji yet I don't need words. All his rooms are full now and he watches the chatter.

I visit just after dawn, the sun yet to peek from the mountain. I take my place by the fire. Babaji greets me as if every day is a first. Nodding and smiling. 'Behtou, behtou.' Falling again to silence. The ashram wakes and the dhuni room fills.

'Breakfast making.' He stirs a pot of porridge, throws in raisins, a few almonds. No more chapatti or leftover rice for breakfast. His attention and care to all that he does flavours every mouthful.

Spring falls to summer with skies so blue I want to reach and touch them, a sprinkle of gold dripped on all creation. My visa will expire in one month. It is already June and the days are washed in warmth, rejoicing with birdsong and wild flowers. I have been away eighteen months. Time to go home for a visit and, of course, renew my visa for India.

He sits on the verandah for the afternoon sun. He has his spot against the wall where he can reach into the garden or watch the blue butterflies land on the sunflowers. The afternoons are for sitting, 'letting mind go to sleep'. He oils his hair with coconut oil, and takes off his t-shirt to feel the sun. Malas lie against his chest, flecked with hair. The Bhagavad Gita is by his side. His presence, his company, fills me with peace. Sometimes I worry that I visit too often, but these thoughts vanish and my disquiet disappears as he offers a pearl. 'This Atman, God inside, no wanting. No liking this, but not liking that. Atman inside knowing – all no problem, no problem. Only mind making problem.'

For the evening meal there may be six or seven westerners, some awkward on the floor, unable to sit cross-legged for long; others are like me, comfortable sitting and at ease eating with their fingers. The silence is broken with laughter and chatter. 'Babaji, you are such a good cook! What is in this?'

He laughs shyly and gives his usual answer: 'Me no English understand.'

The garden is replanted and dahlias stretch towards the sun. Bushes of orange and yellow marigolds grow among the potato and radish crops. He makes strings of flower malas to hang over the entrance to the temple or on the trishul by his fireplace.

As I take my seat against the wall, he barely looks up, but always a 'Namaste'. I want to tell him my plan. 'Babaji, me humara desh jana.' [I am going to my country.]

'Accha? Khub jana? [Yes? When are you going?]

'Dho upter,' [Two weeks] I say, happy I have these little bits of Hindi. The cat sidles up the steps and sits by my side, licking her paw. My stomach tightens and eyes moisten. This haven has become home. This ashram, Babaji and his simple ways, is a place where I sit comfortably within myself. I think of the expression 'Home is where the heart is'. The ashram is a place I feel my heart.

'You country going, no India coming?'

'I go to England then come back. I want to see my family and I need new visa for India.'

'England same like India?'

'England! No, Babaji, very different. In England there are not so many people and the streets are more clean.' It isn't that though. How can I explain? Babaji is lighting a beedi and takes a pull before speaking; smoke streams out with his words.

'Same sky, same prakriti. This God's world and Atman is everywhere.'

'True, Babaji. And the grass is also green in England and birds sing and it rains and the sun is the same sun that shines here in your garden.'

Babaji chuckles. My concerns evaporate. 'Chai piou?' he asks. Of course, it is all so simple really.

My Guru H.W.L. Poonjaji, known as
Papaji to his many devotees

Rishi Bhawan, where I stay in the hills above Mcleod Ganj.
Babaji's ashram is nestled in the valley behind the house.

Babaji by his dhuni

Babaji in the ashram garden.

Babaji

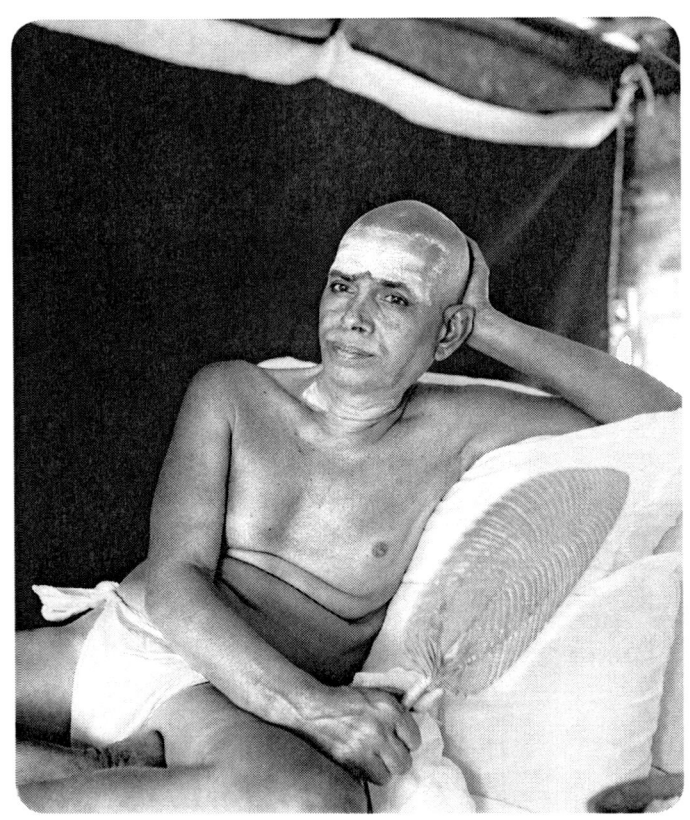

Sri Ramana Maharshi, the great saint of Arunachala

CHAPTER TEN

—⁓⁓∘⦿⦿∘⁓⁓—

Returning

'If there is peace in your mind you will find peace with everybody. If your mind is agitated you will find agitation everywhere. So first find peace within and you will see this inner peace reflected everywhere else. You are this peace! You are happiness, find out. Where else will you find peace if not within you?' Papaji

England is neat and tidy, ordered and empty. White sheep dot the verdant green fields and there is a lullaby of sounds as bleats and calls mingle with birdsong. Clouds race their shadows over gently undulating pasture.

My parents live in quintessential England. Creamy sandstone walls enclose yellow stone cottages with window boxes spilling purple and pink petunias. Hollyhocks and roses adorn neat, manicured gardens. Elegant horses graze in paddocks and villages nestle amidst narrow country lanes. The Cotswolds are home to the wealthy. Park-like estates with wrought iron gates and golden stone homes surrounded by gardens bursting with flowers. Old oak, chestnut and weeping willow – the beauty of the trees of my homeland amplified by the magnificence of summer.

'Darling! Darling, is it really you?' My mother almost suffocates me in her embrace. 'Let me see you! Oh darling, it's so good to have you home again!' Her face is rosy and tears mist her steely eyes.

'The great traveller has returned! "Is there anyone there? said the traveller! Knocking on the moonlit door!"' My father strikes me as childlike and eccentric as he hops from foot to foot in his obvious delight. He quotes from a favourite poem of my childhood. He is a great source of poetry, his genius brain retaining hundreds of lines of the classics that he memorises as he cycles each day to school to teach advanced maths.

'Here I am!' I stand in the kitchen with my short floppy hair, and my green and red skirt, which I have sewn myself, trails to the floor.

We sit in deck chairs in an English country garden. Pots of velvet pansies stand as art works on the patio. After a moment I sit on the grass, still slightly damp. It is one of the things I have difficulty readjusting to – sitting on chairs all the time. A family of blue tits perch on the wire and provide a distraction. Poppies in the field beyond the garden wave waxy red heads against golden corn, ripe and perfect. I miss chapattis dunked in sweet milky chai.

'Why don't you get a proper hairstyle while you are home?' my mum asks. 'You could look nice with a proper short hair cut. If you don't mind me saying so.'

I stay for seven weeks in England but cannot find a purpose. Perhaps it is more than this – more that I cannot find myself here any more. I left my homeland to 'find myself' in India, yet as I sit here in this green and pleasant land, I worry I may have lost myself completely instead. I left eighteen months ago, believing I was from a normal family who ate big lunches together of nut loaf and roast potatoes, blackberry and apple crumble, while wearing paper hats from Christmas crackers containing lame jokes and little plastic gadgets. This same family feels alien now – parents, and a sister who has for now, it has been tearfully explained, cut herself off from the family. Apparently she has recently sent a letter explaining she no longer wants contact. My mother is devastated and my father bewildered. Surely not in my family. And where does this all leave me?

It seems the only reason to be here is to renew my visa for India. It's as if a current pulls me and I cannot rest anywhere. I dream of walking in the mountains and sitting by Babaji's dhuni. It is to the mountains I will return but first I want to sit in satsang again. Here in England that all too familiar feeling of deep distress has reappeared. I cannot help but fall into chaotic confusion whenever I look at my father. I find myself studying him as he washes up, or carefully cuts up his meal before eating. I want to find a clue, a suggestion of anything to make sense of what I have been remembering. But all I find is an eccentric school teacher, admired by many, who attends church and sings in the college choir, is up early each day to say his prayers. Who clearly adores me and is still so affectionate. Yet I squirm as his lips brush my cheek in a morning kiss. My father loves to walk, and often after supper he and I stroll around the village where my parents now live. The formal gardens and elegant homes, the overwhelming neatness, accentuates my own internal chaos as clearly as sun and shadow. He swings his arms and recites poetry to me and as we pass another walker, or someone in a garden, he calls out a cheery 'hello, lovely evening'. He is a man who lives each day with an almost childlike enthusiasm, at times slapping his own hand declaring, 'What a naughty boy I am.' The effort of pretending all is well wears me down.

Whatever it is I am searching for, I have clearly not yet found it: instead, I have found a pit of snakes slithering in the deeper recesses of my mind. I was not looking for a guru yet the urgency of my quest is suddenly amplified. As Papaji says, hold on to the raft that will take you across the ocean of samsara. 'Your freedom is my job. Simply stay quiet,' he has often said. His offer is too good to miss.

Where is the peace I felt sitting in satsang? Where is the bubble of joy I held in my heart as I walked among the great deodars? What is that recognition as I sat by the dhuni in the ashram? The soft caress that lifted my heart like a feather when I heard the muttered 'Hari Om Hari Om'.

*   *   *

Lucknow in September is hot. I stay away from the growing colony of westerners. After the stifling order of England I want the extravagance that is India. I step again on her soils and breathe her all in.

The Maha Bodhi Society is a Buddhist temple offering modest rooms to pilgrims. Located in the older part of town, the streets around the temple are jammed with people. Vendors push carts laden with fruit and vegetables, or plastic kitchenware, or boys' shorts and bright, frilly dresses. Pigs wallow in the flowing gutters and cars and trucks push their way through. Kids on the rooftops fly home-made kites with long tails that flutter colour in the sky.

An Australian man is staying at the Maha Bodhi Society and when, after a few days, he returns to his country, he leaves me his bicycle. Every day I cycle through this chaos. The worst is the main road up to the centre of the city. The traffic is intense, with trucks, buses and cars heaving and snarling through the mass of auto rickshaws, gushing thick black smoke, and the buffalo carts and hundreds of motorbikes and bicycles. Motorbikes often carry the whole family, the man driving, the wife sitting sideways, a kid on the handlebars and the other kids squashed in somewhere. Likewise a bicycle may be laden with plastic pots or dragging iron poles behind. A cow ambles along in the middle of it all, or a huge bull gazes off into space while the traffic swerves at the last minute to miss him. Cows in India are sacred and their place in the chaos is assured. I keep my direction clear and don't hesitate. It is a lesson in going with the flow. And trust.

Exhilarated from the ride I take my seat on a cushion on the floor at Papaji's satsang to wait in silence. The heat and humidity of post monsoon keeps the numbers down. The small, air-conditioned room is a welcome break from the temperature outside.

Satsang is mysterious. There is no doubt thought is reduced to a vast quiet landscape. 'The well of silence', as Papaji describes it. It is deeply restful to sit in his presence, listen to him talk: 'Peace does not belong to the past, peace is instant Presence. Just stay here with me. Your freedom is my job. You are not to do anything, simply stay quiet, giving no rise to a single thought.'

One morning as Papaji leaves after satsang he turns and asks if anyone needs a lift to Hazrat Ganj, in the centre of town. I hesitate but he seems to be looking at me and I hear myself say: 'Yes, I do!' He nods as I climb in the back seat behind him. Papaji speaks a few words to his driver, a Scottish man called Patrick, who then asks my name and where I am from. He repeats this information back to Papaji. I can see the top of Papaji's bald head. I am startled by his nearness, his vastness amplified in proximity. His energy is consuming. His presence is all around, like a fragrance so sublime I want nothing else. I close my eyes and feel a spinning in my chest. It is as if layers of blankets clouding the truth are being whisked away.

As we reach Hazrat Ganj, Papaji again talks with his driver.

'Where do you need to go?' Patrick asks.

'Anywhere is fine.'

We pull over at an intersection. I step out of the van and thank Papaji profusely. I bow with folded palms and he taps me on the head through the open van window. I stand and watch as they then drive away. How can it be that to spend twenty minutes driving through traffic with this elderly man has left me in such intoxication? Suddenly everywhere I look is dancing energy; spirals of light mass together to create form. I walk down the main street through the people and bustle and almost drown in a feeling of great love. It's as if I have taken a step backwards into myself and from this place I can see only perfection: the arc of water spraying from the pump as a woman fills her bucket, the ox with his head hanging low as he pulls a cart of iron posts. The shoe cleaner squatting on the filthy pavement, the endless roar and throb of life. I have heard many times that God is Love; the perspective of 'God' just needs to shift from outside to within. The feeling lasts most of the day.

Three weeks later Papaji's wife dies. Following the Hindu tradition, he travels to Haridwar on the river Ganga, to hold a ceremony for her ashes. Satsang is cancelled for a couple of weeks. I take a night train to Pathankot, wait in the familiar bus station, before the four-hour bus ride to Dharamsala.

CHAPTER ELEVEN

———⌇〰️⌇———

Babaji

'Still your mind in me, still yourself in me, and
without a doubt you shall be united with me, Lord of
Love, dwelling in your heart.' Bhagavad Gita

The forest is damp, battered and trashed by the monsoon. Branches and leaves lie across the muddy path. The air is cool and clear after the pollution of Lucknow. The bridge at the bottom of the garden spans a torrent.

I am sure he knows I am coming. My heart skips as I poke my head around the door. He looks up from his seat at the fire.

'Namaste, Babaji!'

'Ho ho! Kub ayaer?' [When come?] His face is full of smiles and his dark eyes hold mine; I feel suddenly shy and I falter. 'Today coming, Babaji.'

'You here staying?'

'No no, I have my room at Rishi Bhawan.'

'Accha tikhai, chai piou.' [Okay good, let's drink chai.]

He fusses with the fire, smiling quietly.

'Monsoon finished?' I am compelled to speak. The age-old tendency to fill in the spaces is loud against his silence. As if this simple expression of being is not enough and if not cemented with the known may vanish all together.

'Ah finished patanahi, aaj monsoon nahi. Bahut barish too much rain coming.' [Finished I don't know. Today no monsoon. Too much rain coming.] 'England you going?'

'Going and one month before coming back.'

'Accha. You coming back good.'

And now I have the known – with words, our connection forged. I drink the dim light of this room, the fire dancing as it has every day since I was last here, Babaji clothed within his own serenity in his simple task of brewing chai. He glances up as if to speak but smiles instead. My own smile is wide and I cannot hide my delight.

My eyes are drawn to him like waves to the shore. I allow myself snatched glances and pull my gaze back to the fire. Every sense is heightened. The wood smoke tingles in my nostrils with a hint of sandalwood. I sip his chai and my mouth rejoices. I hear the garden and the sounds of birds and if I listen very carefully I am sure I can hear the flowers open towards the light. My eyes are in heaven, feasting on dark, dark skin, eyes that speak of the beyond. I loosen within and give myself completely to the task of being here. The gentle roughness of the sack cloth upon which I sit, dirt floor swept smooth. Simply being here, as the words of Ram Dass float in my mind: 'Be here now.' Nothing more and nothing less. And as Papaji himself says again and again: 'Simply keep quiet. Do not stir a single thought.' How subtle these words are.

'England tikhai, Judit?'

'Tikhai, Babaji, family tikhai. Then Lucknow going. Papaji satsang.'

'Accha. Bahut accha you guru having. Guru finding sub se lucky. This life very lucky life.'

Let's leave it at that. How could I begin to explain to Babaji that my parents are devastated by my sister refusing to have contact and that in my homeland I felt as displaced as a rabbit in a lion's cage?

I sit by the fire, wrapped in silence. Slowly the world returns with thoughts of unpacking, settling in. 'Babaji, me going.'

'Tomorrow come?'

'Accha, Babaji.'

'Tikhai chello, joint piou then going.'

Halfway up the hill I have to sit and just take in my surroundings. The damp fragrance of the deodar pines, the massive sky beholden with white clouds, the naked peak of Triund rising up between the trees. After the confines of the city this world looks vast: the air pure, and my own self a tiny dot on this magnificent landscape. I remember Babaji saying sometime before 'Smoking mind same same just different' and I giggle.

*   *   *

A big festival is coming up. Diwali is the Hindu New Year, signifying the return of light, and it is celebrated according to the moon, always falling on new moon. The ashram is full and the days are full too – full of warmth, blue skies and autumn colours.

Babaji loves Diwali. In his home place of Bengal he tells me Diwali is, 'Sub se number one festival. Here mountain people not caring so much.' He is planning and preparing. Spring cleaning sadhu-style.

Whenever I visit the ashram I bring a flower or stick of incense for the temple. As I place the flower at the base of the lingam an idea is formed. After breakfast of semolina porridge, I wash the pot and Babaji places the kettle back on the flame. It is our habit to sit a while before the day unfolds. The idea has taken root.

'Babaji, can I paint the temple? It looks a little like it needs new paint.'

He looks at me then looks away a moment. He studies the fire and the smoothed silver ash. I wonder with a sudden anxiety if I have insulted him.

'You temple painting no problem.'

I can hardly hold back my feet as I stride down the hill to Dharamsala. I buy a big tin of white paint and a smaller one of red for the Om sign. Babaji is pleased, telling everyone staying there: 'Temple painting accha hai. God very happy. Accha hai.' It takes me two days to finish, just in time for the celebration. I keep 'Om Namah Shivaya' in my mind all the time as I paint under a sky tinged now with steel.

Diwali is celebrated in the evening and I spend the day at the ashram. Village kids bring baskets of yellow and orange marigold flowers and we help string them together in long malas. Babaji remakes the dhuni and the earth floor. He mixes wet cow shit and earth together in a cracked plastic bucket, smoothing the mixture with his hands around the fireplace and then the floor. It dries quickly and feels as clean as any floor I have sat on. The tape player is out on the verandah and devotional songs to Laxmi sing out. He sings along, every now and again stopping to give us the meaning. 'Ma! Ma! Only Mother can bring happiness to this heart.'

Laxmi, like all the goddesses, symbolises the divine mother. She is also the goddess of wealth and prosperity. It is her night and the ashram sparkles. We put wicks in little clay lamps and carefully place them all down the steps through the garden to the gate, so the goddess can be welcomed home.

Babaji wears a new lungi, his hair neatly combed and oiled. Locals come by for a blessing, bringing fruit or sweets. He has been cooking a special dish made with a yellow dhal, yogurt and curry leaves. Curry is a tree and grows throughout India. The leaf has a pungent irresistible fragrance, subtle at first, but when I smell my fingers after rubbing the leaf, the scent is rich and aromatic. All day the pan has simmered on the fire. There are eight of us for dinner. As he lights the lamps, mumbling prayers, it is easy to imagine the gods are pleased.

I stand behind him as he performs evening puja. The other ashram guests join us too, standing to the side, one with his camera poised. Babaji lights the camphor resting on the brass tray to circle the flame around the lingam. The temple shines with its new coat of paint and I have placed extra flowers at the base of the lingam. I suddenly hope that it is okay, that I have not been too familiar. Babaji always tells me Shiva is very kind. Not so much fuss with his worship. The mantras are longer tonight, and Babaji has placed a picture of Laxmi in the temple also. He sings to her then lights incense; the fragrance reaches in to me and for a moment I fear I may faint. I reach out to hold on to the temple pillar and the cold beneath my hand brings me back. Babaji stands before me. His eyes are asking and I nod. But all I can see is a host of temples clouding my vision, golden domes and haloed light. The shimmering image of gods walk towards me, arms outstretched. He finishes his puja with 'Hari Om Hari Om'. I can hear the words but my being is still clothed in the vision. I stand to one side and find myself in the sight of the deodar forest. I focus my gaze on these ancient, sturdy trees. Tears are coursing down my cheeks and it takes me some moments to come back to my centre.

I rejoin the others by the dhuni. I am thankful no one appears to have noticed my emotion, except Babaji who nods again as I sit. And in his glance I have the sense that he sees into me and he too has experienced the thin veil of reality lifting for a moment to reveal other worlds.

Babaji fusses over us all as if we are kids. Everyone gets a dollop of ghee and no one refuses the second chapatti, another spoonful of 'curry', his blessing tasted in every mouthful.

After sweets, one by one the ashram guests retire. I sit with Babaji out on the verandah. The night is black, the new moon long vanished, and the air is cold. The last of the oil lamps flicker and fade, like fairies in fairy tales.

'Babaji, your ashram is so peaceful.'

His face is illuminated for a moment as he lights a beedi. 'You inside heart peace, then whole world peaceful. Ashram place helping to know peace, more strong peace. Ashram place many thought is God. Temple place same. This God inside you same same, so now you happy. Tikhai?'

I wonder for a moment if I will tell him what happened as he sang puja. I sense my awareness more precise, as if I were sitting in satsang with Papaji, and decide to remain quiet.

'God always with you, Juditji.' Babaji speaks at just the right moment. Later he pats me on the back as I reluctantly say goodbye.

* * *

The day after Diwali a resting quiet shimmers in the air. Each and every leaf still basks in worship. I close the gate and walk up the path. Sunlight falls on the sunflowers, small birds dart among ripening corn. The low buildings gleam from all the preparation, the flower malas vivid against the white. Remains of the oil lamps have left dark patches on the steps.

Babaji sits in the sun. The ashram is quiet and I am glad. He puts a book to one side as I step up on the verandah. He wears his new lungi, bright orange and still a little starchy. His chest is bare, three strands of mala beads against his brown skin. I notice the way sunlight highlights silver hairs on his chest.

'Namaste, namaste.' His murmured voice echoes the quiet as he smoothes his beard with his fingers.

'Namaste, Babaji.' I sit against the back wall looking out on the garden, moving a cushion to make the most of the sun. He unfolds his legs, yawning. I unwrap myself from my shawl, fold it neatly beside me, tuck my legs together and rearrange the long shirt to cover my lap.

Babaji yawns again.

'Diwali good feeling?'

'It was so beautiful, Babaji. I enjoyed very much.'

'Diwali accha hai. Bengali people like to welcome mother home.'

I smile. He looks so pleased, as if for sure the goddess has returned. 'Babaji, you still worship Kali?'

'Kali is mother, Shiva is father. My job only karma yoga. God looking in many form. These foreign people coming, same God coming. All for time pass. Bas. Only for thoughts of God.'

He falls silent and I stay listening. 'Time pass only for God,' he declares again, and picks up his book. 'This Bhagavad Gita. You looking sometime.'

Leaning forward he shows me the script. His fingers gently smooth the pages, tracing the words like a beginner. Then he wraps it into a cloth and places it under the cushion. He folds his hands back on his lap – big solid hands, slightly crinkled. Yawning again, he then laughs, a melody I now know well.

'Tired feeling today, some tea drinking.'

He stretches and stands, stretches again, patting my head as he passes. His hand feels warm and the tenderness with which its rests, just for a moment, remains. I watch him disappear, then work some more on detangling my hair with my fingers. I have no mirror but here in the ashram a small one is hung on the wall and I am startled sometimes to see my reflection: my hair is growing now of course and if I am not careful it seems intent on turning into dreadlocks. I can hear Babaji muttering to himself as the cat slides out, pausing to wash her tail.

He is back with two tin cups balanced on a plate, some sweets from the festival. He sits, putting the plate on the floor between us. 'Some sweet is good. Mother likes to give children sweets so children happy. Children happy then mother happy. You happy – then God happy. Same same.' He smiles again and he holds my gaze. 'Tikhai, Juditji, tikhai?'

'Sub tikhai, Babaji.' A thread weaves between us, lingering like an early morning mist.

*   *   *

October days are glorious. Warm sunshine pours in pools from above. I know his routine: he is up early for ablutions and returns to his room for japa meditation. As dawn breaks he arranges the fire for its day of service, boiling water and brewing tea. Everyone staying at the ashram comes together for breakfast. He tends to the garden, sits for a while in the sun, reads words from the Bhagavad Gita, mala at rest against his chest. Mid-afternoon he prepares for dinner, eating at sunset.

I visit before breakfast when the sun sheds light high on the mountains but is not yet seen. I mostly find him sitting alone, still wrapped in his shawl. I take my place with barely a word spoken. Other days it is late afternoon when I turn up and I stay for dinner, into the evening, walking home by torchlight. The ashram is bursting, every room taken. Dinner is a social event, westerners unaccustomed to silent eating.

I sleep again under the stars, on the rope bed I move to the edge of the trees. I wrap myself in my sleeping bag and blankets as the black heavens host a changing nightscape strewn with stars. When the need for solitude is irresistible I take off with a small bag on my back. I have my place by a river rushing from the snowfields, a steep-sided valley, almost a gorge, where a large rock overhang gives shelter. A flat earthy space before boulders and rocks guide the water downwards, swirling through channels of rock, falling over in a frenzy of falls, and emerging to a wide clear pool just below. The water here is turquoise and in spite of the freezing cold I plunge in. A dip in ice-cold water is a remedy for everything. If my mind is troubled, it clears the moment I plunge under. Alone and alive, I make a fire, cook a little dhal and make a chapatti with the flour I have brought. At night I climb into my sleeping bag and my companion is the rushing water.

Once I walked here along the narrow zigzag path that clings to the valley wall, traversed rock slides, climbed an almost sheer rock ledge, and came upon a milling mass of bleating goats and sheep, with three shepherds and a dog. The shepherds gave me milk for my chai and I stayed just one night with the animals bleating and grunting their stinking breath all around me. The shepherds are mountain men and take their flocks up to the meadows at more than 3000 metres. The monsoon is milder up there and they stay until they descend for the winter. Mostly when I visit my place of retreat there is no one, just willie wagtails darting on the rocks, and the endless sound of falling water.

*   *   *

Mid-November the nights are cold. I buy thermals from the Tibetan shop in town. Babaji wears a shirt and in the evening a woollen waistcoat of rust red. Only one westerner is still at the ashram and he has plans to move on now the sun is losing its strength. I too have plans – to travel to Delhi then back to Lucknow.

December skies bring snow to the higher peaks, sprinkled white against the grey. In the morning the water from the tank is icy. I leave buckets of it in the sun to wash with in the midday warmth. My breath trails like dragons.

Another week and I am leaving.

My feet tread the well-worn path to the ashram. The woods are quiet now, as nature turns inward for a time of rest. I find Babaji sitting in a patch of sun scrubbing the soil from a pile of potatoes. He finishes his job then settles against the wall. He lights a beedi, cursing the matches that fizzle and die without a flame. A breeze is a murmured whisper in the trees. Small wren-like birds with bright yellow breasts flit as they sing and a crow lands on the temple roof, black against the white.

The silence is easy, my breath a welcome companion, following its rhythm to settle in the quietening.

'Chai piou, Judit?'

He is watching me as I turn my gaze to his words. He bundles up the potatoes.

I sit still and my heart pounds. He is back in a moment.

'Babaji, very sweet chai!'

'Yes, yes, too much chini putting. Cold coming more sweet is good.'

He slurps with little noises.

'Tomorrow going mountain side, one cave place staying.'

My eyes hold his.

'You coming?'

His question is a relief. 'Sure, Babaji.'

He explains how to find the cave just below the ridge at Triund and that I should come in the afternoon. I watch his hands as he talks. Hands that are rich brown like the earth, strong and familiar. With the knowing that I will visit him in a cave high up the mountain comes the awareness that a path has been forged. The afternoon almost drags and I wish we were leaving right now rather than tomorrow, just so I won't need to go through this waiting – this discomfort, now the snake is out of the bag. Doubt creeps in too. But I can find absolutely no reason why not.

*   *   *

The next day, dusk is almost descending when I finally see him, a silhouette on a rock. He stands as he sees me, and watches this last exertion up the scree that slips and slides, scarring the silence. I am breathless when I reach him. All around, the sky is streaked in orange, and the charcoal peaks point upwards against a pale lemon. He nods his head in the abstract way I love.

'Very late coming!'

I catch my breath from the steep last climb. Babaji stands with his arms folded across his chest, his head thrown back slightly. He is looking at me in the way I always feel he looks right inside me as a smile spreads slowly. He puts his hands briefly in 'namaste' and mutters 'Hari Om Hari Om' in welcome.

We stand together on the boulder. Rocks fall steeply away to a world below. The mountains wear their silence in a poem to creation, broken only by the harsh call of crows. The light fades to reveal the slither of a crescent moon – Shiva moon – Venus by her side. This vision could not be more perfect.

The cave is spacious, the rock roof high enough to stand. On the fireplace in the middle of the cave, Babaji has already cooked dhal with the mountain leaf, bitter and pungent. We eat and the air is thick. Another note has joined the silence and it crescendos and falls between us. I am full with anticipation … this unknown meeting away from the safety of the ashram. The fire gives a circle of orange light and shadows dance to the black night.

Babaji sits motionless until the fire quietens. He places a gnarled log that the flames eagerly snatch. 'You blanket bring?'

'Ek hai.'

'Tikhai, ek nitche dho upper garam hoijayaga.' [One under, two up we will be warm.] I pass him my blanket and he arranges it on top with another blanket of his. He takes a torch from his bundle.

'Outside going?'

Outside is a nightscape brilliant with stars, the moon long gone after her short display. He walks a few yards then disappears into the absolute black and I hear the hiss of pee against the ground. I do the same before returning to the cave. The entrance is tight and I have to lower my head. A beckoning flame twists and swirls as I crouch and squeeze through the opening. The cave is cosy, a womb within the vastness. The silence is surreal.

Babaji fixes up the cloth at the opening to hold the wind away and the fire has lost its enchantress. The flames subdue and concentrate on their burning. I can feel the heat on my cheeks. Babaji takes a tin from his pocket and inside is a piece of charas and a few cigarettes. With a stick he pulls an ember from the fire and rests the charas by its side to soften and warm. I watch him empty the tobacco out of the cigarette so the paper is still intact. Then after he mixes the charas and tobacco well, rubbing and mixing, he fills up the cigarette again.

'Cave place accha?' he asks.

'Cave place bahut accha. When did you find it?'

'Many years before. Sadhu people like cave staying. Sometime western people staying. Last year one Australian boy staying one week. Liking silence and meditation also. Good cave. No water inside coming. Wood hai, pani hai upper.' He lights the joint with 'Om', lifting it first to his forehead. He holds it like a pipe so his mouth doesn't actually touch the filter. I do the same, letting the smoke course down my throat before slowly letting it out. The effect is immediate – maybe because of the walk and the higher cold air.

Babaji lights a beedi. 'Ah, smoking mind, crazy mind,' he chuckles. 'One smoke, two smoke, always want more smoke.' And he chuckles again.

'Hungry? Little eating? Some chapatti hey.' He rummages in his jhola, his shoulder bag, and finds them wrapped in paper. 'Maybe some jam, hey. Little sweet good.' And he pulls a tin from the shadows and opens it. Inside are a few old jars and a jar of strawberry jam. 'This Australian boy leaving.' And he chuckles again. He passes me the chapatti spread with jam; the sweetness is good and brings me more to myself.

'One more eating?'

'Sure, one more.' I smile and want to say, *Hey we are having a party.* Instead I eat the chapatti; the jam has crystallised a little into crunchy sugar.

'Babaji, pani hai?'

'Pani hai,' and he passes me a lota of water. The sense of unknowing again creeps in. I have no idea how the script is going to unfold.

'Tikhai sleep going,' he announces as he settles in the blankets. I lie next to him, folding my shawl for a pillow. The dying fire throws golden warmth across his face. His nearness startles me. I close my eyes and smell his fragrance of wood smoke, lingering incense, sweet spice. I can feel the rough wool of his waistcoat, the softer blanket covering us both. Firelight falls to faded shadow as the dark creeps in, completing this timeless world.

He softly murmurs a string of 'Oms'. The vibration resounds within the chamber of rock. His hand pats mine, briefly. 'Sleep going,' and he turns on his side. My heart pounds at his nearness. Have I misunderstood? Have all the gestures and intricacies been of my making only? *He is celibate*, my mind insists, as if I had forgotten. What are you? The modern day Eve tempting Adam? Will he fall from grace? Is his God as wrathful as mine? Lying here next to him in unfamiliar intimacy, in a cave above an already wild world, my mind has a mission. Have I misread the situation? What did I expect? I make myself comfortable on the hard earth floor. As his breathing changes and sleep is sure, I let the thoughts go and snuggle as close as I can, for warmth as much as anything, then I too lose myself to the night.

In the morning, Babaji is already gone. I did not feel him stir. The early morning air freezes my breath, crystalline vapours in a hint of light from the outside. I remain motionless to collect my dreams but they too have vanished.

As I step outside the cold slaps my face. I take a blanket from the bed, wrap it around my shoulders and stand on the boulder stamping my feet. This is my terrain. Mountains burst with energy in motionless form. In the eerie silence, the winds whip by with ice. I raise my arms to the heavens, juggling the weight of the blanket, humbled yet again by the magnitude of such wild nature.

Scree bounces over rock. Babaji makes his way down with his kamandal in one hand, lungi tied up around his thighs. He strides with ease down the steep mountainside, his head held high. He too looks unrestrained as if even his role at the ashram can be left behind.

'Ho ho! Tikhai tikhai?' His hair streams around his shoulders and his face, his skin, glows like polished teak. He joins me on the rock, pulling out a beedi and matches from his woollen waistcoat pocket. He wears no more than this woollen waistcoat and a t-shirt underneath, as he does at the ashram.

'No cold, Babaji?'

'Cold, no cold. Fire inside hey!' He smiles and lights up even more. 'Bhagwan sub atcha hey! Prakriti, God's world, this God world. Bahut accha.' [God is the best. This universe, God's world very good.] The beedi keeps going out. 'Matches karab hogaya. Man making problem always coming.'

The air itself holds a thickness and the smell of snow soon to come. The rock face above is littered with shapes as the sun sprinkles its light in pristine arcs of gold.

'Alone place going sub accha. Nature place then good feeling coming.'

'For me too, Babaji. One time I went to the Parvati valley and lived high up away from people. It is a gift to remove from the world.'

'You sadhu life living no problem.'

He squats down on his haunches. I too sit and the rock is cold beneath me. Close enough to touch, a minute space between. I could pour myself into him and become one.

'You know energy, Juditji? Everything energy. You, me, this rock, this sky, all same energy. Nature place gives good understanding. Shiva living mountains place why? Energy strong, body strong, mind clean. No mind problem.'

All I know is that to be here, alone in such magnificence with Babaji, is tying me up with anticipation. As if I am sliding on ice.

'No eating good feeling. Light coming.' And he laughs as if it is absurd anyway. I laugh too and our eyes hold.

'You sometime fast, Babaji?' I have to break the spell.

'Fasting, many time fasting. Body rest sometimes giving, very good.' He smiles again. He is freer up here on this mountain, off duty. 'Come, upside going fresh water take. You sometime this place alone coming, then water place knowing tikhai.'

The spring is thirty or forty metres further up. Grassy knolls make easy steps, and we zigzag up the steep slope to a ridge of soft grasses

145

where little plants creep over rocks. The spring trickles out from beneath a rock, smooth and slippery from the constant wet. We sit back with legs outstretched, soaking in the welcome warmth as the sun moves higher. Eagles ride above, a slow circle round and around. As we watch, cloud forms appear out of nowhere to spill over the mountain ridge, voluptuous white formations hurried across the vista by darker, more ominous greys.

'Barish aigar, patanahi. Wood hey do muskil nahi.' [Rain coming, wood have so no problem.] The sun is swallowed by black cloud almost as he speaks and the air falls to a chill. We scramble back down after filling the container with pure spring water. A small pile of wood is stacked outside the cave. 'Spring time up side going, wood taking. Now winter time no more coming, this wood using. Big fire making and warm coming. No bear coming.'

He is laughing that little chuckle as if he is the only one who knows the joke. I know very well bears live around here. I've seen them myself. Just a few weeks ago, walking up on the path not far from here, I saw a mother bear and two young just above where I sat. And in the other valley – the wild place, as I like to think of it – there are bears too.

Babaji still chuckles as he piles pieces of wood in his arms and crouches through the entrance. He builds up the fire, squatting on his haunches, smoking a beedi, watching the fire roar to life. He is the master, I think, and I am his devotee. My cheeks colour and blush as I again stumble over myself, the complete and utter starkness of him and me.

'Khya?' he is asking. [What?] What indeed.

A pot of water steams and little bubbles rise to the surface.

'Doud nahi, kali chai abi.'

He is making black tea. He pours and sits again in silence. Enough, I tell myself. Enough. I too pull inwards, rearrange myself on the hard earth, warm my hands around the tin cup and keep my eyes firmly down. My request of enough is not enough. A thin slippery finger twists a little tighter in the darker recess of my guts. A finger of guilty shame, or shameful guilt, I am not sure. The thin finger grows, mutates to a serpent, its mouth gaping, coiling and recoiling, whispering of my badness.

I step outside, claustrophobic, mouth scalded from sipping too-hot black tea. The vastness claims me and I find myself flung far and wide. The sky is heavy and almost upon me, cloud so low and laden. For a brief moment I want to vanish. Wish that the dense cloud all around could suck me up and lose me forever. As if from full breasts, raindrops leak and the wind has hushed. I turn my face upwards; rain and tears sting my flushed face. My lungs receive the cold air as I breathe fast, in out, in out, holding a finger to block a nostril. It is a practice Babaji has shown me, as a way to quieten the mind. I do not like this onslaught. After a few rounds of pounding my breath, I find the rhythm again, letting my breath come as it pleases, focusing my attention. Coming back to just this: standing on a mountainside with rain as cold as ice touching my flushed cheek and a darkened sky above.

I am driven in by the cold and increasing rain; the cave is dim and the small space noticeably warm. I can hide myself in this dimness, shrink to the shadows. Babaji puts a tavar, a chapatti plate, on to warm, balancing it on a couple of stones. From a tin he pours flour onto a plate, mixing dough. Strong, firm hands, moulding the dough with ease – hands I love to watch. I notice the flame, the arc of changing orange-gold, the deep burning of coals – patterns and landscapes created and burnt before my eyes. I drop back into my body, feel the hardness of rock beneath my sit bones. I sense the serpent, the slippery finger, return to its hiding place.

Babaji often speaks of all action being yoga. Karma yoga is service to God. Watching his hands, I want to hear him speak. He does not waste words on idle talk. Besides, his words have a poetry of their own – a lyrical mix of Hindi and English, and always the perfect antidote to a thought buzzing in my mind. Sometimes as we sit on the verandah at the ashram, sunlight pouring and pooling, flowers enticing birds, the warm drone of life around us, he can speak just a sentence and it is as if he knows where I am. Knows me through and through. Not now, I pray, not now. The flush creeps again. *Speak*, I urge myself. *Speak!*

'Babaji, you are always doing karma yoga?'

Flattening a roti between his palms, he places it on the hot plate. 'This cave place coming then bhakti yoga. Bhakti yoga only for love, God-love. Cave place then world chello. Only God. Nature place very strong place for looking only God.' He stops mixing the dough and sits back on his heels. 'Gyan yoga then mind looking to God. Gyan mutlub [means] knowledge. Gyan yoga then God looking with mind. Bhakti yoga is God looking through heart. Same same.'

He pauses, watching the greys outside. The small opening is like a birth canal to the world. Time turns away for the briefest moment and every movement becomes the subtlest dance. He turns to me and in a voice so soft and quiet tells me: 'This love feeling inside heart, this bhakti.' He reaches over and holds my hand, just for a moment, then lets it rest.

We eat the warm rotis outside on the rock, with sweet black tea to wash them down. The sky is slate, the wind again relentless. The swollen rain clouds lift enough to let us see the peaks surrounding us. Perhaps this is how it is with God: always here but obscured by clouds of beliefs, emotions.

We have eaten little during the day and I feel a lightness return, buoyant, and an abundance of energy. Retreating again to our cave, Babaji fixes up the sack cloth against the wind that blows in gusts. He piles more wood and the fire reaches high, spreading her warmth in a moment. The wind whines and moans and sways the sack-cloth door. Enclosed in our haven, Babaji sits. Eyes almost closed, motionless. Firelight highlights gold and I imagine he could be an angel. I join the silent vigil; focus on breath, the steady rise, fall in and out, this duet of me.

I hear his cough, a low rumble to herald his return. He shakes his head in that singular move; just a small movement that declares all is as it should be. Still with no words he smoothes out the blanket and lies down. I sit for a moment feeling the flame on my face, unsure yet sure, so I lie down next to him and he pulls the coarse wool blanket over to cover us both. Flames play in patterns. Seductive swirls lick and tease in the shadows.

Babaji turns slightly, raising enough to look at me. He runs his hand slowly down my face. His hand feels like leather. I want to unzip his skin and ease myself in. Our eyes hold. 'You trouser off taking, tikhai?' Almost a question, but more an instruction.

I undress completely, folding my clothes in a pile. He unwraps his lungi, pulls off his jacket, shirt and t-shirt, leaving only his malas and loincloth. We lie again in the firelight. The cold air reaches in and I have no doubt I am alive. I pull him to me, and he wraps me in his arms in a tight embrace. His eyes hold me until mine drop away. He reaches down and unties his loincloth. Bursting for release. I feel my body loosen, a slight shudder as I nestle into his beard, his hair and smells. Slowly, tentative, he enters me with a little gasp, shivers rippling through his chest. My body responds as if parched and this is the purest spring water pouring forth. It is as if I am making love for the first time. I pull him deep inside and cling to him, nestled to his chest, his malas against my cheek. He opens his eyes and I become still, as still as the earth beneath me. I let my arms fall to my side, surrendered to him, and he covers my hands with his, pressing me down, filling me again and again. A veil of energy sculpts us as one. Poured into his form, his very being, melted away to the grandeur of the mountain upon which we lie.

It cannot last and slowly but surely the shift occurs and now there is he and there is me, and a sudden shyness. He burrows himself into my breast, then raises himself up, whispering, 'Om, Hari Om,' sealing the sacrament with his words.

The fire recedes, shadows reach in. He pulls the blanket over and I snuggle in to him. His body is perfect, his penis still hard. We lie bathed in silence till the fire dwindles and the air is too cold for naked skin. Babaji wraps his lungi, smoothes his beard with his fingers. A low muttering: 'Hari Om, Hari Om.'

The fire is greedy, snatching and curling over the wood he carefully adds. The flame glows orange and I see his face lit with gold. The hiss and whisper of the fire play against a silence so vast it roars in my ears.

'This sex doing bahut accha! Good feeling.' He breaks into a smile and I reach over to him and briefly stroke his hand. Oh, too soon to part, the void too stark. I'm somewhere in between, floating in the still-fragrant union, embedded still inside.

He sits now, pulling into himself; he breathes long. My body feels loose, like a stream of viscous liquid. I too sit, with the fire our focus.

'Babaji, how long since you making love?' I am bold, I know, but I want to know.

'Many years before one wife having. Me nineteen years, marriage to girl from village. Good marriage. Two, three years no baby coming. Doctor going speaking she no having children. This wife good person saying, "You going no problem." This life me no like too much, household life tight feeling. Actually wanting sadhu life. No baby coming then husband free. More wife take, or going and sadhu life coming. Marriage time then sex doing, liking very much. Sadhu life no sex doing, sometime problem, so hing [asafetida] eating. No onion eating. Some breathing doing, power coming and then no problem. Now you here and big problem coming.' He looks at me so playfully then folds his palms together and closes his eyes. 'Om, Om, Om.'

The heat rises across my cheeks as he again opens his eyes and takes me with only a glance. I lower my gaze but a small voice whispers, *There is only now, and here you are far above the world in your secret lair.* I rest my hand on his thigh. And he is uncrossing his legs and I am letting my hand slide itself slowly through the folds of cotton and then again we are lying, firelight, darkness, the wind outside howling in response. Have I ever wanted someone as much as this? I cannot remember. A hundred lovers I may have had but here on a stone floor, only now, can I give all of me.

*   *   **

I sleep with the lightness of awareness filling my being. The cold keeps me curled against him, pressing into his smell of earth and goodness. Somewhere in the cold night I dream of wandering through a house cluttered with people. Every room I enter is the same: hands outstretched, fingers clawing, wanting. And then there is Babaji, walking towards me. He leads me through a doorway to an empty room. Just silver light and emptiness. I wake and listen in the complete dark to his soft, even breathing before sleep collects me once more.

We wake to a world hushed in silver. The first snow has fallen early this year. Naked rock is silhouetted against heavy, grey skies. Our world is bathed in the purity of millions of unique crystals. The last of the wood feeds the fire. Black tea, sweet and strong, a roti to fill the stomach. Our world is lost in a cocoon of grey ... timeless, silent. The blankets are still laid out. Wordless and wanting, we move as one. It is too cold for nakedness so I take my trousers off and he unwraps himself from his lungi. He enters me almost immediately. His breath pulls me to him and then we are naked and the heat rises up and singes my soul.

There is no need to linger. The fire is spent, just the glow to remind of what has been. Babaji tidies the embers, finds a few sticks where the pile has been. He places them over the orange coals, the last burst before this cave will be lost for the winter in a world of white.

'You alone going, tikhai?'

'Tikhai, Babaji. Babaji, thank you.' My hands are together in prayer.

He folds his hands over mine and leans towards me. We rest for a moment with our foreheads touching. He will wait a while before his own return later in the day.

He watches me go, standing on the rock, stamping his bare feet against the cold. I walk quickly, carefully, scrambling down to meet the main pathway back down the mountains. The snow is thin, worn only by the higher hills, and as the village comes into sight below me, the path is bare.

*　　*　　*

Four days later my rucksack is packed. Tears fall down my cheeks as I walk the path down through the forest. I pause a moment, long enough to pull myself back, dry my tears, wipe my eyes. Suck my breath deep inside. My feet are heavy, reluctant to take the steps for a last chai, a beedi on the verandah. Yet it is already written: train ticket bought, the journey mapped out. There has been no talk of staying, moving into the ashram, anything ongoing. Babaji does not belong in this world of relating, and nor would I want him to. Ours in a love shared high in the mountains, in a cave soon to be hidden under a blanket of snow.

He sits on the verandah, as I knew he would. He is quiet, still, and offers barely a glance as I take my place. Slowly he creeps back in, becomes more solid, yawns and stretches a leg. He unfolds himself and smiles. 'Tikhai, Juditji? Tikhai?' I find myself unable to answer.

He reaches for my hand, patting it gently. 'Going time?'

I nod. 'Going time.'

'You when coming back?'

'Spring time coming back.' I imagine returning just as the snow melts and the sun throws light again for the new shoots to push through on the grassy hillside above the cave.

'Tikhai you going. Coming back tikhai.'

I have bought him a pale orange shawl. His pleasure shows in his eyes, dark eyes that shine with the radiance of God. 'Chello, one chai drink, then going.'

He brings the tin cups and in the cold air, steam wafts and curls. He slurps noisily, lights a beedi, and throws me the pack.

'Joint smoking, Babaji?'

So we do, passing it often, sharing it between our lips. I sit some more. I am not in a rush, but then it is time. 'Going is going' after all, as Babaji often declares.

He stands and we embrace, loosely at first then he holds me and I feel his slight nervousness, then a growing hardness and my body replies with a soft whispering tingle, a deeper breath. He draws away to stand by the steps, looking out into the garden. 'Come, temple come, blessing give.'

Side by side at the temple he stoops down and takes the lamp, burning as it always does. He waves it over my head, with his eyes almost closed, muttering mantras barely audible. I stand and receive with my hands on my heart. He dabs his finger into the vibhuti powder and places a dot of red on my forehead. He leaves his finger for a moment and I can feel an energetic swirl between my eyebrows.

Trees shed their last leaves, spindly fingers point upwards. The sun, relaxed and dreamy, lies low in the sky. 'Winter time good time. Quiet. Bas.' He wraps his shawl tight around him then folds his hands together. 'Hari Om, Hari Om.'

CHAPTER TWELVE

The Guru

'God is not hiding! When you don't see God it is only because you are looking elsewhere. So you must absolutely see God and nothing else. Then it is God who is looking through your eyes.' Papaji

Pathankot station is a vortex of commotion. I find my carriage as the train pulls in late. My heart sinks when I realise there is no women's compartment for the night ride to Delhi. I find my compartment, already a swarming mass of activity as mothers settle children while small babies cry, men mill about in the narrow walkway and others carry suitcases and bundles as they push through, searching for their berth. I find my seat number and squash into the lower bunk. On the top bunks, four or five men sit, swinging their legs. The lower bunks are packed. A beggar pushes his bandaged stump through the bars of the window. Soldiers watch from the bunk across the aisle. I try out my Hindi and stern faces melt to smiles. They usher away the handful of men to find another place as the train rushes off through the night. I lie out flat on the top bunk, my shawl tight around me. The noise, the people all around, press in on me. I pull my woollen hat firmly down. Across from me on the other top bunk a man lies amidst suitcases. His family below jostle, a baby cries. Two women talk loudly above the clatter of the train. I close my eyes and let myself return to the mountains, the vast rock of ages cleft for me. Sleep comes in intervals, peppered with remembering the feeling of anticipation, a sense of trepidation, as I walked up to find Babaji in the cave, and how I thought I might not find him as the clouds were swirling lower, and how the cloud lifted just at the right moment to reveal him standing high above the path on the rock. I replay the days spent in the cave, the perfect location for our romance. It was sex with a difference. No foreplay, no tentative kissing, no awkward rearranging of myself to feign interest. As I remember the way he entered me, and the way my whole body wanted him, I realise how healing it has been for me after the confusion with Helene. It is as if high up there in our cave, the world, with all its troubles, could not reach me. But it did reach me, I remind myself, and this thought is unwelcome, as if staining the perfection of how I want it to be. Pure. Untainted.

The train pulls in to New Delhi station as the winter sun struggles free of the smog that blankets the city. The chaos is extreme. Police and army spill from everywhere, guns in hands or slung over shoulders. Batons and sticks tap the ground. Outside, the traffic moves slower than ever and the queue for a taxi is a jostling scrum. A porter finds me a yellow and black cab, an old Ambassador with torn red leather seats. The cab driver tells me the news. Last night a mob of militant Hindu nationalists burnt a mosque in a place called Ayodhya. Widespread rioting has broken out between the Muslims and Hindus and a night curfew has been called. No trains are running to Lucknow which has a large Muslim population and where the violence has left several dead.

Ayodhya is sacred to Hindus, the birthplace of Lord Ram. Lord Ram is an incarnation of Vishnu and is worshipped as a god. Not unlike Jesus to the Christians. Hindu mythology is full of stories of his life in which he is joined by a pantheon of other gods. Many temples have statues of Ram with Sita, his beloved, and Lakshman, his brother. Often Hanuman is there, the monkey god, Ram's faithful servant. Ram is said to represent the perfect human, living in devotion to God with his wife Sita by his side.

No one knows when trains to Lucknow will resume. I have time on my hands.

In my hotel room I read the Bhagavad Gita. The version Babaji has given me has both the Hindi script and the English translation. It is the dialogue between Krishna and Arjuna, Krishna being another incarnation of Vishnu.

Look to me alone for comfort, refuge, strength. You are forever dear to me, hence be in peace.

I imagine him sitting by his fire. At night, as I lie between the starched sheets of my hotel bed, I can almost feel his rough wool waistcoat, feel his hand sliding down my back, the tickle of his beard against my cheek, the musky smell of coconut oil and juniper wood. Never could I have imagined when I first met him, more than a year ago, that this meeting would lead to a mystical union in a fire-warmed cave. I scrutinise the weeks before, when lingering glances would be sealed with a hand resting on my knee – just for a moment, but resting nonetheless. It was his hand, I reason, not mine. Did I in any way lead him on? I wonder now. My attraction to him has been much more than the physical, as if his presence is infectious, addictive, and I can never have enough. Babaji embodies something I want – a master of his own mind, his day-to-day focus on worship, on karma yoga. As he so often says: everything for God. His words resonate within me, his presence and life of renunciation, of contemplation, affirms my own commitment to this path, and the rewards lived out before me. Just being in his ashram allows the ceaseless chatter of my mind to subside and I like who I am, and rather than finding endless faults with myself, worrying that something is amiss, I am awed that my life includes such a friendship. 'Not my mind,' he often says, 'mind is mind, that's all. Only Atman is real.' Babaji is a teacher to me in so many ways. Explaining a passage from the scriptures, or simply telling me neti neti, 'not this not that', to my questions of Shiva, the supreme reality of consciousness. How often he will say 'all for looking to God', that his life is 'only for service to God'. His habit of repeating 'Om', and the pervading quiet, his attention to the fire and the temple, the way he quietly serves, and the rituals that reach into me with a known familiarity, give me the sense of being home, that I have found my flock.

*   *   *

Four days later the curfew is lifted.

The train to Lucknow pulls in to the familiar station just after sunrise. A smoky landscape of steam and fog greets me in the cool air. I take a tempo to Indira Nagar, the area of town where Papaji lives and where satsang is held. Police stand in groups around the main intersections, the only sign of recent troubles.

I sit at the little chai stall opposite satsang house, dunking a stale bun in cardamom chai. The chai wallah is tall and thin and wears the white skull cup of a Muslim. He smiles and nods his recognition. I watch the procession of westerners arrive by rickshaw and scooter, wrapped in shawls against the cool foggy air. They all look so ordered, together, well dressed. The women mostly wear matching kurta and trousers, shawls tucked neatly around shoulders. I notice the ingrained dirt on my feet and how cold they are in the chappal, my only shoes.

The policy at satsang house is that the first to be let in are any newcomers and those returning after a time away. This allows them to take a seat in the front, close to where Papaji sits. I leave my rucksack under the stairs and sit on a yellow cushion to wait for Papaji.

The hall fills up with about three hundred people. Now the climate is comfortable, this is the busy time of year for spiritual seekers. We all stand as Papaji walks through the crowd to take his seat. He wears a blue wool hat and a long shirt and pants. As he walks in, a tear slides down my cheek. Before settling himself on his seat, a wide bench with cushions and white cloth to cover, known as a tucket, he stands before the photo of Ramana – Ramana Maharshi, his own guru, from the sacred mountain of Arunachala.

Once he has folded his legs into the cross-legged position and arranged his glasses and handkerchief to one side, he begins satsang. I sit on the yellow cushion, overawed by the feeling of immense love that springs and bubbles from a well I didn't know was within. I am always amazed how spontaneously this arises when in his presence. It is definitely from a realm far from rational thought.

'Om shanti shanti shanti. Let there be peace and love amongst all beings of the universe.' He is quiet for a moment before speaking again. 'How this universe comes out of emptiness? Let me tell you. If you carve an image into the rock, before the image is carved the rock had the capability to hold the image. A gold necklace is made out of the gold. This gold has inherent nature to be made into any shape. When necklace is made, then gold and the necklace are together. Gold has inherent nature, you can bring it into any shape, will not lose goldness.

'Likewise this consciousness can take any form. Whatever it thinks so does it become. Consciousness creates this universe without losing its own nature. It is inherent nature of the ocean to create waves. Waves are not there then ocean doesn't lose anything, if waves are there then ocean doesn't gain anything. When plenty of waves the ocean is not troubled by this. Ocean remains ocean.

'Like this emptiness, consciousness will never be disturbed. No such thing as multiplicity and unity. No difference. Consciousness was not lost.'

I shuffle on my cushion and unwrap my shawl. All around people sit motionless. Inspired by the hall of meditators, I focus again on his words.

'Question is, "Why this creation being created to give trouble to all these beings that stay in it?" This same question, "Why God created the universe to give trouble to so many people?" You have to see what is the trouble now?'

He leans forward, smiling at us all.

'In darkness, in the forest, you see a stump of tree and you think it is a dacoit, a robber, and it is going to attack you. With close reasoning you see it is only a tree. How fear arises in you! You call it a bandit, going to rob you. Where do all these things come? It means you were not aware. Therefore the rope looked like a snake. Snake never was present. Out of ignorance you called it a snake and fear arose. There has been no snake at all. On close investigation you find there was no snake.

'On very close investigation you are going to investigate in the consciousness. Where does this universe abide? Looking closely it will disappear. On close investigation you will find never did anything arise and this is the ultimate truth.

'Without knowing this, your troubles are not going to end. Wherever there is duality there is trouble. Wherever there are two there is fear. Wherever there is oneness there is no problem. Hence you have to investigate here and now without any postponement. Who am I right now? Then you will find your own inherent nature of your own beingness, your own peace, happiness, eternity.

'"I am bound" then you are bound. "I suffer" then you suffer. "I am free" so you are free. Here you do not agree. If I say you are free, from the beginning you are free then you don't agree. Here you are confused. If I say "you suffer" then you say, "Yes, yes, we all are suffering." This is why the religions were formed for all the suffering. Who has seen hell first of all? Who has seen the mind? All is imagination so rid yourself by one single question: "who am I?"

'This question has to be solved by every human being. This birth has to be respected, adored to win freedom from this hallucination, imagination that you have been suffering. So that is the end. Om.'

He closes his eyes, sits again for a while. Then a small cough, sips some water, and wipes his mouth with a cloth. There is a thickness in the air, a silence that slowly rearranges as people shift position, stretch a leg or cough.

Papaji puts on his glasses and looks at the letters people have written to him with questions or experiences they want to share. A young German man sits at his feet. After an exchange, filled with laughter, another question is read and the questioner comes to the front to sit at Papaji's feet. He answers with such love and kindness I melt a little more.

'Find out who is aware. It will show you all by itself. Lift your veil of ignorance is all you have to do and you are in light. That is all. This is the diamond.'

The German man's girlfriend joins him, touching Papaji's feet. He seems to delight in her joy, his face full of smiles. She sits up next to

Papaji and sings the mantra 'Satyam Shivam Sundaram'. We all join in and I sing with adoration. Even Papaji is singing, until he says: 'This girl is singing very well. You come here. I like her singing. Yes, you come here.'

I open my eyes and he is looking at me, gesturing to me to come forward.

'Come, come!'

I do so with no hesitation. My body responds. No thought, no doubt of whether I will or not.

'Yes, yes, you sit here.'

I sit on the tucket with him and my floppy wool hat hides my crumpled hair.

'Where do you come from?' he is asking me, his face full of smiles. His energy ripples through me, leaving my mind completely blank. I don't know how to answer, so he plays with me, full of his infectious laughter.

'England,' I say, then I laugh; it all seems so absurd.

'Sing, sing!'

I do, just for a moment: 'Shiva Shiva Shambho Mahadeva Shambho'. I struggle to whisper the words then I fall at his feet and remain there till the end of satsang.

After satsang I go straight to the small room where he sits for a while before leaving. The room is already full. One of the attendants stands at the door.

'I want to see Papaji!' I say.

She waves me through. 'It's already full in here but you can find a place.'

The only space is by his feet. I tread carefully among the others sitting on the floor and I am there. He looks down at me with his sparkling eyes, taking his glasses off as if to say, 'Yes?'

'Papaji, can you give me a new name?' The words slip out and surprise me. I had not considered this before. Yet as I hear them it makes sense. I want to name this connection. I want to be his disciple.

'Very good.' He chuckles and takes a pen and paper and writes something before handing it to me. 'Prem Kumari. This is your name.'

I refold the piece of paper and put it in my pocket, and I realise I feel unworthy of such a name. It sounds so grand, formal even. Two words instead of one. I know that Kumari means virgin and it touches a deep disquiet, a shame … yes, unworthiness.

My thoughts sound loud and I sense myself watching them as if they are subtitles in a foreign movie. 'Kumari! Kumari! Virginal princess!' Prem means love, divine love. From Judith to Prem Kumari! Maiden of love. Instead of gratitude and wonder at such a name, the same sense of exposure as when I shaved my head clings to me, like the vulnerability of a newborn.

*   *   *

I want to stay in Indira Nagar, the neighbourhood of the satsang house. Kavitha Lodge is where I find my room: a bricked-in area on the roof, with no door. I hang a curtain and it suits me fine. Four other people stay there too and I introduce myself as Prem, a comfortable compromise. The Kumari part I tuck back in my pocket for another day.

I know I look like a hippy among all the neat and tidy westerners. I wear my woollen hat and a blanket with a hole cut out for the head, like a poncho.

It is now two years since I left my life in London. It may as well be an eternity.

One rainy evening I walk to the Public Call Office to make a phone call. Sitting in the booth cradling the phone is a woman with long black hair. Our eyes lock. Later she tells me she had seen me through the glass as I shook the rain from my hair.

Her name is Hania. She is short, round, and wears a long purple shirt over loose white trousers. Her long hair is black and her skin suggests she may be Native American. She looks like a squaw and I tell her so.

'No no! I am Italian stock, first generation American from Italian immigrants.'

She found her way to India after following the Hare Krishnas. She has been in Lucknow only a couple of weeks. When we met she had been calling her lover in America.

'How come some people call you Prem and others call you Prem Kumari?' she asks, as we eat lunch together on the roof outside my room. I like to cook my own food, often kidgeree with a vegetable or two.

'Well. Recently I changed my name. Actually I asked Papaji for a new name and he gave this name Prem Kumari. It is taking me a while to settle into it. Sounds a bit grand, don't you think? So for now I am just going as Prem. It means love.'

'What does Prem Kumari mean?'

'Well, Kumari means virgin, or maiden. So I guess it is maiden of love.'

'I think it is a beautiful name. I would be proud if my Guruji gave me a name like that.'

'I find it all a bit of a mouthful and really, it's a bit uncomfortable having a name that means virgin.'

'I understand Kumari to mean princess. How delightful to have a name that means love princess or princess of love.' I blush and barely look up from my bowl of kidgeree, watching the way the ghee melts and forms almost a river. Hania is quick to add: 'Hey, I really didn't mean to embarrass you. I'm happy to call you Prem, or Kumari or Prem Kumari, whatever you are comfortable with.' She reaches over and holds my arm.

'Thanks,' I tell her. 'Look, I never thought I would even be here with a guru and all this scene. It isn't really me, if you know what I mean. I guess I'm just a newcomer to the whole thing of satsang, gurus and devotees.'

'That's okay, I understand. It's the same for me too in a way. You are here for his teaching and also because he is a living guru who asks nothing of his devotees. Except to find out who we really are. And that is why we are here.' She lets go of my arm and helps herself to another spoonful of kidgeree. Her words are true. I know it. Since my encounter with Papaji on my first day back I have kept pretty much to myself. I certainly don't write him letters or feel brave enough in any way to put myself forward, so to speak. I did make a card for him soon after he gave me my name. I drew Shiva and a small lingam and on the back wrote the words from the Ashtavakra Gita, a favourite scripture of mine. After I had handed it in, Kavita – whose room on the roof I stay in – returned from his house one evening and came to find me. I was as usual sitting up on the roof enjoying the small taste of the night sky.

'Papaji was asking about you this evening. Talking about the girl who made the card with Shiva on. He really liked it. He was asking how you support yourself to be here in India and I told him you were a nurse. He said, "Ah very good, her patients would have loved her. They must miss her." As she tells me this I almost swoon. I can feel an energetic swirl or spin in my chest. It banishes again any doubts I may have as to why exactly I find myself in this polluted bustling city with a couple of hundred westerners sitting at the feet of a guru.

Hania is a gift. 'I'm so glad I have met you,' I tell her. 'I have always felt a bit of an outsider at satsang with so many westerners coming straight from the west or Pune. I have India in my bones like you do.' Of course I have made connections, with a few women in particular. Hania is different. She feels like a warrior, a bit of a loner, and a long-time lover of Krishna. She is also gay.

'I had a sort of affair with a woman last year,' I tell her. 'We spent two weeks together on a beach and after a few days we became lovers. I'd never been with a woman before, other than a few kisses.' I didn't tell her that our loving was exclusively on my terms. I find myself blushing and knotting up inside as I remember how I was with Helene, how I thwarted the potential with my insecurity. Maybe I am not really attracted to women, simple as that. I have just been lovers with Babaji and had to almost hold back for fear of throwing myself into him all at once. And as I think of making love with him I realise it is just different – from women or from any of the countless men I have slept with. It is like our souls are joining and our bodies simply reflect that union. A merging, almost, into him.

'Mmm, will you go back to men?' Hania is smiling and fortunately her usual sense of perception is not tuned to my thoughts right now.

'Well, I already have. I have a lover up in the mountains.'

'Do you? What's he doing up there in the winter?'

'He is a sadhu, has a small ashram.'

'You've been lovers with a sadhu? I've seen that before.'

'Really?'

'Yes, of course. Can be a nice Shiva Shakti. And some of the babas are so beautiful.'

I'm glad she's not fazed. 'I've known him a while. A long time before we were lovers.' I want to sanctify our connection, ensure she does not think of it as anything casual. That this is the real deal, so to speak. Nothing flippant, nothing casual.

'I'd like to meet him sometime. He's a lucky man.' And she reaches across and kisses my cheek. 'I'm glad I have met you too! I would have no one to eat out at the street stalls with. Most westerners here are too wound up about getting sick to enjoy what is here. Later, let's go and eat aloo tikki and take a rickshaw to the Hanuman temple in town. It's Tuesday after all and the puja there is beautiful, with bhajan afterwards!'

*   *   *

My visa finishes at the end of February. I visit the immigration office in a government building in the centre of town. I fill in many forms then wait a long time in a corridor splattered with red betel stains. If I didn't know better I could think there had been a slaughter here recently. The immigration wallah is a small man with a round belly on top of which he rests his hands. He slides my passport across his desk with a shake of his head, tucking the paan that he is chewing to one side of his mouth. He speaks as if he has a golf ball in his mouth. 'One month more, madam. Then you must be exiting the country.'

*   *   *

Pilgrimage is an integral part of Indian culture. Hindus embark on a pilgrimage to ensure a good marriage for their sons, to cure a health issue, or simply to worship a deity at a particular time auspicious for blessings. Vedic astrologers prescribe a pilgrimage of different temples to visit, pujas to enhance certain planetary influences or to lessen the impact of unfavourable planetary aspects. Arunachala is such a place. Papaji speaks often of Arunachala. This mountain is said to be a manifestation of Shiva. It is where Ramana Maharshi, Papaji's own guru, lived since the age of sixteen and Ramana Ashram nestles at the feet of this holy hill.

The south of India heats up by late March. Now is the time to visit Arunachala. I will take a pilgrimage to the holy mountain and then renew my Indian visa in Sri Lanka. April will be the perfect time to return north, and to Dharamsala. I send Babaji a card telling him my plan and that all is well. Every morning since I have been here in Lucknow I light incense and place it in front of a photo that I took of him, sitting by his dhuni. He is smiling a wide smile. I also place a flower before the photo. It has become a ritual.

CHAPTER THIRTEEN

Ramana Ashram

'There is nothing to attain and no time within which to attain. You are always That. You have not got to attain anything. You have only to give up thinking you are limited, to give up thinking you are this body.' Ramana Maharshi

Every day Ramana Ashram feeds the neighbourhood sadhus. A large untidy group line up in the shade of an old gnarled mango tree, a scruffy bunch with faded orange clothes and long beards of black, grey or white. Smeared with ash, they provide a perfect welcome. Arunachala rises above. My first sighting of Arunachala, outlined in the distance from the bus, invoked tears of reverence that slid soundlessly down my cheeks. As we drove closer the form took shape until here I finally am, standing on sacred soil.

Ramana Maharshi is one of the last century's greatest saints. The dining hall has a large photo of him sitting cross-legged, eating with his hand. Every morning a fresh flower mala is strung in devotion to this great sage. We sit in rows on the floor, ushered in by a host of attendants, who serve us each two idlis on a banana leaf and a cup of milky coffee in a stainless steel cup. Idlis are steamed buns of slightly fermented powdered rice. I prefer idlis plain and decline the ladle full of soupy dhal known as samba, spicy with chillies. This is traditional south Indian food, along with dosa, which is a fermented mix of rice and dhal made into a thin pancake. Samba is served with everything, watery and sometimes burning with chilli.

Ramana Ashram is a place of presence. Puja begins before dawn, and throughout the day bells can be heard from the temple and from the main hall. A statue of Ramana in the main hall marks the Samadhi – where his body was entombed almost sixty years ago. A lingam is placed in front of the statue, covered with flowers. Brahmin priests attend to its worship. Devotees walk slowly around in circumambulation. I too join the walking, savouring the cool marble beneath my feet, the haloed joy. Walking meditation in action. The air has a thickness that dissolves me at my edges – sinking in to myself, and floating at the same time.

The mother temple houses Shiva: a lingam in the sanctum, attended by a Brahmin with an ample hanging belly and white hair in a thin topknot. He barely smiles and sloshes water from a bucket to wash the floor. The temple is black granite and the walls are thick. Incense pours into the dimly lit interior. I watch the preparations for puja, the low chanting and preparations for worship as the bundles of flower malas are unwrapped and carefully placed around the lingam. Incense plumes and swirls and bells clang, resounding off the walls where deities sit in niches with yellow and orange marigold flowers. An oil lamp is always burning, invoking a mysterious realm removed from time, and I wonder if a coven would perhaps feel similar.

Lunch is a feast. We line up outside the dining hall to take our place on the floor with a banana leaf as a plate. Attendants move up and down the rows with steaming silver buckets to serve a splash of yellow dhal, a dollop of very cooked vegetable, a pile of rice. Buttermilk from the ashram cows deftly served in a cup, then sweet halva to finish.

My attention is pulled again and again to the mountain. Arunachala is said to be Shiva himself. I wonder whether the aura of presence that emanates here is from this age-old collective belief and that creates an energy field itself. Or is it truly an aspect of God? Presence is unmistakable, like a wave breaking against virgin sand, and I settle for the mysterious unknown.

On the fourth night of my stay I wake to a vision. My room is lit up with an iridescent golden light that changes before my eyes to the outline of Arunachala. Fully awake, I sit up in an instant. The vision is like nothing I have ever experienced and lasts some minutes. Everywhere, everything is this golden image of Arunachala. The light slowly fades to a glow before reality returns to the form of a darkened room. I lie in a state of communion with God, a complete absence of thought, only a deep extraordinary silence. I fall back to a state of sleep, with the recurring thought: 'I am sleeping', and watch the play of sleep happen to this person I know to be me. I know to be me simply because from the moment I was born into this body I have been given a name. Every experience, every shape of my life has either name or form. And this is how I have identified as myself – lifetimes of belief in myself as a separate being. I hear the voice of Papaji: 'Ask yourself just once: who am I?'

I stay eight days in Ramana Ashram and do very little but immerse myself in the routine and sanctity offered. The experience of the vision of Arunachala leaves me in no doubt as to the glory of this mountain. No wonder Ramana, when he was sixteen years old, left his home and travelled here. He never left. After living in a cave for some years he moved down the hill to where this ashram grew. The old hall, as it is known, has the tucket where Ramana used to sit. There is a photo of him reclining, his gaze unflinching. This is a place of silence, no bells or puja, just the essence of self-inquiry. I sit against the wall in here, close my eyes. I hear the puja from the main hall and temple and the diluted sound trickles through me like a cool mountain stream. Thoughts still play havoc, the ceaseless commentary and chatter. Yet much of the time there is a silence so thick it leaves no room for anything else. The space between my thoughts is amplified and I know that this is the realm that I glimpsed when Henry left his body. Sitting here in this cool hall – a refuge in itself from the chaos and noise of life outside the ashram gates – I find it utterly mysterious that the presence of a sage, whose photo seems to wink and shine, can be felt so strongly some fifty years after his death. So what then is death? I have heard many times over this last two years in India that the self, the Atman, the soul, is the foundation of eternity. Now as I experience for myself the wonder that arises when thought is absent, it allows me to be more discerning about how much attention I give a thought when it does arise. I smile to myself, remembering how often Papaji tells us: 'Simply keep quiet; do not touch a single thought.' I believe my thoughts are real, have never ever questioned further the reality and nature of thought. It suddenly seems this is a bad habit picked up from the general consensus of my life so far. I think of the punitive God I grew up with and how death was to be feared. Yet death is surely just a continuation of being. The simple words of a song we used to sing in Sunday school creep into my mind and I realise in essence there is no separation between the God of Christians and this presence all around me. *Be still and know that I am God.* I rearrange my sitting position on the tile floor, follow my breath and concentrate my awareness again to bask in this silence. It isn't long before my lower back twinges and my legs desperately want to be uncrossed and stretch. I bow down before the photo of Ramana and pray for his grace.

*　　*　　*

On my last day I venture out of the ashram. I take a rickshaw to visit the main temple, one of the largest in south India. The busy main street gives the first sighting of the temple gopurams, four huge pyramids sixty metres tall. Elaborate carved stone pillars, tiered in layers, stretch upwards into the blue sky.

The rickshaw turns down a side street where lean-to shacks rest against the high granite wall of the temple complex. Black tarpaulins stretch over posts and a woman cooks on a fire while bare-bottomed kids play in the dirt. Cycle rickshaws sit idle. A woman sweeps dust to a pile. The street is narrow and jammed; horns blare and bicycle bells ring. After sitting for too long with the black exhaust filling my nostrils, I pay the fare, wrap a scarf over my head and walk through a throng of people. Stalls sell statues of the gods, brass bells and urns. Conical piles of red kum kum powder shine in the sunlight. Mala beads, pendants on red string, coconuts for offering in the temple are all available. Around the corner the street widens for the main entrance. A music stall opposite plays Shiva bhajans so loudly the sound is distorted. A pale creamy coloured cow picks through a pile of garbage swept up against the temple wall. A bowl of fire raised on a stand burns with orange flame, black smoke threading through the air. People bow then wave their hands over the flame. I pause to say a prayer before entering the temple.

Women sit with baskets of orange and yellow flowers, jasmine and tidy piles of deep pink roses, already fully open, straining for their own darshan. Malas coiled, already made. I leave my chappal with the flower woman for one rupee. As she hands me the change from her wrinkled fingers, beggars surround me. Black eyes pierce their gnarled faces and they plead with outstretched tins. I search my pockets for rupee coins and place something in each tin. Sadhus beg too, and offer a low 'Om Namah Shivaya' as they hold out their bowl.

As I step into the temple compound, the certainty that I have been here before is unmistakable. I can see myself here but not with normal vision. It is as if I am watching an old movie, the colours and images slightly faded. I sit on the stone floor and lean against the cool granite wall, overwhelmed by the energy all around me.

This temple of Lord Arunachaleswara is much bigger than any I have visited before. It is a massive, thick stone-walled compound with a bathing pond, several temples and the auspicious Shiva temple. Pujaris sit in twos or threes on the steps, threading yellow flowers from woven baskets. Sadhus sit alone or in groups, dots of orange against grey granite. Kids run to me with wilted strings of tuberose still holding their fragrance.

'Five rupees! Five rupees! Flower, madam, flower!'

Families of monkeys run by with babies clinging to their bellies. Three sadhus sit on a ledge of stone, their legs swinging idle. 'Om Namah Shivaya!' one of them calls to me and I return the salute.

'Om Namah Shivaya!'

The sadhu smiles and holds his hand up in a blessing. He has a thick string of malas around his neck and his forehead is smeared with grey ash. His hair is three thick jutta and he holds a stick in his other hand. Above it all, presiding over its worship, is Arunachala. The sanctity suggests the anchor of the heavens.

Where there is Shiva, his goddess is never far away. Shakti: the great energy of creation. A very subtle vibration from my toes through to the top of my head keeps my attention exactly in the moment and I am filled again with the overwhelming sense of love and desire to worship. 'Take all of me,' I whisper to a goddess carved of stone – a goddess who has been dressed in a gold and yellow fabric, whose face glitters with diamonds in her nose, her ears, and necklaces of jewels around her neck. At her feet, oil lamps burn. A golden bowl overflows with fruits and a coconut cut in half displays its white flesh. 'Thou shalt not worship idols', the Bible says. I take darshan: drink the water offered, receive a dot of red between the eyebrows and stumble out.

I gaze up at the mountain; the sun is lost in its own brilliance as the heat falls on my upturned face. It feels impossible that I will leave the following day and I realise that actually I am free to come back if I wish. I decided there and then that I will, after my trip to Sri Lanka for the visa business.

CHAPTER FOURTEEN

Arunachala

'Are we not at peace in the interval when one thought ceases and another does not yet arise?' Ramana Maharshi

U nawatuna has all the ingredients of a tropical paradise. White-sand beach lined with palms, water as blue as eternity, just a suggestion of a wave as if even the ocean is too relaxed to make a fuss. A reef off the bay gives shelter to turtles, which swim side by side as I take my many dips. I stay in a local guesthouse with a voluptuous mama cooking up a storm every evening. By chance, a couple of women I met in Bodhgaya last year are here and the company fits the scene. I turn twenty-eight and celebrate the day with them. We walk through the jungle over a headland to another beach where we collect shells, create mandalas in the sand ... just us all day with our picnic of pineapples and bananas.

'How delightful to spend my birthday with women in paradise!' The last time my toes touched sand, my body swam in warm waters, was of course in Thailand. I haven't heard from Helene in some months now. Last I heard she was back in Amsterdam. I wonder why I haven't heard more recently. Of course I know how it is. Travelling brings so many experiences, encounters and meetings that in the moment of relating feel that they will last forever. I look at the women before me now, Annie from Switzerland and Kasha from America. Kasha is Philippino heritage, exotic and gorgeous. Two women linked by a man, who was Annie's partner and is now Kasha's. They speak of him with concern. He's been meditating too much and apparently his feet have lost touch with the earth. I envy them at times, the sisterhood they share and their obvious care.

I am becoming a loner. Who do I wish was here? Helene of course, although who knows what could have changed over the time since we met. It could be awkward, confronting even. Hania is the one, with her solid wisdom and dark almond eyes. We would sit and chant together as the sun receded, creating altars in the sand to worship.

I sit on the sand before the flat blue ocean. I'm twenty-eight, on a beach in Sri Lanka, and have I found what I am searching for? I consider this question and imagine how Papaji might smile and say, 'If you have a gold coin in your hand will you even question if you have found the gold coin?' No, of course not. I think of the night I woke to a shimmering golden Arunachala outlined before me, how there was a quiet in my mind, an absence of thought that had lasted all the day. It flavoured my time at Ramana Ashram with nectar like honey. The overwhelming love and outpouring I felt at the Shakti shrine in the main temple. The mysterious presence of Papaji and the way my whole being is pulled to him. Perhaps the question of a search is now outdated. I have bought the ticket, so to speak, and I am in for the ride. India is carrying me to places I could never have dreamed.

Still I am troubled by my mind and its ceaseless comments. Here on the beach it is my body that is under scrutiny – *can't believe you have been travelling in India so long and you're not thin. Look at those thighs, you really should think about exercise.*

So when Annie comments how healthy and great I look, I can only mumble, 'Really, I don't think so.' A German man joined us on the beach the other day and clearly kept his eyes on me as I retreated to the ocean and swam and swam in the velvet water.

Late afternoon we sit with a cold Sinhala beer and watch the sun dip low in the sea. I send a prayer of thanks to all the gods for casting me adrift. As if in response, the heavens herald the passage of night with a display of fiery red.

'Perfect for an Aries!' Annie laughs. We wait till the sky is full of stars before heading home to a dinner of potato curry cooked with green beans, spices and coconut milk. Annie is into astrology and warns me that twenty-eight is Saturn return year. 'Can be a big year.'

*   *   *

Arunachala shimmers red and stark against a faded sky. Tiruvannamalai in April is hot. Sweat runs down my back and the dry dusty air catches in my nose and throat. What am I doing here, I wonder momentarily, in the south of India, in a polluted town, when I could be up in the mountains amidst cooler climates and towering vistas – with Babaji. Yet I've sealed my fate, even arranged my accommodation before I left for Sri Lanka.

My cottage is one room with a kitchen and a bed. I pull the bed out onto the verandah, secure the mosquito net and spend most of the day and all of the night in various states of recline. The heat lulls the mind and from eleven in the morning to about four or five in the afternoon it is just too hot to do anything.

This is retreat time with a difference. There is no structure to follow, no bells to guide me. The mountain pulls me to gaze almost unblinking, as shapes take form with the changing light, but the heat pins me down and there are limited possibilities for activity. I try to concentrate on reading. The teachings of Ramana offer a place of quiet to rest within and savour. Yet it isn't long before thoughts creep in, out of the ether it seems. *What are you trying to do? Why don't you get a purpose to your life? If you had stayed with Mark you would probably have a family by now. And live in Cornwall. You are part Cornish after all. Would have been perfect. Instead you're trying to be something else. Not doing too well either, hey?* I try to ignore the thoughts and read another paragraph. *You'd probably be like Sabine screaming at the kids all day.* Jesus! Give me a break! I have no interest in thinking about Mark, a doctor I dated for a while, yet here he is in my mind. It was the most serious relationship I had and my mother was heartbroken when I ended it. I abandon any idea of meditating and doze until the heat of the day passes.

In the late afternoon I hop on my bike and ride to the chai stall on the main road. It's serene around this side of the mountain with many sights to fill my hunger for entertainment. Neem trees line the road and the chai stall is a plastic tarp flung over a wooden structure. Chai in the south lacks the finesse of chai in the north and often I opt for coffee – a milky brew that jolts me from the slothful heat.

Coffee finished and energy restored, I ride on down the road. My favourite temples are here: a Shiva temple with the Parvati temple next door, across the road a Hanuman temple. Women sit on the steps, insisting I buy tulsi and camphor to offer – the herbs fresh despite the wilting heat. The pujari has a round belly and a soft lovely face and when he sings, after giving me a pat on the head and a splash of water in my cupped hands, he sounds like an angel. His voice echoes in the cool chamber as I bow before the orange monkey image.

*   *   *

The custom in India is to circumambulate a shrine or holy place and so it is in Arunachala. It is considered auspicious to walk pradakshina – clockwise around the mountain. It is only possible in the early hours when the relentless heat is dormant. I wake before light when darkness enfolds the heavens and the streets are almost empty. The village is deserted except for the dogs, which growl and bark.

Dawn creeps across the sky. Women carry pots to the water tap, men head to the fields for their toilet with water jars in one hand, coughing and spitting as they go. The pathway winds through a young juniper forest behind the village. Fresh shits steam and stink by the path. Mudbrick huts stretch all around this side of the mountain, joining with the edge of town after an hour's walk. I walk quickly, intent on my pradakshina. Walking barefoot encourages me to be present to every step. A sharp stone, fresh excrement, a thorny twig – all require vigilance. Papaji speaks of vigilance, of bringing one's attention to the content of thought, to witness thought, rather than be swept along in a seemingly endless chatter. 'Do not let anything disturb your peace.' Why then is it so hard to disengage from one's own thought?

I notice it depends on the thought content. If I find myself busy with trivia such as revisiting a conversation I had in Sri Lanka and what I might have said differently, or whether or not to stop for idli at the ashram today, with this sort of chatter I catch myself, pull myself back, take notice of what is happening around me until I feel myself present again. It is the self-recrimination that seems to entwine in a way that never gives an option but to collapse under the weight. When the bullet hit its mark on the Bodhgaya retreat I was right with my response. I do not love myself. Or at times even vaguely like myself. Not easy company to keep when options are limited.

Every day I set out religiously in the pre-dawn night for pradakshina. The village dogs growl and snarl as I walk faster, praying they leave me alone. As day unwraps herself from night, village kids take up the pressure. 'One rupee, one rupee. Hello school pen, school pen.' I smile, shrug or ignore them as best I can. It's not the company I want. Then there is the path behind the village where the stink is really bad and I have to watch the path for fresh steaming turds.

In town the dusty air is choked, the tempos, buses and trucks in full swing. The sheer mass of India weighs on me: unrelenting crowds, the overflow of traffic, cracked and broken roadsides. I weave and turn, swept along with the tide. Eyes turn and men leer. *For fuck's sake*, I want to yell, *I am walking around this mountain! I'm a pilgrim, can't you see?* Instead I keep my eyes to the ground, the dirt, the grunting pigs wallowing in slimy gutters, garbage piled up everywhere.

With the first sighting of the towering gopurams of the temple, my step quickens and my thoughts refocus. The chaos and clutter and noise and filth recede into the background. I step into the ancient world and the walls surround me with the sense of coming home. It is the Shakti temple that entices me. Every day the goddess is adorned in different cloth, saris of gold and pink, red and turquoise. She wears rings on her fingers and toes and sparkling jewels fall across her breast. The precision and devotion with which she is worshipped has been unchanged for millennia. The air is thick enough to hold, full of the sultry perfume of incense and camphor and oil lamps. The inner chamber hums with her tune.

Darshan complete, sometimes hours later, I resume my pradakshina out through town, walking on the edge of the road with rickshaws, bicycles and trucks racing by. I stop in at the ashram, sit for a while in the hall, the welcome feel of white marble underfoot. The sublime quiet, the presence that thickens in my breath, delivers me back to myself. There may be a puja happening or chanting in the main hall.

I walk past bathing kunds where monkeys sit in the trees and a sadhu washes an orange cloth in the green-brown water far down the steps. And then the last stretch, after turning off the busy main road to Bangalore. Neem trees filter the sun. Shrines and sadhus are everywhere. Monkeys spill from the trees, to stroll down the road, or sit on the stone benches watching the world pass by. This is my neighbourhood – the temples and collection of chai stalls. Nothing much happens; sadhus attend to the temples and others add their presence by doing very little other than sit by the roadside turning mala beads through their fingers.

* * *

Restlessness creeps in between the slats of thick hot air as I rest during the heat of the day. I think of Papaji and pray to him. The heat, mosquitoes in the evening, walking alone with eyes following me, is getting to me.

I still religiously walk pradakshina. I stay longer now in the main temple in town, unable to pull away from the force of energy emanating from the Shakti shrine. I take a rickshaw to the ashram; the sun is already high in the sky and it is just too hot to finish the walk. It is early May and the heat is extreme. My shirt sticks to my back, the sun pierces my covered head, and my feet are sore on the hot dirt of the road. I arrive back home ready for the quiet, white walls and fan, a cold bucket bath to wash the lines of dirt from my feet.

Temperatures rise to the high forties. In the afternoon hot breezes bring red dust and the earth is baked crimson. The mountain shimmers, all definition lost, as if it too has melted with the heat. It is going to be months before it will change.

As the heat wears on, the ants build up. One morning I find a swarm of them, everywhere, covering every inch of the floor and surfaces of the house. They crawl up my legs – tiny black ants – and as I sweep them away, brush them from my legs, I burst into tears.

The next afternoon, as I sprinkle the lawn and water the laden papaya trees, I almost stand on a snake. It is as thick as my arm, long and black. It slithers away inches from my bare feet. I guess it is a black cobra. A shiver runs up my back as I realise I was so close to a highly poisonous snake. I watch it disappear through the wire fence. Snakes are symbolic. It is time to leave.

The rising irritation with my inability to just be quiet, truly quiet, is growing to a distraction. The experience of sitting in Ramana Ashram, or in the main temple, is a spacious opening, like the petals of a flower touched by the sun. The contrast with the distracted me – the one who feels like I am under attack from another part of myself – is unbearable. It seems stubborn and entrenched, as if two distinct people are in residence. I want to return to Papaji, a raft over troubled waters. This time here alone, with the heat, with the majesty of the mountain, has been a pilgrimage indeed.

*   *   *

The man behind the desk at a travel agent near the ashram looks bored and half asleep; a fan whirrs above his head, papers weighted under a statue of Ganesh.

'Phone now not working, you later come,' he tells me so I give him my request to book a sleeper train to Lucknow and in the evening time I return.

'Not possible. Trains full, next month going.'

'No, no, not next month going, this week going. Or next week is okay.' I'm sure my beseeching will work.

'No, all train full. No booking possible.'

'But I need to leave!' I realise the futility as I speak.

'Then maybe you bus taking.'

Bus! Is he mad? It will take days to reach Lucknow by train. By bus it could be a week. I hold on to myself and suddenly feel so foolish. The man has already lost interest. The heat is getting to the locals too. I accept the facts. All trains from Madras up to the north are full for weeks. There is no way I will take a bus for days on end. I obviously need to stay.

'Thank you, ji,' I offer and he responds, 'Welcome, madam.'

Like all the scriptures state, it is great good luck to meet a teacher who can reveal the truth, a guru, the dispeller of ignorance. I decide to leave anyway and see what I can do to find a train in Madras.

The express train north to Delhi leaves on a Friday and Tuesday, so Monday is my last pradakshina. Monday is the auspicious day for Shiva worship and I feel a blessing in my plans. I spend hours in the main temple, sitting in the inner sanctum of both the Arunachaleswara shrine and the Shakti shrine. I know I will be back to this sacred place. Arunachala, Shiva in form. I sit in the shade, content to watch the myriad scenes of pilgrims, sadhus, children, families. Worship and devotion is so entrenched in the Indian culture. This culture has remained unchanged for thousands of years: the gods, ritual and devotion exist hand-in-hand with everyday life.

*   *   *

Madras railway station is thick with people pushing, queuing, waiting. It seems impossible. The train departs at 6 pm and by 4 pm it looks hopeless. The queue is almost unmoving, with a noisy fan stirring the hot stale air. Sweat pools and runs down my back, across my forehead. I focus my thoughts and pray. Lucknow is my destination and I pray for help. Literally some minutes later, a man appears. Some hours before, we had spoken a few words when I asked him for help in finding the right queue.

He returns at this moment, squeezing through the lines, gesturing frantically. 'Madam, please come, madam, please you coming ticket buying. This Delhi train soon leaving.' He hurries me through the queuing crowds straight to a ticket booth.

The ticket seller behind the counter wipes his forehead with a dirty looking cloth. 'I want a ticket to Lucknow on the New Delhi express.' I'm almost shouting through the opening.

'Madam, train is full. All trains full. You getting ticket for next week.'

'No! I need to go today.' I am suddenly unable to deal with the heat, the buzzing flies, the incredible disorder. I can feel a slither of panicky claustrophobia, and fear momentarily grabs at me. The ticket hall is packed, my helper squashed by my side. He spits a thin stream of red betel against the counter wall then speaks rapidly to the ticket seller.

'Okay, okay! Take ticket on train to Jhansi. Jhansi–Lucknow no problem.'

I hand over the rupees, snatching my ticket. The relief that floods me is filled with gratitude. 'Thank you, thank you,' I whisper.

'Train soon coming! This express train. Jhansi big station, many trains for Lucknow.' He rushes me through the throng, across a bridge to another platform. Minutes later, amidst a billowing plume of black smoke, the train shrieks into the station, pulling up to a clamour of whistles and shouts. He even finds my compartment.

With a slight shake of his head he smiles, 'Namaste, madam.'

I want to hug him. I fold my hands together. 'Thank you, thank you, ji!'

He beams at me. 'You are my guest in this country. It is my duty, madam.' He disappears into the swallowing crowd.

Two nights later we reach Jhansi mid-morning. The ticket seller in Madras was right. The next train for Lucknow leaves later in the day.

*   *   *

The deadly heat at the end of May keeps westerners to a minimum. It is the season of bael, a pulpy round fruit with skin that needs to be

181

peeled. It is cooling for the body and full of vitamin C. It's mango season too – piles of green-skinned local ones, a few rupees a kilo, the orange flesh juicy and sweet. I feast on them every day. I have a small, two-room apartment in the neighbourhood of satsang house and already a week has passed.

I wake with dawn to sit in front of my altar. Meditation has changed now to asking the question: who am I? If I find a household of thoughts wanting to engage, I ask myself, 'Who is having these thoughts?' The teaching of Advaita is to trace the source of the perceived 'I', to find out what inherent reality the individual self has. Thought is the basis for everything.

'Just keep quiet for one instant, and don't stir a single thought in your mind. Peace does not belong to the past, peace is instant Presence.'

Devotion overwhelms me. Such a love for this man who patiently listens to us and diligently tells us we are already free. That it is all such a great illusion of the mind to think we are anything but Self. He loves to joke about the name Lucknow: 'Luck Now! How lucky to be here in satsang. There are many preachers in the world, but here in Luck Now we find out: Who am I?

'The grace of Self gives rise to the desire for freedom. The grace of God brings you to the Guru. The Grace of the Guru removes all doubts and leaves only freedom.'

One week merges to one month, another week, another month. In early July, clouds gather in the afternoon and the heat builds up till even at night the air is barely breathable. The pollution sits in a heavy swathe and the sun fades to a dirty red, long before reaching the horizon. Sultry forms creep across the sky, the air charged with the promise of rain. Finally it falls, in big steamy drops, to the shouts of children splashing in the streets, and continues till the lanes are a mushy slush of mud and slime.

At the beginning of September I have another six weeks of visa and the pull to see Babaji is impossible now to resist. It is time to head to the hills. How gracious India has been to me. I have met my guru, and can sit by the fire of a sadhu who lives his life in service to God.

CHAPTER FIFTEEN

The ashram

*'Fix your mind on Me, be devoted to Me, offer service
to Me, bow down to Me and you shall certainly reach
Me. I promise you because you are very dear to Me.'*
The Bhagavad Gita

My feet fly down the pathway through the dripping woods, across the little bridge, a roaring stream beneath. Smoke mingles in the mist as I push open the wet wooden gate. He sits by the fire as if he has never moved, neatly wrapped in the orange shawl. I think it's the one I gave him all those months before. For a moment he looks shocked then gives me a big smile. My heart surges upwards as he speaks. 'Judith hai! Accha hai, Judith!'

'Namaste, Babaji. Namaste.' My folded palms unravel.

'You when coming?'

'Just now, Babaji.'

'You here stay no problem. Accha tikhai.' Our gaze rests for just a moment before he pulls his eyes away to meet the flame. 'You long time no coming.'

'Long time, Babaji. Now I am here.'

'Tikhai tikhai. You now here stay.'

Babaji is just the same. His delight in my company is clear in the smiles that spill from him, the glances of such tenderness. I share a little of my adventures since I saw him last, of changing my name and travelling to Arunachala. 'Very good, very good. Prem Kumari bahut accha name.'

Three other guests stay at the ashram. After dinner is eaten and plates cleared away, the others leave the fireplace and I stay and smoke a beedi. Babaji tidies the fire, speaking very little, yet a communion occurs. The fire is the common focus. I notice how it caresses the smooth brown of his skin and lights his beard with golden highlights. He looks up too and always his eyes hold me for just a moment before we both look quickly away.

My room is next to his. A low bed, three shelves of planks balanced on stones. The pillow is musty and the window bare. I hear him cough and mutter in the early hours; the smell of beedi smoke mingles with incense and the low chanting of his prayers. As dawn slips in between the trees he attends to the temple, the clear tinkle of the bell a definition for the day. I join him by the fire as he uncovers the embers from the night before, the white cat asleep in her place by the woodpile.

I have been here a week.

'Tomorrow this valley place going some wood taking. Early going, night time home coming.' Babaji looks at me with his eyes full. I know, of course, the valley he speaks of, where I have sometimes camped. There is a rock overhang by the river which rushes from the snowfields above.

'Tikhai, Babaji.'

'You going, this top ridge waiting.'

*   ×   *

The next morning I go to where the Durga temple on the ridge faces valleys of mauve. The sun is an orange ball far away and I watch its form soften to gold as shadows recede and light fills the world. Babaji suddenly appears through the pines and although I am expecting him, waiting for him even, I am startled.

'Short cut.' He nods and hardly pauses so I scramble to follow. I catch up and fall into place behind as he strides along the path, machete tied with a rope over his shoulder. As the pathway narrows and the lips of the valley press in, he stops.

'Kumariji, tikhai?'

I can only smile – a shy smile – and I keep hold of myself in case joy bursts me open as I step close enough to smell the mix of coconut oil and sandalwood on his skin. He holds my face in his leathery hands, our foreheads touching just for a moment.

The path weaves down to the river below, crossing over the boulders to the cave ledge beneath the rock overhang. Shepherds have camped here recently; the stone fireplace is blackened and the smell of goats lingers. I squat on one of the massive boulders and watch the clear water pour between the smoothed opening, its silken sheen surging to white as it tumbles, crashes and glides.

Babaji gathers sticks for a fire. From his bundle he takes a small pot and a packet of rotis wrapped in a cloth. He brews sweet black tea and we sit on the earth. Our knees touch. Tiny wrens with red bodies and silver heads flit and flirt amongst long tendrils of ivy that falls in curtains from the rock high above. Ferns tucked in amongst crevasses; a constant rush of river behind the boulders. Sunlight pours from the slash of blue above. The fire burns to a smoulder before us as the sun moves on, throwing us into shadow. I stand and stretch then find a spot on one of the boulders where the sun warms me once again. Babaji follows and takes off his shirt and folds it neatly beside him.

'Sun good feeling. Body happy coming.' His malas rest where I want to be.

The water is turquoise. I take off my clothes and slide in. The iciness shocks me. I want to yell and shout with sheer delight but instead I submerge for just a moment then climb out, wrapping my scarf around me like a towel. Babaji laughs.

'Ganga ki darshan!' I declare. [Blessing of Ganga.]

I dress and lie on the warmth of the sun-baked rock. He rests his hand on my forehead, lightly brushing a strand of wet hair. I look up at him and then follow him to the fireplace. He holds me again and my cheek presses against the beads of his malas, the soft brush of his beard; I am surrounded by his scent of coconut oil and smoke and incense ... and him.

He watches as I let my trousers fall to the ground, then pulls me to his lap and I feel him grow, harden. He holds me close and I fall in to him, his smooth brown skin like amber beneath my fingers. Our eyes hold as he enters me with a groan, pulling me closer, rocking me on him; then he becomes still, unmoving, until his whole body trembles. Holding me, moving again, a low groan. I give a little more and I can feel him deep inside; I want to rock and rock but I let him be the leader. A subtle greater pleasure spreads and pierces and I muffle my sound; his body responds and again the stillness. He pulls back just enough so I can still feel his breath, his eyes dark liquid pools to dive into again and again. I move slightly and he shudders again, closing his eyes. I close mine too, breathing as deep as I can. Malas brush my breast, nipples as hard as him.

Later, when I am dressed, we sit side by side. 'This liquid, no out coming.'

'Better not, Babaji.' But I have wondered how he can be so controlled.

'This very good feeling, Kumariji. Too much good, Kumariji. Sometimes now me problem coming. Before, mind only God thinking, now half God thinking, half you thinking. This problem coming.'

I have no answer. I do not want to hear these words. I have entombed him in a vault untouched by everyday relating. Our loving has a purity that I do not want to tarnish. I hold his hand as the flowing song of water rushes all around.

He squeezes my hand then takes his back, smoothes his beard, searches for a beedi. 'Chello tikhai, sub Bhagwan. Sub Bhagwan hey.' [Enough – all is God.] I'm surprised at how I need to hear these words. To know he has returned to being a man who dwells in a place beyond the duality of mere mortals, a man who has no need or want of me.

He leaves before me, to gather wood on the way, and of course walk back alone through the village. I watch him climb up the steep grassy bank then throw my hand in salute as he turns to raise his as he always does. Any words are lost over the roar of the water. I return the salute and smile. Yes, it suits me, this uncomplicated coming and going, joining and parting. I watch as he vanishes through the trees.

A stupor falls everywhere I gaze. I can smell Babaji still on me and I lie back on the earth with hands pressed to my heart. I think of his words earlier. Maybe I can live here in the ashram with him, let our relationship be known and public. Somehow I don't think that is what he wants, and I would never dare ask. Is it what I want? Perhaps some time in the future, but not now. My wings are beginning to unfurl and I want to remain weightless. I wonder again how it would be having Babaji in Lucknow, joining my life. It is an abstract thought and instead of following it I pull back into myself and listen again to the rush of water, forever moving, free falling down this valley.

*　　*　　*

It is almost dark when I return and Babaji is serving dinner. Conversation flows as we share our days. No one is at all interested that both Babaji and I have been out all day.

The ashram at night is silent in her velvet robe. We sit on the verandah and smoke a beedi. Babaji crumbles up a piece of charas, rolling it into a joint – the perfect moment to smoke. I watch his face, illuminated by the glow of the match, fall back into shadow, night poetry written under a galaxy of a million stars.

Without a word I follow as he opens his bedroom door. A candle burns on his altar and the room is cold. The heavy blankets press us close. Somewhere in the early hours I wake and tiptoe out back to my own room, slipping into the cold musty bed to sleep again.

After breakfast we are again alone. 'Kumariji, you cloth buying and Indian dress making.' He fumbles in his box by the dhuni and pulls out some rupee notes.

'Babaji, you don't need to give me money!'

'Me money giving same like you my wife and new cloth giving.'

'Dhanyabad, Babaji.' My voice is small and this smallness surprises me. A tiny contraction in my gut and a sudden remembering of his

187

words: 'Now my mind half God thinking half you thinking.' I push it all away. No, I don't want anything to spoil this.

'You my ashram stay then Indian dress me buying. You my place stay, no problem.'

I brush the twinge aside and lay my hands on his feet. 'Thank you, Babaji.' And he pats my head.

Every town has a Khadi shop. Khadi fabric is handloomed local cotton. The designs are simple with a distinctive thread. I pick a light coloured fabric with a weave of blue. The tailor takes rough measurements and a couple of days later an outfit of long Indian shirt and loose trousers, tight around the ankles, is ready.

I wear it immediately.

'Accha hai! Khadi cloth bahut accha.'

I'm surprised by his request. For years now I have been wearing Indian dress, a long shirt to my knees and loose trousers tight at the ankles. In the south of India I wore a sari, loving how the length of cloth could be wrapped around my head as well. I don't wear scarves very often but I certainly wear only chappal – thongs or flip-flops – or bare feet. If Babaji wants me to wear this Khadi cloth, I am happy. His pleasure is infectious.

*　　*　　*

After the evening activities are finished and the ashram is quiet, it's our habit to sit a while outside, with a cup of hot water and a smoke. I spend the night with him, creeping back to my room as dawn threatens to reveal what no one knows.

Embraced by the dark we lie together and the energy claims us, insists on union. I cannot resist him. I want to weave myself into him, join with him forever. Before sleeping, he lies on his back, chanting 'Om', then breathes with increasingly long breaths. I lie close enough for his warmth, his smell drawing me to a dreamless sleep.

I help in the garden and clean rice for dinner. We sit in the sun on the verandah, oiling our hair with coconut oil. Every morning he reads a chapter from the Bhagavad Gita. He reads aloud in Hindi and I watch the way his face lights up and his eyes swoon with the words of scripture.

Sometimes he gives a rough translation: 'Mind only for looking to Krishna, to God, then peace coming. This world samsara, world looking then no peace coming.' He looks at me for a moment. 'See, Kumariji, world looking, me you looking thinking, then no peace coming inside.' And then his smile is so warm my cheeks singe and I feel the blush spread through my whole being.

'Inside, my heart always with God. This knowing, so no problem. Samsara coming, samsara going. Atman alone is. This you knowing; Tat Tvam Asi. You coming, you going, only mind problem. Atman never problem.'

He holds me so tenderly with his gaze that I sense a tear pricking. 'Love no problem, Prem Kumariji, no problem.' The way my name rolls off his tongue allows it to land somewhere inside me it previously had not, by my own sense of unworthiness. Papaji, in a satsang recently, was giving a new name to a woman sitting before him. He had said to her 'we already have Prem Kumari, Prem Kumari means beloved of God', and as he spoke my heart had spun and the invading overwhelming sense of grace and gratitude seeped into every cell of my body, every pore of my being.

I glean more of Babaji's story. Years before he lived in a temple by the ocean and every year the spring tide came up so high it washed part of the temple away. Some had said there was a curse. At that time he was heavily into the practice of mantras and magic, offering puja to the goddess Kali, endlessly repeating her name. The four years he stayed in the temple, the ocean lapped just at the edge. He left that place after a man had 'spoken bad words' to him. Babaji had thrown a curse at him and the next day the man became sick and died. 'Then no more tantric practice and Haridwar going.'

In Hardiwar, a sacred city on the banks of the Ganga, he met an older swami who became his teacher. One of this swami's devotees had given him the land where the ashram now is. Babaji had come with this swami up to these mountains. Together they built the ashram then the swami died, leaving Babaji to take care of it. That was possibly fifteen years ago, he wasn't sure, but he has been here ever since.

'Mountains good energy. This place stay and no more travelling. Slowly western people coming like this cooking so karma yoga time. One place stay, good feeling. No interest in outside. Plant potato, watch potato grow. Bas. Visitor come through the gate, same like God coming.'

'Babaji, how old are you?'

'Birthday not keeping. July time born, maybe forty-six or forty-eight. Sadhu people not so much birthday looking. This body only for death, Atman inside, no birthday.' He laughs to himself. 'This knowing then no birthday.' And he laughs again.

Sometimes we speak in Hindi, and as I am always asking him what something means, his English improves with my Hindi, which is still very basic. Whenever the others are around he speaks mostly in Hindi. I pretend to understand even though I am not always sure.

I have ten days left of my visa and again I have to think of travel. I will go to Nepal. It is easy to get another six-month visa for India there.

'Kumariji, you December coming and ashram staying. Me Ganga Sagar going for sadhu time. Tikhai?'

I like the idea of taking care of the ashram while he is gone. He has spoken before of Ganga Sagar, an island in Bengal where the Ganga flows into the sea, the river returning to the source. It has many temples and is another of the numerous sacred places of this auspicious country.

'Babaji, sure, but maybe too cold!'

'Cold no problem, more clothes putting and fire burning no problem.'

I chuckle to myself. With Babaji it is always just so simple. I like the idea – more retreat time and a chance to look after the temple and fire. Simple days. Sadhu days.

Three more days now before I leave. This is the plan: long train ride and bus journey to Nepal, a trek in the high Himalayas while waiting for my visa and then back to Lucknow for a visit and up here again for the end of the year.

Babaji sings softly as he sweeps the path, talking to the cat as if she is his love. My bag is packed. Our foreheads touch. Babaji takes my hand in his, squeezing it hard as we say goodbye.

CHAPTER SIXTEEN

The roof of the world

'If God dwelt in the mosque, who dwells in the rest of the earth? If Ram dwells in the holy places and also in the idol, how could he dwell in two places at a time? To the east is Hari, to the west Allah. Search the heart within – Ram and Rahman live there. All the men and women of the world, your form is in all.' Kabir

The bus from Kathmandu is crowded. The cackle of local music dies to leave darkness, inside and out, and the rumble of the engine as we bump through the night. Men slump in their seats, the smell of alcohol on steamy breath. We pull into a small town, the bus stop deserted.

'Dumre! Dumre!' the driver shouts and I stumble out. The street is black and silent, the houses closed up. It's 1 am and the dogs begin to bark.

As my eyes adjust, I see a sign offering 'best room'. A light glows yellow from an upstairs window. As the dogs bark again, a woman calls: 'Hello! Room! Room!'

Saved by a woman again! As I cross the road, she peers out into the night.

'You have a room?'

'Room, huh! Huh!'

She holds a lamp and I follow her up steep narrow stairs to the attic. The bed is hard but I am not going to complain. I breathe long and hard, trying to settle the nerves. First the bus, full of drunken men, and now no choice but to trust, after being left alone in the middle of nowhere. I climb fully clothed under the pile of lumpy quilts and sleep.

Morning sun is flung like a blanket across the bed. I peek outside to a day full of brightness. In sunlight the woman downstairs is all smiles and I see her wrinkled face and thank her for finding me the night before. I give her a hundred rupees and she tucks the note into the fold of her shirt.

I am walking to Muktinath, a holy site for Hindus and Buddhists, through the domain of the Annapurna range and over the Thorong La pass at 5416 metres, 2000 metres higher than I have been before. Trekking to a pilgrimage site sacred for Buddhists and Hindus alike is perfect. I can cover my bases in one go, so to speak. Hinduism is claiming me but I want all that I can get of God. The two main leads in my search are both steeped in tradition: Papaji, a devotee of Krishna all his life; Babaji, and his life of renunciation. That small nagging nausea of guilt rushes in my gut as I worry again that I have pulled Babaji from his union with God. Perhaps when I return to care for his ashram he will withdraw back into himself, will not want the carnal satisfaction of sexual union after tasting the forbidden fruit. Maybe he seeks this retreat time at Ganga Sagar to be among his own – sadhus, temples, swamis and prayer – to re-take his vows. I quicken my step, lengthen my stride and watch as eagles circle high above, searching for prey far below.

Manang is the last village before the pass. Five days of walking through vistas of rice paddies strung out like emeralds in the lower valleys. In the forests are the first colours of autumn, yellow and deepest reds, as leafy patterns cling to their last days of glory before spiralling back to earth. The breathtaking sight of snow peaks far, far above. Soft white clouds hug the mountains, patches of light drift upward. Sounds of water amplify the great silence beyond. I remember words from the sage Vashista: 'Even this, the blueness of the sky, is an illusion.'

Laid out before me is a vast, treeless valley divided by a wide churning river. Steep mountains rise in a distant circle, huge snow peaks on the misty horizon. It is a land of enchantment and as the sun touches the peaks like a prayer in the morning light, the cold is intense.

I set off early as my knee is giving me trouble. The path traverses down the ridge to the riverbed below. The valley is still in shadow, and as I walk I watch the sun, a painted line on the mountainside, move slowly down until finally the valley floor also receives the warmth. I battle an icy headwind and a knee that seems to have had enough. The wind blows scree, tiny pieces like knives that bite into my face. I struggle across the vast landscape, insignificant, nothing, a mere dot on this vast, harsh and bare terrain. The contrast to the lush and vibrant landscapes of the previous days could not be more extreme. Clouds swirl high with the wind blowing down from the north. There is no one else in sight – just stark, desolate wilderness. I still wear only chappal. Trekking to high altitudes in thongs! The cold is extreme, and when the sun is banished, even momentarily, it is freezing. I hope that Manang offers shoes at least.

The shape of life further ahead forms into an old woman walking alone. She is wrapped in blankets like a hooded ghost. She stops just before me. 'Tashi deley!' she greets me; her upturned face, curious and smiling, peeks out from the hood of blanket. I join my hands together. 'Tashi deley!'

She pulls out a couple of potatoes, still warm, from her pocket and gives one to me. I eat it with gratitude. Right now I would give anything for a hot bath and a lie down. My knee screams for me to slow down but I want to reach the village and then rest. With the pain in my knee, and the change of terrain to harsh and clearly freezing, I am suddenly aware of how unprepared I am. I am wearing chappal – thongs – and am walking up to altitudes of over 5000 metres. I do not even have a warm thermal jacket. All of a sudden I have no idea what I might have been thinking. Why can't I be normal and take a trek with a tour group, instead of battling away alone up here in forgotten worlds. I take strength and sustenance from the old lady and follow a herd of yaks for the last few miles into town, massive animals with hair to the ground and big feet leading the way.

Manang is full of promise. Medieval buildings of thick stone, square and solid; prayer flags, long faded and torn, strung from flat roofs. Washing on lines tugs in the wind and every available space is stacked with wood for the coming winter. High above on the shaded mountain clings a monastery, shrouded in billowing flags.

At the Mountain View rest house the owner shakes my hand with a grip strong enough to crush, and tells me his name is Tengba. Tears prick my eyes at his welcome. I flop on the hard bed and let my knee rest. Across the valley is a glacier that spills in a muddle of greys to a lake so blue I am mesmerised. The cold is beyond what I thought possible. The air is thin and thready. This is the highest I have ever been. An American doctor working at a small clinic here is giving a talk on altitude sickness. I go along to listen. Apparently, each season many trekkers need to be rushed back down the valley. I take heed of his message to take things slowly and am happy to spend a couple of days here acclimatising and resting my knee. I am hopeful I will make it, as this is the last port of civilisation.

*   *   *

The shopkeeper has bright turquoise earrings, as the men often do, and, like all the locals, a very wrinkled face. His eyes are long and slanted from too much squinting in the bright sun. I guess him to be at least sixty years old. His shop sells a few pairs of Chinese army boots and I find a pair that fit well enough. I splash out on a bar of Cadbury's chocolate and we both laugh at the inflated price. He then tells me he is thirty-seven years old. The woman, who smiles and nods but speaks no English, is his sister, not his mother as I had thought. A harsher climate I could not imagine up here in this world of white and greys.

I think of Tenzing Sherpa's words: 'People come looking looking, some people come and see, but what to see? Only silent stillness.' These mountains are as ancient as the world itself, bearing witness to our insignificant appearance on their landscape. A brief entry onto the stage before death consumes us once again.

This altitude brings a stark reminder of my own mortality. I have a dull nausea and a pounding headache. My hip has joined my knee with complaints. From the abundance of beauty below, as the path wound up from vistas of glory, I am now entombed in grey. This stark valley, this treeless wilderness, reflects the transience of all things. Joy is replaced by a humble realisation of the task ahead: the climb over the pass. I have to confront the fact that I am absolutely not prepared for a high altitude climb.

*   *   *

I eat dinner with a German couple fitted out with ski jackets, boots and woollen hats. I give myself with ease to the conversation. Jan and Oliver have trekked several of the routes in Nepal. 'Walk over the pass with us, better than alone.' I accept with gratitude. Jan hardly speaks English but Oliver does. 'How did you hurt your knee? I have a support bandage you can wear.' I am surprised by how much I like his concern, his desire to know about me.

'How come you are up here alone?' he asks. 'Is it your first time in the mountains?' So of course I tell him a little, that actually I have been in India for a few years now and that I only want to renew my visa and take a walk while it is being processed. 'I always run off to monasteries,' I say. 'So I thought I would take a pilgrimage to Muktinath. And this back way is less popular. I always prefer to stay as much away from tourist routes as possible.'

I try to draw Jan into the conversation, with my very few words of German, a language I never cared for. Oliver translates for me but it all seems too much effort so I just keep quiet and instead listen to Oliver tell tales of their previous treks. Not a couple, I discover, but brother and sister.

We eat potato momos, like dumplings, noodles with yak cheese and thick Tibetan bread. Yak cheese is like good vintage cheddar, with a rancid smell. Outside the sky is moonless and alive with stars.

*   *   *

After breakfast of tsampa porridge we set off together for the long walk to Phedi, the last rest house before the pass. The path is narrow, following the side of the steep valley, across scree and wild grass, rock falls and waterways. Wild flowers poke tiny petals from under rocks, mauve and pink, little splashes in the stony ground.

Oliver and Jan walk at a fast pace; I go slowly as my knee does better this way. It is much improved from the day of rest and with a bandage for support, but still I can feel it with every step. The path climbs a gradual incline until my world is one of grey swirling cloud and even the bravest wild flower has long been left behind. The valley sides are tight, covered in rock and scree, and a trickle of water winds its way down.

Phedi means foot of the hill and I have to laugh – hill? It hugs the mountains at an altitude of 4400 metres. We will leave before dawn to maximise daylight for our climb over the pass.

*   *   *

'Kumari, are you sure that knee is good for this?' Oliver asks the next morning. He is concerned and I can understand why. I smile bravely and nod. I hope it is. The cold is now my main concern. I have a woollen scarf around my head, four layers of clothing with a thermal next to my skin, woollen leggings I bought in Kathmandu, the long Indian shirt that Babaji gave me, a long skirt of thin cotton that I wear on top of my trousers, and then a long woollen poncho on top. Another scarf is wrapped around my neck. I have a walking stick from the autumn-clothed forest and my bundle of bare essentials is light. My feet are unused to being encased, but are much warmer. It is, after all, freezing.

At 4 am I fill my stomach with porridge. I fall into step behind Oliver over silver scree and slate stone. His head torch gives a reedy film of light to follow. Jan walks behind me and the light from her torch also

196

reaches my feet. I concentrate on one pace at a time, one step at a time, breathing heavily with the thin air. My feet are numb and each step is marked with a gnawing pain. Light creeps in and shadowy silhouettes reveal a vast array of mountain peaks spread out like an ocean – above and below, naked to the horizon, further than the eye can see. Peaks crowned with heavy white cloud reach up in splendour, shaking off their blankets to embrace the heavens. There is not one sound except my breath and the scurries of stone displaced by our steps. I am completely frozen and it is only going to get colder. I have no choice but to turn back. I cannot go on. Oliver supports the decision and no one hangs about. I watch them disappear in a moment, swallowed by the cloud.

I stand alone to savour this moment. A vast unending landscape of mountain and clouds of light, greys and silver above and below, desolate and barren. Yet there is a beauty so profound, silent tears run down my face. The cloudscape and the way the light falls in shafts of white – a far away snow peak illuminated as if by the hand of God himself. And it all is at eye level, spread all around and far below. Too cold to linger, I begin my descent. It's not long before my knee is screaming. Walking down proves far worse than walking up. I question my decision to return; at least I wasn't alone before and I had nearly reached the pass. But 700 metres in this high altitude is a vast difference. Anyway, now I have no choice. I am alone in this terrain of infinity. Tears again fall down my face, but without emotion, as I concentrate on one step at a time. At regular intervals groups of trekkers pass me, slowly climbing up, clad in woollen hats and proper jackets, boots and gloves. Surprise always on their faces when they see me limping out of the mist.

The first sight of Phedi brings a moment of joy, a rush of relief that I've made it back to civilisation, people, and shelter from this mountain wilderness. It is empty now and quiet, the workers still cleaning up from the night before. Afternoon will see the trekkers arrive from the pass, having walked from Muktinath on the other side. Stories to tell, stomachs to feed. My knee and both feet are paining badly. The big toe on my left foot is rubbed raw by the boot and I wrap tissue paper around it before setting off again. Resting here alone all day is pointless. The workers feel unwelcoming, suspicious, afraid that maybe I am injured. And the desolation does nothing for my mood. I am in pain and very alone. This is not what I had expected of my trek. Phedi is a stark display of wooden buildings with corrugated roofs and rusty water tanks, half hidden in the swirling mists. Manang is the place to rest. I swing my bundle on my back, take my stick in my hand and walk slowly downward.

*　　*　　*

The yak sellers are in town, apparently the reason why the men are all drunk. I ask Tengba for a room; he laughs hysterically and then stumbles, clutching at the table. He picks himself up and gestures to the stairs: 'Yes, yes, same room free!' Every step up the narrow stairs could be the last. My knee can hardly bear an ounce of weight. I push open the door to see a man snoring on the bed. I almost scream in surprise. Thank God he is asleep – an Indian policeman, of all people. Tengba's wife takes control. 'Oh sorry, so sorry, too much drinking, this husband drinking, everybody raksi drinking.' She smiles her round smile and I am too tired and cold to think anything. She shakes the man violently and moves him downstairs. 'Festival day!' she explains.

Collapsed on the bed under a pile of quilts, I look out the window to take in my surrounds. Sunset creates high drama in the skies as massive cloud sculptures reflect deepening red. As the clouds scatter, a crescent moon – the Shiva moon – is perfectly positioned just above the ridge. I watch it creep behind the mountain.

Next morning the herds of yaks are still tied in the streets, the sellers nowhere to be seen. The American doctor fixes up my toe, noticing a patch of dark on the other big toe.

'It's very foolish to trek at high altitude without the proper equipment. This patch of dark here is actually frostbite.' His disapproval is clear. 'You were at my talk a few days ago. I remember seeing you. I suggested then that only those with proper equipment should attempt the pass.'

I decide to keep quiet. I can sense the age-old pattern of wanting to justify myself, convince him I am really a decent person. The truth is I have been foolish.

'Will I lose my toe?' I ask.

He looks up and I can see his face relax. 'Unlikely. No, of course not. It is only a small patch. A dot really. It's good you turned back when you did. How come you are up here alone anyway? There are plenty of groups to join.'

'Well I came to Nepal to renew my visa for India and just thought I would do a quick trek.' It is the truth.

He sighs. 'I guess you like adventure, hey?'

'This has been more than I bargained for. Worth it though. Have you been up over the pass? Wow, the magnificence up there is beyond imagination. It's another world!'

'Yes, I have trekked over. Some years ago now. I always wanted to come back so here I am working the season up here.' He looks like he could say more but decides not to. I follow his cue and remain silent.

'Well, take care and walk slowly. The only way is down!' He gives me two antibiotic tablets and a handful of painkillers to take over the next few days till I am down the mountains.

*   *   *

The screaming wind as I walked up to Manang now blows against my back, as if the spirits of these mountains urge me on my way. I hobble with my stick till the path at last winds up the ridge. I look back at the last sight of the pass far away. The skies have cleared enough to reveal a jagged line of peaks resplendent against the horizon. I bow with folded palms and turn downwards. The vista changes to forests, and green, abundant, gushing water. Rock and scree underfoot are replaced with more yielding earth. The golden feast of autumn as slanting sun highlights a walnut tree robed in yellow.

Mid-afternoon I reach the village of Pisang. I take the path up to Old Pisang, higher up the valley, across a rickety wooden swing bridge and up again through terraced fields to the village. Across the valley, Annapurna – the mother of the world – stands magnificent, as snowfields glisten in their virginity. Next to her rises Gangapurna, well over 7000 metres.

The village is a string of wooden houses perched on a ridge. Faded prayer flags laze in the still air. It is well worth the extra walk. I stay in a family house with a big room upstairs that opens to a tiny rickety wooden balcony, enough space to sit and revel in the magnitude all around. Annapurna rises against an almost cloudless sky and I want to fall to my knees and prostrate to what is surely the best view in the world. It's all been worth it, just for this.

Kids play noisily in the bare earth fields. They wear sweaters that are too big and torn trousers. They all are barefoot. A tall lanky boy, after seeing me from the field, knocks on my door and comes on in. 'Madam! Best charas, you try, no problem!' He thrusts a small piece in my hand.

'Okay, I give you twenty rupees.'

'You want more? Five tola? Ten tola no problem.'

'No, thank you. But chai possible?'

'Yes, chai.' When he reappears I also ask him for a cigarette. In a moment he is back. I give him another five rupees for his trouble. The charas is soft and crumbling and I enjoy the smoke, perfect medicine for mind and body. The mountains before me take on a surreal, otherworldly vision and I want to stay forever in this kingdom. The throbbing in my foot subdues and I feel every tired muscle relax. The afternoon sun is warm and soothing. Patchy clouds send shadows before them then cluster on the peak of Annapurna, resting a while as if they too are in worship. The feeling that these Himalayas are a vault holding God, like no church ever could, plays again in my mind. Is it the reaching up into the heavens, nearer to God? Or is it that the majestic presence suggests omnipotence? Ah, of course! Shiva himself has his home here, at Kailash, but clearly his devas are nearby.

*   *   *

Tonight the fireside scene is of women. Not a man in sight. Mayagru is the woman of the house and sits here with her three daughters, various sisters and relations, eleven of them in all. Mayagru wears the biggest nose stud I have ever seen. They talk constantly, laughing and drinking tea. The fireplace is vast, with logs piled to the side, and sends warmth through the low room. It's dark inside, lit only by lamps. The women take no notice of me and anyway no one speaks Hindi. The dialect here is strongly influenced by Tibetan. I eat on the floor, with my fingers – dhal bhat with pickles too hot to even smell and a small spoonful of subze, spinach and potato. I savour this safety of women. I threw myself to the elements and they won. Tossed back to walk the way I have come. I breathe the frozen empty night air for just a moment, then roll up another smoke and wrap myself in a quilt to huddle on the balcony as the night reveals nothing but stars.

The next morning, after tsampa porridge and chai, I swallow the last of the painkillers and set off, using a walking stick. I am in no hurry. I am heading to Koto. I pass apple orchards and chai stalls, cross endless meandering, falling streams. Reds and gold are sprinkled like fairy dust over the landscape. Koto is busy, and the kitchen where I stay for the night is small and smoky. Porters drink raksi and the party becomes wild as the kettle is passed.

A policeman makes an entrance, demanding quiet, and the partying pauses for a moment. Suddenly he sways and begins an elaborate drunken dance; the porters all clap and cheer and some also start dancing. A woman, busy at the fireplace, refills the raksi kettle, watching the scene with tired eyes. She lifts a toddler and perches him on a surface. She pulls up her shirt and he grabs her sagging breast, suckling from her as she stirs a steaming pot.

In another room a group of French trekkers cook dinner on kerosene stoves. It's the porters' night off, hence the party. The trekkers cook chicken and grate real cheese and open a bottle of French wine. I am amazed to see such food up here. Children sit on the floor and watch; I eat dhal bat and also sit on the floor and watch. I feel more of a connection with a group of barefoot, grubby-faced kids, with whom I can barely exchange a word, than with the trekkers. I can speak French well enough to have a conversation, yet what could I say? These are trekkers who fly in for this tour, all organised and tidy. As I try to conjure up sentences, the French is muddled with Hindi, so all I can find myself thinking is the sort of things I would say to Babaji. I wonder if I will ever return to the west.

I am tired of these drunken boyish men. I again watch the festivities; the policeman is still dancing. A porter close by, smiling and laughing, tries to pull me by the arm. 'Dancing dancing, you me!' Another also sees me and pushes his way to where I stand. I know I am an oddity, wearing my long woollen coat and talking a little with their women. I remember with gratitude last night's scene of the women, where there was such a different vibration. I sat for only one evening in their dark kitchen, yet there was a sense of belonging that is the core of connection. I shake my head at the drunken porter and retreat for the night.

*   *   *

The bus ride back to India is tedious; a small child, sitting on her mother's lap on the seat in front of me, continually vomits out the window. Thankfully my window has glass, which is smeared now with yellowy splatter and drip.

I have no reservation for the train from Patna to Lucknow and find myself in a compartment filled from floor to ceiling with men. Groups of them wear blue bandanas tied around their heads and I guess they are on their way to a political rally. I leap off and try the next carriage. Same deal: every bunk filled with men, all decked out in a sort of uniform, and not a woman in sight. Eyes stare, and I feel like a piece of meat about to be fed to wild dogs. I run up the station to the end carriage and jump on. The compartment is full, as usual, but the presence of military in shining uniforms gives a sense of safety. I notice families, an old man with thick-rimmed round glasses, and hear a baby crying.

I squash in next to the window, amongst a family, women at least, the children wide-eyed and staring. Men sit up on the top berth, swaying with the lurch of the train as it pulls away from the station. The army men are the worst. Their eyes never leave me and I am not dealing with it well. My foot throbs from the run up the platform; I pull my scarf over my head and look out the window as the afternoon clatters by. Whenever my gaze is free, I am met with stares, leering stares, and I feel a rising paranoia as my vulnerability gets the better of me.

Suddenly I just hate men, all of them, especially these dark-eyed skinny ones, with their plastered down hair and their tasteless polyester trousers and unblinking stares. I almost wish one would brush a hand against my shoulder so I could smack him hard in the face. I want to stand up and scream at them all that they are dirty bastards and deserve to rot in hell. My jaw hardens and my throat tightens until I fear I may choke.

I let the feeling rise and subside. I pull deeply on my breath to regain a sense of calm. A packed train steaming across the Indian plains is not a place to lose control. I actively meditate, and through closed eyes, tears slip and slide down my hot cheeks.

Diminished to an emotional wreck, I shiver inside myself. What have I done? This is no good, no good at all. *It's okay,* I tell myself, *you will be back in Lucknow soon. Just hang on. It's probably the painkillers you took for your foot, making you feel like this. I expect they were strong ones.*

*   *   *

Seven hours later, landmarks, even in the dark, are familiar. It's already 9.30 pm when the train pulls in. I fight my way through porters wanting trade. 'Yes, madam, bag carrying.' 'Madam, rupee rupee.' A beggar hangs on my sleeve. I am in no mood. 'Chello! Chello!' I jerk my arm away, swing my bag on my back and limp through the crowds into the waiting throng of bicycle rickshaws, motor rickshaws and taxis. 'Madam! Where you go?' 'Madam, cheap hotel, yes come on!' 'Madam, you sit down!'

I know enough by now to limp out onto the street, and I take the first auto rickshaw that screeches to a stop beside me. The pollution is dreadful as we zoom through the dark streets, still alive with activity, all the way to Hazrat Ganj. The thought of another hotel for the night is just too depressing. I feel unwell. A friend of mine I would sometimes spend an afternoon with during the hot season is still in Lucknow. I hope she is anyway.

'Bhaisaab,' I utter in my best Hindi. 'Indira Nagar jana!'

'Indira Nagar?'

'Ji, Indira Nagar.'

'Accha tikhai.'

I know it is late but I need a friend. Dogs bark in the back lane of Sundari's home, an apartment above an Indian family. Lights are on and I call, softly at first, over the locked gate. 'Sundari! Sundari!' No answer so I stand back in the laneway, disturbing a mother pig that grunts and snuffles from her sleeping place.

'Sundari!' *Hear me please*, I silently plead. A face looks over the balcony, sees me, and she is down in a flash to open the gate. 'Prem Kumari! It's you! Come, come.'

'Sorry it is so late but I need to crash on your floor tonight.'

'No problem! Come! Good to see you back! My friend from the States is staying also. You look dreadful. What has happened?'

We climb the stairs, whispering. I dump my bag on the porch and head through the door. A woman with reddish hair sits reading on the mattress on the floor. A candle burns and incense sends sweet fragrances my way.

'Hi!' She looks up and smiles.

'Prem Kumari, this is Janaki, my friend from California.'

I burst into tears. My jaw aches from the effort of holding myself together, although by the looks of me I have anyway failed. Janaki is up in a moment. 'I'll put water on to boil; you need a cup of tea.' She disappears into the kitchen. Sundari is soothing and sweet. She makes appropriate sounds as only girlfriends can, and waits till I calm down. I look a mess: my clothes are filthy and my foot is wrapped in a bandage that suddenly, in this light, I am ashamed of.

'Honey, let me fix you a hot bath. I think we have enough water left.'

She returns from putting the immersion coil into a bucket to heat water. Janaki brings a pot of camomile tea. Out on the porch I smoke a beedi, telling the tale of the train ride.

'But what about your foot – well, feet? Looks like these bandages need a change.'

'I went high up in the mountains and got frostbite in my big toes. This one is a bit of a mess.'

'Mmm, you have been on an adventure.' Janaki disappears and returns with a bag of medical supplies. Sundari checks the water and calls out, 'It's ready!' She has added fragrant oils and the smell is heavenly. She lends me clean clothes and Janaki fixes up my foot. The nail is hanging off and the nail bed is a mess of yellow pus. I suspect I have a slight fever.

'Let's see if this powder does the trick. It's an antibiotic powder.' She cleans with Betadine then dusts the toe generously and re-bandages it. The other toe looks like it is on the way to healing itself. I take in my surroundings. The small, enclosed room, the soft light of candles, the scent of lavender oil as Sundari fixes a bucket of water, the altar on the shelf with photos of Papaji, another of Ramana, flowers in a vase, all invite me to safety. I can feel my nervous system unwind little by little and realise how tense, how tight my jaw feels. I remember the scene of the men in the train and how it felt like a pack after the prey.

'The train I caught from Patna was intense. It was full of men on a political rally or something. It was scary.' I slump back on the floor, suddenly so tired I am not sure I can manage a bath even. But of course I will. I am filthy. 'Sometimes travelling alone is not fun. I was the only westerner on the whole train from what I could see and even in the carriage where I was I couldn't cope with the stares.'

And now here I am in the caring hands of women. I am pleased that I came here, that I didn't check into a hotel and wait the night out alone again.

* * *

I stay a whole week with Janaki and Sundari, sharing the small space. We cook lunches of kidgeree running with ghee, grated beets and carrot, tomato and cucumber salad. Evening time we sit outside on the porch, drinking tea and sharing stories. Janaki is back here in Lucknow after her youngest child graduated. 'Now it's my turn! I have time for me!' She has two kids and is a single parent.

'It's tough,' she says. 'Parenting takes you out of your comfort zone and shows you sides of yourself you maybe would rather not see. At least that has been my experience. Don't get me wrong. I love my kids and will do anything for them, but right now it feels so good to be doing something for me.'

Mothering is her instinct. We will be sitting on the verandah, candles burning before a photo of Papaji and suddenly she hops up and says: 'Mmm, let me fix us all an oat straw tea.' Then she reappears with herbal teas or warm milk and honey. I wonder whether I would be so receptive if I hadn't just climbed to the roof of the world and almost fallen off. In the past, if anyone fussed around me it sent flecks of annoyance through the air. It must have been good for her kids, though, to grow up with a motherly type fixing their hurts and rubbing their feet.

'Let me see if I can take some of those tangles from your hair,' she tells me. 'They are looking like dreads.'

I tell her that I like that I have three dreadlocks forming and have decided to keep them that way. My hair is easily long enough now to tie up and I keep it pulled back all the time, in a knot on top of my head. Janaki fusses over me and I lap it up. It's been a long while and I rest and relax while she re-dresses my toe, which heals well under her care.

The trek was more of a pilgrimage than I realised. I didn't make it over the pass but I have crossed into another valley within myself. I no longer strive to meditate, to be alone and focused; something inside me has relaxed, let go. As my toes heal, my energy becomes buoyant; the high altitude left its mark. I will stay in Lucknow until the end of the year, this is clear. Satsang with Papaji is the perfect antidote to it all.

Hania is back with her girlfriend and they join us for lunch one day, and the three of us decide to find a flat to share. 'I'm only here till the end of December. I need to be back up in the mountains to look after the ashram while Babaji has a retreat time away. Let's see how it goes till then.' I like that I have this mission; the commitment before me brings a sense of importance.

'So you're still seeing your sadhu lover?' Hania raises her eyes.

'Yes, I am. It's quite amazing actually.'

'Maybe we can come up for a visit, when you're taking care of the ashram.'

'Do – it will be great to have you both come stay.'

I can picture the scene already, sitting by the dhuni kneading the dough, turning out chapatti after perfect chapatti while the dhal simmers away. Yes, I like the idea.

Right now I want to settle, put my feet down, buy paints and a canvas. The trip to Nepal finished any desire to travel and the hassle of being a woman alone on the plains of India is getting to me. Even though we are in a middle-class suburb where most people are used to westerners, I still feel someone staring; or a group of young guys will walk just a little too close, elbowing a breast or nudging a shoulder.

I perfect the art of wearing a sari, holding the folds in neat pleats, tucking the thick wad of cotton into the sari skirt, then another wrap around with enough cloth left to throw over my head and shoulders. I blend in more and more, walking with confidence, at ease with the surroundings. I am accustomed to the smells of drains, and the sight of kids half naked shitting by the side of the road, or dogs eating the flesh of a dead pig. Speaking a little Hindi adds to my confidence and at the market I understand the price, and can barter and exchange a few words. Every trip I learn new words till all the vegetables roll off my tongue with glee. 'Chokanda', 'gazza', 'bund gobi'. The stall keepers love it. And so do I.

*   *   *

The same day that we move into our flat Sita Sharan comes to town. Sita is an old friend of Janaki and has visited Lucknow several times over the last couple of years. Towards the end of satsang she is chatting away to Papaji in perfect Hindi. She is wearing long silk robes and pearly pink lipstick. I like her immediately. Papaji asks her to sing a bhajan and her voice is divine. Janaki invites her for lunch. Sita has strict religious practices that include mantra and offerings before eating. She enthrals us with her stories of the gods, of Hanuman and Ram.

I buy a mattress from the Khadi Bhawan, have sheets made up at the tailor, and move in. My room is the smallest, at the back of the flat, as I am the temporary one. It is quiet and cool and has everything I need.

The following Monday we arrive at satsang house to the news that there has been an explosion in the kitchen. Rumours are rushing that maybe it was a bomb. One of the caretakers has been hurt, but not seriously. Anyway, there is no satsang the whole week.

We meet back at Sundari's. 'Let's go to Chitrakut!' Sita's enthusiasm makes it the obvious decision. Chitrakut is the small town by the holy hill where Sita and Ram were exiled and lived for seven years. Already in the few days I have known Sita, Chitrakut has become a place of legend and mystery.

'Sure! Let's go today!'

So we do, on the afternoon train to Karvy.

CHAPTER SEVENTEEN

———— ·∿∿∘·⟨⊙⟩·∘∿∿ ————

The land of Ram

'You are my mother, my father, my brother and my friend. You are my knowledge and my only wealth. You are everything to me, my Lord of all.' A verse from a prayer that I first heard in Chitrakut

We are a mandali, a group on a pilgrimage. Sita floats through the turmoil and squash of the ticket office. Her creamy silk robes billow and rush around her moving form. We jostle and push to keep up. Our guide for this journey knows what she is doing. At the front of the queue she takes command of the ticket seller with her precise Hindi. I stand to one side, happy to let another take charge for a change, with the noise and cacophony of chaos around us, a surging sea also wanting urgent tickets. I watch as she argues and then pulls money from her bag that the ticket seller pockets with a nod of his head. We strike our way through the station to wait for the train.

Generous baksheesh allows the six of us into a cabin with only four berths – as if the exact number of passengers had mattered on any of the journeys I had taken. The train is on time, unusually. We pile into the compartment, all excited, chattering like kids going on camp. We spread ourselves out after Sita meticulously wipes the berths with a cloth, kept in her bag for just for that purpose. She knows how to travel – no more crowding in a compartment full of staring, leering men. We travel first class 'non A.C.' in a compartment with a door that locks and windows that open, behind the bars.

'I always travel with my kit,' she explains as she spreads a lungi over the bottom bunk on which she now sits. The berths are blue and padded, and the barred windows are open to the noise outside. Steam hisses, vendors shout and beggars plead.

'Chai chai chai chai.' The wallah stops when he sees our white faces and sings for us alone: 'Chai chai chai.'

Sita pulls out a stainless steel cup. 'I prefer to use my own,' she tells me. I don't mind the clay cup myself; it has no handle and is not much bigger than an egg cup. I don't mind either the thin silt always found at the bottom. The cup is then thrown out of the window, recycled back into the earth. The chai is watery and very sweet and I leave the last slurp as the train heaves from the station.

Cool air rushes in and dusty dark spills across the sky. Hania and Juliana snuggle up on one bunk and Sundari and I squash together on another. Sita and Janaki, being the elders in the party, get bunks of their own.

Sita wakes us at around three, just as the train pulls in to a deserted station. Our plan has been to sleep the few more hours in the waiting room but it is firmly locked and there is not a person around to help. No taxi, no rickshaw, until finally Sita finds a driver sleeping in a rickshaw in the street, wrapped in a blanket. He coughs and spits, then drives us all squeezed in the back for the twenty kilometres to Chitrakut. The roads are empty and black and the beam from the rickshaw's headlight is often dim. This is bandit country, and, as Sita explains, the driver is nervous until Chitrakut appears and Sita directs the driver down narrow dark lanes.

We follow her down an alley, then down steep narrow steps, through a courtyard and into a little room with no door. It is dark and empty but for a smouldering fireplace at one end. The room smells of sadhu – incense and wood smoke and maybe ghee.

'This is Laxmana Swami's ashram and his dhuni room. We can make ourselves comfortable here.' We lie on the hard mud floor and sleep the couple of hours till dawn. Temple bells ring in symphonies; we hear muffled voices, a man's low cough and another voice chanting 'Ram Ram' somewhere outside the wall of this dark and unknown room where we rest.

Hania and I are old hands at roughing it. She has lived in the rainforest of South America as well as years in a Hare Krishna ashram in India. I suspect Sita prefers a little more comfort. Although in the seventies she stayed for seven years here in Chitrakut, living as a sadhu and following austerities and rituals I am fascinated by. As for me, I have spent nights on a railway station platform with a huge mail sack for a bed, waiting for a train that never turned up. Juliana stretches and takes a moment to smile at those of us already awake.

'Prem Kumari was the first awake. She was about to sneak off by herself when I woke!' Hania leans over and kisses her.

'I'll come too and show you where we can bathe.' Sita wakes as elegant as ever. 'Come,' she says.

The Mandakini Ganga is said to emerge from an underground river flowing from the Ganga herself. Shadowy figures float in the thin dawn light as the narrow cobbled lane emerges on the ghats. The Mandakini lies before us, a silent smudge of black. Steps lead down to the water and the creamy stone is cold to my bare feet. A woman hugs a wet sari to her rounded form, long black hair loose and dripping. Orange flowers, already offered, sway with the crease of movement in the still water.

I watch Sita shed her long robe, her lungi already tied around her body. She stands knee-deep in the water and folds her hands together in prayer. Somewhere close by a man's voice rises in lyrical harmony as he sings in the stillness. Bells ring out and the air hums with 'Ram Ram, Sita Ram'.

The cold of the water is a surprise. I pause and offer my prayer, submerging to my chin, my lungi riding up around me. The water is thick and silty, squelchy mud between my toes. As in the baptism of Christianity, something new is born.

*　　*　　*

Sita is well connected in Chitrakut. What a blessing to be part of this trip. Since returning from Nepal I have been held by the two arms of the crone: Janaki, as the wise woman and mother, and Sita, the high priestess, full of ritual and mystery.

The mahant of Yagna Veda welcomes us with delight. He is a small man with a radiant face, delighted to host this mandali of western women. 'Deviji! Deviji!' he greets us. Sita calls him 'Dadu', an affectionate term for an elder. After a brief reunion she leads us up steep stone steps that spiral up to a wooden door. Our room is almost round and completely empty; it is light and airy with three arch-shaped windows with bars to stop the monkeys. It is the perfect room for our pilgrimage.

Hania is brushing Juliana's hair. Juliana has skin like a pale moon and her eyes are the lightest blue. High cheekbones etch her face like a painting, and her lips are full. Her long flaxen blonde hair is usually always tightly tied; when she shakes it loose it transforms her. She and Hania have, to my eyes, a relationship grounded in respect and care. They like to wear the same outfits, today a long shimmery peacock-blue fabric. Intimacy, as Hania likes to say, is in-to-me-see. Yet how confronting that feels, how easily a sense of shame creeps over and into me. The haunting confusion of self-doubt.

A small boy brings a pot of chai with six stainless steel cups and a pile of puris, still warm and wrapped in a cloth. Sita offers a corner of a puri to her altar, already assembled on a shelf: a little statue of Krishna, another of Hanuman and a small black rock. 'Remember that it is Grace that has allowed this journey. Our longing for the divine has brought us here so let's pray to Lord Ram that our pilgrimage will be fulfilled.' We all offer our own silent prayer as Sita lights incense and I pray that indeed my pilgrimage will be fulfilled. What exactly do I want from this pilgrimage, this unexpected journey to this other realm, one where sadhus and rishis practise tapasya and SitaRam presides? I decide it is enough to just be here, to sit on the stone floor of a room, with this group of women and Sita, whose name this town endlessly repeats. It is said that it was here in Chitrakut that the gods descended to earth. I suspect their footprints may still be visible.

Chai and puri finished, we take an auto rickshaw to Kamadgiri – the holy hill and forest that has been home to Ram and Sita. A single track runs from the road to the base of the hill, a perfect mound of forest. I walk barefoot. The rush of bells and chants played through loudspeakers proclaim our purpose. Even the shoe keeper greets us with 'Sita Ram!' and hands folded in namaste.

'Far out! Devi worshippers everywhere!' Hania buys a pile of yellow and orange flower malas and places one around each of our necks.

'I'll give mine to Shiva. Is that okay, Sita, to give a mala if I've already worn it?' I know that details are important to Vaishnavites, as Sita is. The rules and regulations of worship are very strict.

'Shiva doesn't mind. He accepts anything.' She laughs as I kiss the flowers before placing them at the base of a lingam.

Sita is meticulous in her rituals and ways. A certain mantra at dawn, another before eating. Food always offered first before eating, bells rung. I would be anxious half the time that I was getting it somehow wrong. I wonder what the consequences would be? With no warning it is here again, the sickening tightness in my stomach, a palpable quickening of my heart, the age-old fear that the God in the heavens knows all about the many sins I have committed. The devil in my midst, eager for his prey, as I slip from prayer to paranoia and hope indeed that no one can see into me. Surely they would dislike me as much as I do. Caught again in a lasso and the rope is tight enough. I stop a moment and shake the sensations away. Not welcome here, not in this holy land where Ram himself has walked.

A row of stalls display ladus: round balls of chickpea flour and sugar, and white milk sweets, sticky with sugar, cut in triangles. Vats of milk simmer and the steam lingers in the breezeless air. An elderly man with a crooked back leans against his stick. He watches us for a moment then touches the ground in front of our feet. 'Deviji! Deviji!' he exclaims and we smile and murmur 'Sita Ram' as we pass.

'See,' declares Hania as we see a huge statue of Shiva, Parvati and Ganesh. 'When women are worshipped as the goddess the gods for sure are near.'

'Will it turn you from Krishna to a Devi devotee?' I joke.

'Ahh! But Krishna plays with the goddesses; they all bow down to his feet!' She dances a few steps, breaking into 'Hare Krishna, Hare Krishna' until we all are laughing.

'A transvestite lives in there!' Sita whispers as we pass a solid wooden doorway. 'He dresses up as Radha hoping to entice Krishna. He is really wild!'

No sign of him today. It's Tuesday: Mangalvar, or Hanuman day. A Hanuman temple has the Hanuman chalisa playing from a tape recorder. I recognise it now, as Sita and Janaki sing it together, the forty verses in praise of Hanuman. The air is enchanted. The pujari beckons to us. 'Aiyeai! Aiyeai!' [Come! Come!]

The tiled floor is cool as we all sit before the murti of Hanuman – tangerine orange, a mala of yellow marigolds around his neck. The pujari puts a dot of orange on our foreheads, a spill of holy water from a brass pot, and a ladu that crumbles as I bite into it. A monkey darts over to pick up the pieces that fall.

'Hanuman comes to share prasad!' I laugh. We eat ladus with monkeys in our midst.

The path is shaded with trees trailing reddish gold leaves, falling on the ground like confetti. The thick forest twists up the hillside and the birds too join in the song. We are not alone in the walk of worship. Families are dressed in their finest, children with oiled hair and neat plaits, almond eyes lined with khol. Sita is greeted at almost every turn – 'Sitaji, Sitaji' – and I feel like a celebrity just walking beside her.

Men walk alone or in small groups, wearing white shirts and pressed crisp dhotis. Mala beads turn through fingers and sadhus complete the picture: orange cloth the colour of the rising sun. Everywhere I glance is a reflection of devotion. We have only been here half a day yet this untouched world has instantly pulled me in.

We take lunch with Laxmana Swami, at the place where we landed in the early hours. Laxmana Swami is around sixty or seventy years old, with thin white hair pilled in juta that hang to the side of his head in a neat roll. His beard winds down over a sagging chest that rests on his ample belly. He nods and smiles at us all sitting before him. His forehead is decorated with the tilak of a Vaishnavite: a red vertical stripe edged in white.

'Laxmana Swamiji is saying that we must walk barefoot while in this holy place of Ram as the dust on the earth has been touched by his holy feet,' Sita translates, but she then has her own private audience, as Laxmana Swami speaks not a word of English. I hope she translates more but she does not. So I keep my eyes down on the metal plate where his attendant is piling rice and a slop of dhal. I notice the dust and dirt on my feet and I know that barefoot I will remain.

After rest time we sit up on the roof of Yagna Veda. I rest my back against a small Shiva temple. Chitrakut winds down to the river below and the ghats, the endless procession of worship. Creamy buildings and the earthen steps opposite fall down into the black water in a tapestry of shifting shapes.

*   *   *

I wake before anyone and slip silently down the stone steps to the ghat. Darkness conceals me as I dip and bathe, the cold waking me instantly. A bell rings somewhere above and the sounds in the murky dawn suggest others are bathing too. Lamps flicker and sway, mantras are mumbled. The water is viscous, grainy, and I imagine the goddess with her many arms, hair spread all about her, reaching out to receive me.

Sita, Hania and Juliana are on their way for a bath. 'How come you didn't wait for us!' Hania asks.

'I don't know, didn't think about it. I woke early and headed off.' I shrug away her frown. I'd been careful not to make a sound. I wanted the lone experience. Sometimes an experience shared can be diluted. 'I'm not so much a constant group type, you know!' Sita smiles and says nothing.

Back in the room Janaki is just waking. 'Hi there,' she smiles then scowls as she sees everyone gone. 'Where is everyone?'

'Gone for bathing. I already took my bath.'

'How come they didn't wake me!' She looks like a child who's been left behind.

'I don't know, maybe they wanted to let you sleep. No one likes waking people.'

'That's not right. Sita stated clearly we are a group and groups do things together.'

'Well, I'm not a total group person. I woke early and went.' I immediately regret the shortness of my words. This is the woman who nursed my foot and my broken spirit. 'Sorry, do you want me to go back to the river with you?'

'No, no. It's all right. I'll go alone.'

I savour the empty room. For a moment I am tempted to head out into the town, answer the call of temple bells and explore alone, following my intuition, the unseen thread that may guide me to a temple where a puja is performed by an old sadhu, or to a hidden shrine of Hanuman with a murti so exquisitely painted I will want to kneel down and bow before him. Janaki's words linger; I don't want to cause any turbulence so I sit on my sleeping mat, tuck my legs into position and meditate until one by one we regroup, any trace of upset washed away in the river below.

Sita has outlined the program for the day. After pradakshina of Kamadgiri we will visit the ashram of a Naga Baba she knows. The Nagas are the wild warrior sadhus and command great respect as powerful ascetics of Shiva. Hah! Even here in the land of Ram, Shiva can be found. As the sun breaks the spell across the east, we pile into a rickshaw and roar off to Kamadgiri, singing bhajans all the way.

'Ram Ram, Radhaji!' Sita calls to the transvestite who is emerging from the wooden door, open wide enough to reveal a slice of courtyard with red flowers in pots. It reminds me of a Mediterranean compound. He wraps his shawl tighter around his shoulders and sings 'Ram Ram' in a deep male voice. He struts down the cobbled path, dressed in a fuschia pink sari with a gold scarf around his head. His face is boldly made up with blue eye shadow and his lips pucker with a splash of red. We walk slowly behind him, as he minces and twirls, his sari lifting to reveal anklets with little bells that jingle as he walks.

The chai wallah is full of smiles. 'Ram Ram, Sitaji,' he nods as we sit on a wooden bench outside, watching the monkeys in the banyan tree. A boy with a torn shirt and shorts that are too large delivers us chai, holding the six glasses in a wire glass holder. He puts them on the table and smiles a big wide smile.

An old man with thick round glasses sits cross-legged with a book, singing the scripture. His voice sounds like the dawn chorus of a song thrush. Sadhus with shaved heads and carefully marked designs painted in red on their arms and foreheads, sit on benches nearby. Others walk with mala beads twirled in their fingers, repeating 'Ram' with every breath. Another with long matted hair trailing to the ground sits by the pathway, lost in another world.

Pradakshina almost complete we take rest by a bathing pond, in the shade of a huge banyan tree. The roots, spread through the old stone steps, are like gnarled fingers entwined with the stone. I wonder for how many hundreds of years these scenes have remained virtually unchanged. Sadhus tending to temples, monkey gods being fed sweets and deities offered flowers. The name of Ram whispered as incense swirls in golden pools of sunlight.

*   *   *

Our rickshaw driver sleeps with his feet up on the handlebars. It is a short drive to Janaki Kund where the Naga Baba has his ashram. The track ends beside a leafy fenced compound. Bougainvillea spills petals of deep red and soft peach, banana palms hang their fruit and leafy trees conceal our destination. A dog greets us with growls and barks, retreating as a whistle shrills in the quiet. The path leads to a low building with smoke curling from an opening in the stone roof.

A tall sadhu with short grey hair and trimmed beard greets us with curiosity.

'Sita Ram, Swamiji.' Sita bows slightly and proceeds in a jumble of Hindi. The swami relaxes and ushers us to the building.

'Naga Baba isn't here, but they expect him soon. We can sit here and wait,' Sita explains with a whisper. The swami brings mats and spreads them in the shade of a palm leaf lean-to against the wall. Sunlight falls in shafts onto copper earth. We sit and fall into a silent almost-stupor, as if we have been given a potion or cast under a spell.

A motorbike chugs and rumbles as a baba rides into the clearing. The dog that greeted us rides in front of him. I never expected to see a Naga Baba ride a motorbike, let alone with a dog as a passenger. The swami takes the bike and walks it behind the building. The baba glances at us then disappears inside, with the dog by his heels.

'Naga Baba is here!' Sita arranges her scarf and I sit a little straighter.

He reappears, clad only in his white loincloth. The dog follows him as he strides to the fire. Sita takes us up and we sit as she introduces us: 'Swamiji, hamara mandali yatra hai.' He looks amused and nods to us all. Naga Babaji has quite a presence. I find myself watching his every move. His hair is mostly jutta and hangs down his back but some bits are wild with curly tails. His beard is fluffy too and his chiselled face and black eyes are full of power.

'Khub aiyer?' [When did you come?] He looks stern and his eyes are piercing.

'Kal subhe.' [Yesterday early.]

'Kahan reheta tum log?' [Where are you staying?]

'Yagna Veda, Maharaj.'

He is satisfied; the interview is over. He reminds me of Babaji and his greeting, wanting to know the basics. As he rearranges the wood, the fire bursts into flame; then from a cloth bag he pulls out a chillum. 'Chillum piou?' He allows a smile, looking again at us one by one. I take my cue from Sita. Already she is engaging.

'Nagababaji ke darshan kellier chillum abkha prasad hai!' [We have come for your darshan so a chillum will be your offering.]

He chuckles and makes a mix. When the chillum is tightly packed he holds it up and utters 'Om Namah Shivaya', before pulling deeply as smoke spurts from the end. He takes off the piece of cloth he has wrapped around the end then passes the chillum to Sita. We all take a turn. The tobacco is strong and sends my head in a spin. For a moment I fear I might throw up. I breathe deeply and take a sip of water. A tobacco rush right now is definitely not on my agenda.

Sita is in full flow. I marvel at her fluency in Hindi and let their exchange play like a lullaby. After a while they too fall silent and we sit by the fire in this shared moment. I sit opposite Sita, close to Naga Baba, and as the head spin falls away I sense a tangible energy emanating from his being. It is as if my own sense of being is amplified, filled up by his presence.

He speaks rapid fire to the attendant. 'Lunch?' he asks, leaning forward slightly as he looks at us all.

We wash our hands at a tap and sit back on the mats under the shade while Naga Baba eats at the dhuni alone. His attendant places a plate and cup of water in front of us all then piles rice from a bowl before returning with aloo palak. Then thick rotis, still warm and singed at the edges. I eat with my fingers and savour each mouthful. We are all on our best behaviour. I wonder whether they cooked up extra when we arrived or if there was just enough anyway. Back at the fire the attendant brings chai in little tin cups. Sita sits on her heels, smoothing her robes around her. She waits till Naga Baba lights a beedi then speaks to him in English.

'Swamiji, can I ask you what your experience is, of the day-to-day life here, living in this ashram. Do you perform puja or any practice that you may be gracious and tell us about? This mandali here all experience a deep love and devotion to the Hindu ways and maybe you can help us in furthering our understanding.'

He smiles slowly, just the corners of his wide mouth turning up very slightly.

'Sadhu life always way of tapas [spiritual discipline]. Tapas brings great power. All is energy. Great power. Tapas means: overcome the mind, desire: to burn out this illusion. There is nothing but Atman. God. Only "Om Namah Shivaya". True tapas is knowing this.'

Sita is quiet and I wait, wanting and hoping he will speak more. His voice is hypnotic. He lets go slowly of every word as if each sound is a living entity to part with carefully. 'Now my karma is I take care of this ashram. Taking care mutlub, this dhuni always alight. Naga Baba yoga is living oneness with this creation, this energy. Prakriti, this world here in union, this is austerity.'

Sita is bold. 'So, Maharaj, is there one practice you can give us, or advice to help our knowing God?'

Without a pause he replies, 'Keep mind for God. Always keep mind in meditation. Too much energy waste when thoughts allowed. Mind greatest power. God mind.' He raises his eyebrows and smiles. 'You Guruji hey, so this is the best. Guruji best help.'

Sita is taking full advantage. 'Is there a practice that may help?'

He scowls for a moment, fierce even. Sita responds with something in Hindi and he loosens. 'One mantra I tell you. This mantra my practice even as small boy. This powerful mantra. Good health and mind sattvic. You know sattva?' He glances at us all again. 'Sattvic mind, pure mind. Only mind for Union with God.'

I wonder what Sita has said to him in Hindi. I wonder too whether he is used to westerners or if we are a novelty – that is, if Naga Babas find anything a novelty.

He speaks again. 'Sattva is number one importance. To keep sattvic mind you be sattvic. This means no speaking with people quick for anger. Or lazy people. Lazy means tamasic, angry people rajastic. No – only sattvic around you. Same like sweet smells. Don't stay with bad smells. Thoughts not good thoughts. And food eating only sattvic food. Some vegetable, dahi [curd], little milk. Some sweet eating is good. Rice, chapatti. Simple. You body sattvic mind thoughts sattvic. This good for meditation.' And he again falls silent, and I wonder if he is perhaps tired of us all now. After a moment of being lost in that god world where all sadhus, it seems, enjoy to dwell, he rummages around in the cloth bag by his side and pulls out the chillum.

'And Naga Babaji, there is one mantra you speak of?' Sita reminds him, before he encourages us to partake in a smoke and we lose our hold on reality a little more. I find myself giggling spontaneously. I can't help myself. It is all so bizarre that so much of life in our western world is to strive for material possessions – for more, always more. Yet here is this man who is more at home in his skin than any I have met, emanating a great power – and he has nothing, just a loincloth around his sparse, taut body. He sits complete within himself, a man wanting nothing. A man who knows he is a king yet with no need for a castle.

Naga Baba leaves the chillum bag by his side. 'Om Om Om,' he intones and in an instant I am listening. 'Om is like invitation. Om also is number one sound. The sound of all of this.' He sweeps his hand to take in the bougainvillea spilling its crimson, the white- barked gum trees and the sky so blue around. And suddenly he pulls his legs to the lotus position, breathes rapidly a few times and then repeats the mantra for us in a low chant. He sits upright as he does and I straighten my back and close my eyes.

'Om Tryambakam Yajamahe, Sugandhum Pushtivardhanam, Urvarukamiva Bandhanam, Mrityor Mokshiya Maamritat. Om.' After a moment he repeats: 'Om hring hrung yung swaha.'

Shivers rush up my spine. The sounds resonate within. My vision fades at the edges and heat burns in my sacrum. As the sensations dwindle I notice we all sit to attention. He has an effect on each of us. A sudden rush of gratitude floods me as I look at Sita and realise the gift she has given in sharing this timeless hidden world with us. Bringing us to Chitrakut where a world of mystery and lore is the governance, where Sita and Ram played out their leela and left their footprints for us to follow. Where Naga Babas sit by sacred fires doing very little, it seems, yet with all at their command. Self-realisation is clearly possible, here and now, as Papaji so often says.

As if on cue we all stretch, shuffle, glance tentatively at one another. The flame is just a trail of smoke from a burning ember. Naga Baba remains quiet but he studies us all and I try to think of something to ask him, to engage him, but I find nothing in my mind. He stares at me for a moment and I find myself responding with a smile.

We take our leave and Naga Baba walks with us down a narrow path to the back gate near the river. 'Again you may come,' he tells us, shaking his head as if we are dismissed. He stares right into my eyes. I feel that flow of energy again for some moments then it stops as he turns his gaze away.

*　　*　　*

The river is clear and flowing, bubbling over rocks and gliding into wider pools. Reeds line the sandy beaches of the bank and opposite a sadhu washes his orange cloth, the reflected colour streaking between greens smudged in the water.

'Sita, what does this mantra mean, do you know?'

'This is the Mahamrityunjaya mantra. It is performed at Agni Hotra, fire ceremony.' She pauses a moment to gather in her mind the words.

'The meaning is this: We meditate on the three eyed reality which permeates and nourishes all like a fragrance. May we be liberated from death for the sake of immortality, even as the cucumber, when perfectly ripe, is severed from bondage to the creeper.'

We sit around her now on the banks of the river.

'The three eyed reality is Shiva but Shiva as Absolute, or Self we can say. All we can do is keep our minds and hearts turned to God and then, like the cucumber when ripeness is there, the fruit will fall. And all cucumbers eventually fall. This is why the mantra is important and powerful too. This mantra is for purification, for mental, emotional and physical wellbeing.'

'What about the sounds he chanted after?' I ask. The vibration has settled in me and I am curious.

'These sounds are said to resonate within the energy body. They are ancient sounds and do not have an exact meaning. They are known as Bhij mantras, seed mantras. These sounds are purely energetic.'

That evening we arrive back at Yagna Veda as the sun kisses the stones with a lingering rouge. We sit in the courtyard with Shastriji. He taught Sita the Sanskrit she knows, back in the seventies when there was no electricity and she lived as a sadhu with these people who embrace her as their own.

Shastri wears the wrinkles of an elder in his hazel brown face and twinkling eyes. He is small with a round belly and short cropped white hair. He sings love songs to us, keeping rhythm with his upturned steel bucket, clanking the handle in a gentle beat. Evening drops her curtain to bring a display of diamonds high in the black heavens. We sit for the longest time and float back up the stairs to our room in the tower.

Shastri is a bhang wallah; every day he prepares bhang (marijuana leaf), grinding it for many hours. This has been his daily routine for longer than Sita has known him. Tomorrow we will eat lunch at Yagna Veda and then partake in the ritual ourselves.

The sun has already risen as we gather for the ride to Kamadgiri. I have bathed under the cover of dark, unwilling to forgo one moment of ritual. No one minds now about the activities of the others. Chitrakut has banished preference and we follow Sita with easy surrender. Again we walk pradakshina, past the transvestite who waves and sings in his husky voice. He wears bright yellow today with a sequined scarf that glints in the light.

I keep the name of Ram close to my lips, as if whispering to my unseen friend beside me. Beneath my bare feet is the grainy stone of this ancient path. When we reach the bathing kund I sit beneath the banyan tree, waves of bliss passing through my body. Tears pour down my cheeks as the sense of God within spins in my chest. A low vibration fills the air as if all creation chants in unison the sound of 'Om'. It spills everywhere, nowhere untouched.

'You okay?' Janaki asks.

'Yes,' I whisper. 'I'm fine.'

'It is a place of the gods here, Prem Kumari. We cannot hide.'

*   *   *

Shastri sits in the middle of the bare stone floor on a thin cushion, grinding the herb between two stones. A window high on the wall lets broken light fall. He smiles and nods as we watch. He smiles most of the time, unless he is singing. He uses the male leaf of the marijuana plant, grinding it into a paste. He has been taking bhang every day since the age of seven and is now in his seventies. He pours a sprinkle of water from a kamandal, adds a handful of raisins and grinds some more. A dark paste is beginning to form on the smooth stone before him. The bhang is ground for quite a few hours before it is ready. Raisins, nuts and sugar are added bit by bit. All the while, as he works, he repeats a mantra.

I listen hard to catch the words, wondering if they are the same mantra Naga Baba recited for us. They are not; these words, although they are mumbled, sound more like a cascade of water on a warm day. Every now and again he declares 'Om' in a more definite tone, like a full stop in a paragraph. When finally the bhang is prepared to a neat mound of paste before him on the wooden board, he rinses his hands then wipes them on a cloth slung over his shoulder. His face folds again in smiles, black eyes twinkle.

'Pani pina app log. Mandakini ke darshan chello,' Shastri instructs with an authority I like. After drinking water we take darshan from the Mandakini before partaking in our ceremony. He gives us each a small ball of dark green bhang, nods his head then whispers 'Sita Ram' and nods even more as we wash it down with water. It tastes pungent yet sweet and slips down easily. With another nod of his head he eats a ball himself then settles before his bucket, tapping out a rhythm as he sings 'Sita Ram' all over again.

The program is to walk to Hanuman Situ, part of a ruined temple carved in the hillside. A better program I could not have designed. We climb up the long line of steps with monkeys chattering around us. An old swami sits outside and banana skins litter the ground.

Kamadgiri lies before us, bathed in afternoon light. The whole of Chitrakut is laid out to see, the high walls of the temples and ashrams golden and glowing. The bhang takes its hold, slowly at first. We giggle and question each other as to whether we feel anything; then it's obvious, so we sit in a row looking out at the mountain. Sita starts to sing the Hanuman chalisa in a lingering melody that catches hold and we join in with a soft 'Sita Ram' to accompany.

Shadows pull the colours to muted blue then stretch themselves like a bruise across the earth. Back in town the light is fading. Bells start sounding at the Shiva temple and I float up the steep steps to a crush of people.

The bells ring continuously over and over, until I can hardly bear the naked sound. The temple is packed and I stand at the back, grateful for the flow of air in the startling heat of puja. Cymbals crash and horns drone long and low. And then they stop. The silence born from the sudden absence of sound leaves me suspended in eternity itself. And then the raucous worship takes off again. The pujari – who I see through the crowd is a teenager, wearing jeans and a shirt – throws his head back, holding a heavy multi-tiered oil lamp which he waves in slow circles around the deities, all the while singing 'Hari Om Namah Shivaya, Hari Om Namah Shivaya' until I too join with the worship and sing with everyone else in this packed, incense-filled, white-walled temple.

*   *   *

I find everyone back at Yagni Veda, sitting with Shastriji. The mandali shines with a radiant light and the idea of spending a life like this – making bhang for hours each day, singing, washing in the river – feels absolutely perfect. I cannot remember ever being so satisfied. If I was born for any particular moment it is this: to listen to Shastriji singing with a bucket, with no apparent care in the world.

We take a pot of chai up to our room and lie around, sharing our selves, and Sita tells us a story of Hanuman.

'After Hanuman brought Sita back to Ram and they are all reunited in Ayodhya, Ram summoned his army and helpers to him. He gave a speech thanking everyone who helped rescue Sita. He gives the generals lavish gifts of horses and gold. One by one they bow before their Lord Ram offering their thanks and eternal pledge for service to his cause. Then Ram turns to Hanuman and gives him a priceless necklace made of emeralds and diamonds, laced with pearls. It is one of Sita's most precious pieces of jewellery. Everyone exclaims at its beauty. But Hanuman holds it in his hands and a tear rolls down his cheek. "Hanuman! Why do you not give thanks to the Lord Ram for his gift?" "Hanuman! Why do you look so sad?"

'Hanuman crushes the gems between his powerful fingers, throwing the broken jewels on the floor. The onlookers mock Hanuman, crushing a gift from Ram himself. "He is only a monkey! What does he know?"

'Hanuman speaks in a low clear voice. "What is the value of these things that may glitter and sparkle? I have examined them inside and out and nowhere do I find the name of Ram. Therefore let them return to the dust from where they came." Then with tears in his eyes Hanuman looks at Lord Ram, watching from his throne. "The only gift I wish to receive, my Lord, is your darshan inside my heart." Ram embraced Hanuman and then Hanuman seizes his chest and pulls open his own flesh, to reveal Ram and Sita seated inside his heart.'

Much later Janaki and I walk down to the water. We sit on the steps in the dark, the lanterns that light the ghats reflecting in the black expanse of water. It seems to me then – with the sound of bells all around, the nearby temple loudspeaker sending a crackling Sita Ram Sita Ram to the ether – that all paths lead to worship in this magical land of Chitrakut.

'You know, Prem Kumari, being here now in Chitrakut it all makes sense. I haven't been here for seventeen years; so much life has happened in that time, but somehow nothing has changed. Here I am, me myself, listening to a golden bell ring out across the water, as it has every evening for all these years. Sita said to me once when I felt despair at the confinement of my life with kids, that Chitrakut is not only a place of pilgrimage, but a state of mind, a state of communion with God. She was right.'

'Sita must be a wonderful friend to have?'

'She has always been there, even if we haven't been in touch a lot. Somehow her life – dedicated to seeking, to the ways of sadhana and puja – was a comfort to me. Sometimes I was stuck in the seemingly endless routine of lunch boxes, school pick-ups, kids squabbling – it's hard to imagine, I think, if you're not a parent. Anyway, there were times during the years I was raising my kids that I just felt like a black hole was swallowing me up. I would yearn for India, and the freedom of spirit we so easily feel here. Honestly, Prem Kumari, at times I felt my soul was sold. Anyway, when she said that to me, it struck home. Chitrakut for me represents that yearning, the call if you like, to the beloved. Everywhere here is devotion. *Ram Ram, Ram Ram.* Anyway, it stayed with me and I would close my eyes and commune with my own godhead.'

Janaki smiles. She looks still some place far away and I tell her so.

'Maybe. Thinking of my kids. Uma has been here, to Chitrakut. Mothering doesn't end when they leave home, I discover.'

'I can't imagine. I really don't think I will ever return to England, let alone be a mother. Or a wife.' Janaki smiles. 'No, I can't see you being a wife either!'

'I just can't see myself fitting into what the western culture offers; the restraints would be too onerous'.

'You remind me of myself, Prem Kumari. I too walked barefoot on this land. Truth is we just don't know what our path will bring.' The bells increase, ringing over and over. 'The fact is that whatever our thoughts and personal preferences, life is just happening regardless.'

'Thanks, Janaki. Thanks for being here, for staying at Sundari's, for being so kind that night I showed up with the foot. For knowing Sita. All of it.' I turn again to the shifting water stretched under the black night and the chanting seems to come from somewhere inside me.

*　　*　　*

The morning is program free. We are invited for lunch with the Naga Baba and will regroup then. After my early morning bath I take a rickshaw to Kamadgiri. Just as the rickshaw drops me at the steps leading up to the cobbled stone pathway, the sun pricks the east, emerging in a perfect orange ball.

Shastri has given us each a tulsi mala. I play with the beads between my fingers, turning them through one by one. As I walk I repeat the name of Ram with every bead that I turn. This is my first time of japa meditation, as it is called, and I am surprised how much I have to focus to keep up the practice.

The carved wooden doors of the transvestite's world are closed. Even the sweet stall is yet to be filled, bare wooden boards awaiting the trays of sugary balls.

The effort of Ram japa keeps me focused on my step. I pass the chai stall where we normally stop, returning the call of 'Sita Ram Sita Ram' from the chai wallah. I stop in the shade of a big old knarled neem tree. The sounds and shapes of the forest cover the hill like a blanket. Birds sit

227

motionless then suddenly take off, gliding through the greens. Branches twist and curl, inviting me into an enchanted world, undisturbed since Lord Ram's holy feet walked on this sacred hill. *Ram Ram Ram Ram ...* his name plays on my lips as the tulsi beads slip effortlessly through my fingers. Free to wander as I wish, alone on this pradakshina, I let my feet guide me. The old baba who always sits and sings from the scriptures already recites his song. A small temple behind him beckons and I enter the cold interior and sit against the wall, surrender to the song of the sadhu, and the simple stone temple. The deity is Hanuman.

The pujari of the bigger Hanuman temple calls out 'Sita Ram!' as I round the corner. No bhajan crackles from his loudspeakers today. I bow before the orange Hanuman and he dots my forehead with orange tilak. Monkeys jump from the roof and a sudden fight between two big males sends all the dogs barking. I savour my aloneness. Concentrating on each step, on each breath, on each bead that passes my fingers, I chant Ram: the name of the Lord.

I turn off the pradakshina path and begin the walk to Naga Baba's ashram, relaxing the japa. In an instant, 'Om Namah Shivaya' rushes from my lips as if the words demand to be spilled. I touch my rudraksha mala that I have worn since Babaji gave it to me more than a year ago; it is rougher, slightly gnarled, and I wrap the tulsi mala around my wrist.

Bougainvillea falls in thick swathes of magenta flowers, leaving a carpet of welcome. Bhagwan the dog greets me as I open the gate. He wags his tail as if remembering and escorts me to the fire. Naga Baba remains still as I hesitate a moment, but then nods to me so, as effortlessly as I can, I sit at the side of his dhuni.

I hold the mantra in my mind. It is quiet; not even the sound of traffic reaches through the trees that give shade and coolness after the walk in bright sun. Birds sing melodies, wrens flit through pools of sunshine, vivid and precise. A breeze ruffles the shimmering leaves on the gum trees, teasing those ready to let go to spiral downwards in the light. The dhuni smoulders, a neat square of silver ash held within a smooth clay pit.

'Prem Kumari,' he says and suddenly smiles. He looks at me with unblinking eyes. 'Good name, Prem Kumari.' He chuckles to himself. I have no idea what to say. My silence now is nothing but survival.

'Chai piou?' he asks between pulls on a beedi that keeps going out. In the next breath he calls to the attendant who is sweeping the path, the sound of the brush giving rhythm to the ragas of birdsong praising the day. Nervousness has no place to stay.

Bhagwan barks, growls and disappears up the path.

'Visitors!' he says.

'Sita and the rest of the mandali?'

Naga Baba shakes his head. 'No, some other, come for darshan.' He whistles to Bhagwan then calls him, and a few moments later an Indian couple are standing at the steps leading up to where we sit. Eventually they sit at the fireplace, smiling at me and giving him oranges and dried fruits as an offering. Naga Baba nods and says only a few words; he is almost severe. The woman is overweight and sweating in the warmth. I guess they are not from Chitrakut. More words are spoken before they nod again then prostrate full length so their heads touch the earth. The husband helps his wife to stand back up, and she dusts her sari, nodding as only Indians can. Naga Baba lifts his hand in blessing and they are gone.

The rest of the mandali arrive as smells of cooking seep from the hut on the other side of the clearing. 'You're looking very much at home!' Hania sits by me. 'Been having fun?'

'I walked pradakshina then came here. Sitting here all morning.' I smile. Yes I do feel at home.

'Sita took us to another mahant. This place is full of saints, hidden away in ashrams and rooms with hardly any ventilation. Shastri sent his chela over to invite us for bhang again. It's just wild.'

'I could stay here forever!' I whisper.

Lunch is two different subze, one of coarse greens and the other with the bright red chillies like a flag of warning. I pick them out. A spoonful of ghee, tomato pickle, and a chunk of lemon decorate the plate; the thick rotis taste of fire. I think of Babaji up in the hills and wonder if he too has been to Chitrakut. I realise that I will never travel with him, to places such as here, as our relationship would be seen as sacrilegious. Imagine taking a room together. It just would not happen. No, I would travel with him only as a sadhu myself, and we would sleep by the dhuni in a temple courtyard, perform japa meditation together, in silence of course, in the cool predawn of our days.

Naga Baba is fasting today. Stomachs full, we join him again for our vigil by the smouldering fire. He has another five years to live in this ashram and take care of the dhuni, honouring his teacher's request.

'Then will you stay on in Chitrakut?' I ask. Sitting alone with him today has made me bold enough to ask a question.

'Himalaya. I will go walking in the high Himalaya. Himalaya is Shiva place, no people, only Shiva.' He chuckles again.

He puts his hand up, palm facing out towards us all. 'Narayana, Narayana,' he repeats with eyes half closed. A whispered breeze plays with the gold-flecked leaves of the neem tree: the still small voice of God. The attendant brings chai in a lota and Naga Babaji pours it into little tin cups, which he passes to us one by one.

As we stand to leave I put my hands together and say, 'Bahut dhanyabad, Maharajji, bahut dhanyabad.' He smiles at me then replies: 'Why thanks, why thank you. You are my heart.' Bhagwan runs by my side all the way to the gate, licking my hand.

That evening Sita teaches us part of the Devi puja, verses in praise of the goddess. 'Let's sing to Papaji when we return!'

'Yah Devi sarva bhouteshu, bhudi rupena sanstita, namastasia namastasia namastasia namo namaha.' [Oh great goddess, grant me knowledge, grant me peace, grant me understanding ...]

*   *   *

The bathing ghats are lined with stalls selling all sorts of trinkets. There are countless statues of Hanuman, Ram and Sita relaxing on a swing, statues that light up and play music. There are malas by the dozen and bells and bracelets, bangles, beads. There are photos of the gods and red and gold temple cloth. A stretch of stalls at the base of the steps up to the Shiva temple sells lingams. The smallest fit in the palm of a hand; the largest stand tall enough to meet my gaze. I want a lingam of my own, and search each stall. I choose the biggest I can carry back to Lucknow. It has a snake curled around the base and the yoni is solid stone for the symbol of Shiva to rest on. It is heavy but after looking at several closely there is something in the carving of the snake that speaks to me. I bathe it in the Mandakini before wrapping it in cloth and packing it carefully in my bag. It is time to begin my own practice of puja. I want the abidance with god, with Shiva, to be the focus of my day, my life. This pilgrimage to Chitrakut has immersed me with grace and I want the fragrance, the essence, to return with me to Lucknow.

*　　*　　*

Satsang recommences and we write a card to Papaji asking to sing for him. As we gather at his feet he turns to me with a smile. 'You saw Hanuman?' he asks then laughs.

'Yes, Papaji. I saw Hanuman.'

Bliss sweeps me again, erupting from every cell of my being. It is as if this bliss, this extraordinary sensation, is in fact the foundation of my soul. The sound of 'Hanuman Ki Jai!' – Victory to Hanuman – erupts in my thoughts. We sing the Devi puja and he listens, muttering 'Chello chello' as we return to our seats.

*　　*　　*

December brings a misty chill to the early mornings. I send Babaji a postcard with a picture of Hanuman. I write 'Ram Ram' and tell him I will be there by the end of the year. I wonder for a moment whether he even keeps track of dates and months, but the season will be changing, trees losing the last leaves, and the air colder as the sun slides further away.

Before leaving for Dharamsala and winter in the hills, I return to Chitrakut. Naga Baba has come in my dreams and I want to sit at his dhuni once more. I travel alone and arrive at Yagna Vedna, where we stayed last time, to find preparations for a bandhara. A bandhara is a feast prepared in an ashram or temple and the courtyard is full of massive cooking pots, piles of potatoes, vats of rice and women who sit or squat, cleaning dhal plate by plate.

The next morning I bath in the cold of dawn and I feel Chitrakut once again pulling me into her web of magic.

Day is barely here as I take a rickshaw to the foot of the hill to walk pradakshina before visiting Naga Baba. A thrill of anticipation ripples through me as I imagine myself by his fire once again. And then of course the doubt comes. Is he even in Chitrakut right now? Am I welcome to show up alone, without the leadership of Sita and the mandali?

Kamadgiri rises in the dawn. Swathes of gold brush the sky. At this early hour the main temple at the start of pradakshina is quiet and the pile of shoes at the beginning of the walk is small. Inside the temple the deities are already dressed. The cloth is vibrantly coloured against the white marble of the sculptures. Sita stands beside Ram, his brother Laxman to one side. Their faces all have a serene beatitude and it isn't hard to imagine them breathing, or suddenly smiling and reaching out a hand. Hanuman is there too, bowing at the feet of Ram. Since Papaji asked me, 'Did you see Hanuman?' I have found more interest in this monkey god. The Lord's loyal servant. I have started to learn the Hanuman chalisa, adding it to my morning prayers and meditation.

The pujari sits cross-legged on the floor, threading flowers onto a string, the yellow and orange marigolds piled in a basket by his side. He stands as he sees me and rings the bell hanging on a chain, then takes a spoonful of water from the brass pot on the altar and pours it into my cupped hands. I drink it down then rub my damp hands over my head, as is the custom. Not a drop wasted. As I swallow the grainy water I am caught for a moment in the purpose of worship. The water is imbued it seems with the sanctity of the temple, and I taste the subtle fragrance of incense mixed with metal from the brass spoon. *May my speech reflect Your name* is my silent prayer. The pujari then hands me prasad, a ladu that crumbles as I take a bite. It is quite dry and very sweet and dissolves in my mouth. He then presses a handful of tulsi leaves in my hand as he mutters, 'Sita Ram Sita Ram.' I put the tulsi in the small shoulder bag I carry. I will dry and keep it, this sacred herb of India. The leaf has many medicinal properties. Babaji has it growing in pots and always brews tulsi tea if a guest has a cough.

I stop at the first chai stall to wash down the ladu crumbs caught in my throat. The chai wallah sits by his fire, warming his hands on the flame, hot oil hissing in a blackened wok. He wears a woollen scarf tied around his ears and under his chin. Seeing me, his face erupts in smiles. The locals seem to have an innocence I have not seen elsewhere, perhaps because there are few western tourists here. But maybe it's simply because this is the land of the gods.

'Oh Sitaji aienge! Behtou behtou!' [Sita has come! Sit sit.]

'Isalie Sita ji nahi. Me akeli arj.' [Actually Sita no, I am alone today.]

'Behtou chai piou.' [Sit, drink chai.]

A vat of milk heats to one side and he busies himself throwing a handful of tea leaf into a pan, pouring water from a kettle, and letting it simmer for a while. Then he ladles milk into a cup, a handful of sugar and a few cardamoms, which he has rubbed between his palms to encourage the flavour to seep from the fat black seeds inside. He smiles and nods as he gives me the chai: 'Sita Ram, Sita Ram.'

It is good chai, milky and not too strong. I warm my hands on the glass. Chai made, he returns to making jalabies, squeezing squiggly lines of yellow batter into the wok of bubbling oil. They puff a little and turn a crisp orange as he plucks them from the oil and tips them into another pan to soak in sugary syrup. The oil hisses every time he puts in a new batch. A pile of ladus and other sweets sit in trays encased in a glass cabinet. A sudden burst of music shreds the early morning silence as a nearby temple plays bhajans full blast.

A small boy appears as if from the ether and declares: 'One, two, three!' and stands before me where I sit on the red plastic chair. An elderly baba is sitting further along the wall, watching me; he comes and sits on an empty chair beside me. He walks with a stoop and close up I see he has a swelling in his throat, partly hidden by his grey bushy beard.

'Which country?' he asks, in crisp precise English as if he has had lessons just for this moment.

'England.' I pause. No, England is too far removed from all of this. 'But now I live in India.' I smile with the certainty of my words. At moments like this I could clap my hands and proclaim to all around my utter happiness and delight. Delight for this moment of speaking with a gentle old baba who sits beside me on a plastic chair while a man in a clean white shirt sweeps the dust and pilgrims nod as they pass. The temple now changes the tape to a gentle lyrical song, a man's voice proclaiming his devotion to Ram. Yes, this is my home. What other life could offer what I feel right now? What else could pull me to my knees and elevate me all at once, satisfy me so deeply, as this moment right now perfects?

The baba raises his eyebrows and nods as he takes the chai from the boy, who insists I listen again to his counting. 'One, two, three, four, five!' I smile at him and he turns all shy and scoots back to the chai wallah who ruffles his hair. The old sadhu also smiles and it is as if we share a moment of intimacy, of connection, as the old man's face too suggests his love of this precise moment.

'Humara gare idder hai.' [This is my home.] He gestures with his head to the stone wall where he sat beside the chai shop. 'Pani hai, Bhagwan hai, or khya chaiyee?' [Water I have, God I have, what else do I need?] What else indeed? I contemplate drinking another chai, spending the morning here on this seat to watch as the world passes by, but I have a mission. 'Narayana, Narayana.' I say as I stand. The old baba raises his hand in blessing as I leave.

The Hanuman pujari calls to me, 'Deviji', with a familiar smile. After touching the feet of the orange murti of Hanuman, I take prasad, little white flakes of sugar that crunch in my teeth. He puts the dot of orange tilak between my eyes, sending powdery flakes down my clothes. I am dressed in cream silk robes covering white trousers to my ankles. My hair, with three strands of juta amidst the curls, is tied on top of my head.

I visit every temple. I cannot miss a doorway, not even a single wooden arch. A swami kneels. A husband and wife receive darshan. I sit behind the swami and see he has a thick book wrapped in a cloth. He unwraps it and opens the pages with great care. The writing is bold and decorative.

'It is the original script of Tulsidas,' the man tells me, his wife smiling broadly.

'Is this Sanskrit?' I ask.

'It is a mix of Hindi and Sanskrit.'

Another couple join us as we gaze at the words. The swami carefully turns a page. Tulsidas is a great saint in India, said to be an incarnation of the sage Valmiki who was responsible for writing, or channelling, several of the great Indian scriptures. Tulsidas lived in the fifteenth century, which makes this manuscript 500 years old.

'Is this really the original of Tulsidas?' I ask, incredulous.

The man stands now. 'Madam, here it is all presumption. Everything here is based on presumption.' He speaks as if his teeth are loose. I smile to myself. It is true. It is all belief. Then it must be that belief paves the way. The swami carefully wraps up the book now as the man and his wife offer several hundred rupees. The others take photos.

'Everything in the world is based on presumption,' I say.

'Yes, yes,' he says and we all smile some more.

Further along the path a sadhu lies on the ground. He has placed a small statue on the path before him and as I watch, he prostrates, sprinkling water on the stones, before kneeling and placing the statue, which could be Hanuman, and a rock, several feet in front of him. Again he prostrates with his head on the ground, arms outstretched, repeating the practice again and again. I wonder how long it will take him to complete a circuit of the hill and then remember that he doesn't care about time. The act of worship is not to attain a goal: it is all there is. As I walk past I see his hair is matted and his forehead smeared with ash.

At the bathing kund, where on my visit with the mandali bliss had swept around me like a flock of invisible swallows, and where the huge banyan tree offers shade, I sit again on the cold stone steps that have been pushed and cracked by the roots of the spreading tree. The sense of blissful union steals in through my heart, the absolute knowing that all is God. I know that when we open ourselves to the knowing of something greater, when the ceaseless chatter of the mind loses its hold, then just as nothing can stop these roots pushing through stone, so our inherent divinity cracks the illusion.

*   *   *

I walk to Naga Baba's ashram. I have all the time in the world and I enjoy the sensation of earth under my bare feet. The ground is camel-coloured and dusty. At a roadside stall where a group of men sit cross-legged on the floor playing cards, I buy four ruby-red pomegranates and a couple of packets of beedis. I have no idea if Naga Baba will even be here.

It's a longer walk than I remembered, as previously I travelled by rickshaw. As I turn off the main road I am suddenly thankful to be away from the trucks rushing past. Trucks always seem to be in a hurry and are often filled to the brim, with people sitting precariously on top of the load. The quiet of the path brings a sudden relief, a preparation for the ashram that is close now. I am nervous, filled with doubt. My thoughts suddenly seem loud and disordered, clattering about in my mind. What if he isn't here? Who do you think you are just showing up! As I reach the gate I am almost ready to just turn back, to admit it was a mistake, that I have no business knocking on the door of a Naga Baba. I walk through the gate and Bhagwan races up the path, barking. He is an Alsatian type of dog and looks fierce. I stop and wait while he barks at me. My presence will be known by now for sure.

Someone calls, 'Hut, hut!' Bhagwan stops barking and wags his tail. Naga Baba himself comes up the path. His face is stern and I wonder again what I am doing. Turning up unannounced, expecting what? I finger the packet of beedis in my shoulder bag. The dog plays at my feet. I pat his head and rub his back and he rolls over on the ground, smiling in a canine way.

'You came alone?' His voice is stern. I am sure he is frowning.

'Yes, Naga Baba.' What else can I say? I suddenly feel very foolish. What shall I say? *Well, Naga Babaji, I dreamed of you so felt to come and visit again.* Oh my God! What a disaster!

'Sita is not with you?'

'No, Maharaj. She is now in Vrindavan.'

He nods. 'Au, au.' [Come.] And then he smiles, a charming smile, and his wide piercing almond eyes stare for a moment deep into my own. Then he points out the fruit trees in his garden, talking as if I was here only yesterday.

'This lemon tree, two time year giving fruit, and this the best mango.'

He touches the leaves, strokes them almost. 'You like mango?'

I can only nod. Already the tree is full of tiny new fruit; it will be months yet before they are ripe. He points out a papaya and guava, another lemon tree. The guava is full of fruit. It is their season. I follow him up the steps to the dhuni and sit. He arranges his legs and nods to me. 'When you come back?'

'Yesterday, Maharaj.'

His eyes return to the fire and he lights a beedi. I busy myself with taking out of my bag the fruits and beedis that I have brought as a gift. I hope the pomegranates are red and juicy, and that the beedis are the ones he likes to smoke. He calls out to the attendant, the one that served us lunch when we were all here. The attendant comes up the steps and when he sees me, he gives such a welcoming smile that I completely relax.

Bhagwan finds his place on a cushion by the dhuni. He licks my hand and wags his tail. Naga Baba watches and I have the sense that he is the master of all that happens here, in this ashram hidden in the trees.

I settle within my slowing breath, the in and out, in rhythm with my surroundings. I sense the underlying quiet – the consciousness upon which this world is projected – holding creation in its hand. Strands of smoke curl from the hut across from the dhuni. Smells of spices mingle with smoke and I hear steady pounding as a mortar and pestle grinds something to a paste.

Naga Baba turns to me with a charming smile. 'Tum prasad khana?'

'Dhanyabad, ashram bhojan sub se accha,' I reply. [Thank you, ashram food is the best.]

'Bhojan nahi,' he tells me with a scowl across his brow. 'Prasad!' He fixes his eyes as if I must understand. 'Prasad hey. This temple place, ashram place. Spiritual nourishment gives far greater satisfaction than the mere filling of the stomach.'

True. Everything here is sacrosanct. Everything is ritual.

I am served lunch alone. I sit under the palm leaf shade and it seems like yesterday that I sat here with Sita and the crew. Time has its own agenda as it really could be yesterday. In fact it was five weeks ago. Since then Juliana asked Papaji for a name. He gave her the name Shobha and told her it meant grace, the return to grace after your head has been turned away. 'Looking at other things,' he had joked. 'Boys.' He had laughed.

He was often like this in satsang, as if he couldn't help but find it all very funny. The name suits her and I have also heard it means beautiful woman, which she is. Living with Hania and Juliana is nourishing. Often women gather at the house, bearing fruits or sweets or flowers. Sometimes we sing or share poetry and recently we started a writing group. I notice my reluctance at times. I prefer to remain slightly aloof, the first to leave the group. As if I want to be sure that no one comes too close, or I have an agenda to keep to myself. I prefer to read the Bhagavad Gita or just simply sit with the lingam I purchased here, decked out in orange flowers.

And now I am here, back in the ashram of Naga Baba, eating lunch alone, from a tin plate. With my fingers I deftly scoop the rice, break off pieces of thick roti and mix the subze of greens and tomato. As Naga Baba said, ashram food satisfies far more than the stomach. It satisfies me in the same way as did the swami singing his prayer this morning, and the sight of the small boy with his hair neatly oiled and parted, as he stood with his hands folded and eyes shut before the Hanuman temple, and the feeling of energy swirling and available as the pujari touched my forehead with a dot of red. It satisfies my soul. It feeds my soul with longing and renders my lips only capable of softly singing 'Om Namah Shivaya, Om Namah Shivaya' in response. It allows me to ponder that in moments like this I have indeed found the peace, the in-between place that I experienced when Henry slipped from his body, and that heaven can be found here on earth. I decline second helpings when the attendant returns with more rice. He is gracious and I sense again how welcoming he is.

I rinse my plate at the tap and wash my hands and mouth. Returning to the dhuni, I take my place, more sure of myself now my mind is quiet and I have a sense of being present to this experience. Naga Baba does not even move his eyes to acknowledge me and it does not matter. Why would he disturb himself? I too fall into a quietness, sitting on my heels as Babaji showed me, to allow the food to easily digest. I close my eyes and allow time to weave its illusion.

A little later, I change my position and glance again at Naga Baba. I may as well be invisible to him. Settling again in a cross-legged position, I find a small sense of joy at the fact that I, too, am content. I do not want anything at this moment. In my mind I hear Papaji say, as he so often does: 'Simply keep quiet. Do not stir a single thought. Then find out who you are.'

My need to go to the bathroom stirs me from my meditation. I stretch my legs and stand and, as silently as I can, I slip away and walk back down the path and find a place in the trees to pee. Just as I do, Bhagwan bounds up. He wags his tail and wants to lick my hand and I juggle keeping him at bay and straightening my clothes. Bhagwan stands by my side then escorts me back to the dhuni. I am struck again that Naga Baba is the master of ceremonies here and as I smile at the dog, he wags his tail even harder.

Back at the dhuni, Naga Baba is preparing a chillum mix. He rubs the tobacco and a piece of charas rests on the edge of the dhuni. 'Chai lau!' he calls, a barking command. I settle myself and the dog again rests by Naga Baba's side. Bhagwan looks at me with his soft brown eyes; I want to ask Babaji if he communicates with his dog but then Naga Baba says, 'He is good dog. I've had since a puppy. Good guard dog also.' He pulls a small glowing ember from the fire with his chimitas and rests it just by the charas. After a moment he throws the ember back in the fire then takes the now soft charas and crumbles it into the mix. I can smell its subtle aroma. Charas is sacred to sadhus and the Nagas are known for partaking in large quantities of it. It is said to increase their psychic powers and gives them siddhis (powers). I decide this is my moment. I will consume the full offering.

Naga Baba has his own cloth to wrap around the end of the chillum. 'Safi nahi?' he asks.

'Nahi,' I reply. I don't have a cloth so he rips a piece from the yellow rag that hangs from one of the tridents placed in the fireplace. He throws it to me even though he could have passed it.

The attendant arrives with chai and says, 'Bombale Hara Hara Hara Mahadev!' as Naga Baba lights the chillum with a spark from the fire. Plumes of smoke and red cinders fly into the air as he sucks and sucks. I have never seen a chillum smoked with such gusto. It is hard not to smile, so great is my delight, my unfurling joy, at being part of this scene. Naga Baba passes me the chillum after taking his cloth from the end. I have already dampened the safi, the small piece of cloth used to wrap around the end of a chillum, and now wrap it around the end so the smoke is cooled before entering my lungs and so my mouth does not touch the chillum. I draw slowly, tentatively, not wanting a rush from the rough tobacco. The smoke is hot and hits my lungs with a punch. The rush is immediate but I stay in my seat, so to speak, and pull again then slowly let the smoke trail out from my mouth. I pass the chillum back and he then passes it to the attendant who repeats the call of 'Hara Hara Mahadev' before pulling deeply himself. The attendant again smiles at me and passes me a chai. Chai and chillum – the perfect way to pass the day in a Naga Baba's ashram.

The chillum sends me deeper into my meditation. The silence roars now. A cough from Naga Baba and the sound of the birds and the slurping as he drinks his chai all seem to have their place within the ethereal backdrop of silence.

'Om Narayana,' Naga Baba mutters. He is pulling on his beard, returning, it seems, to the company. The attendant still sits on the other side of the dhuni. He responds to Naga Baba with 'Om Namah Shivaya'. The words jolt me, command me to sit straighter. I respond myself, 'Om Namah Shivaya, Om Namah Shivaya,' and Naga Baba smiles, that slowly uncurling smile, and his gaze again pierces me.

And so the afternoon passes. The chillum has amplified everything. The beauty of light falling through trees, the way a bird may flit by in a flash of red. The way the dog will stretch every now and again and look adoringly at his master, the sound of a bell far away and the steady burning of the fire. Naga Baba fiddles and rearranges his chimitas; otherwise he simply sits and the energy from him is that of presence. The attendant has gone and returns with a glass of water for me, just when my mouth had become unbearably dry. He offers the cup then disappears.

Naga Baba remains silent most of the afternoon. Every now and again he turns to me and delivers one of his charming smiles. It is enough. I know I am welcome. As the air becomes cooler, he stretches, smokes a beedi and calls to the attendant. 'Chai lau!'

Again he pours the chai in a steaming arc to a little tin cup. The hot sweetness slips between my lips. He drinks in silence. He rinses his mouth and wipes his face on a cloth hanging from the tridents standing in the fire pit.

'How long stay?' He leans slightly forward, resting his chin on his hand.

'Tomorrow I will go to Benares for a couple of days on my way back to Lucknow. Then I go up to the mountains to take care of an ashram there.'

'Accha?' he says, looking at me again with eyes so piercing I can only look down.

He takes a piece of paper and a pencil from under the rug that he sits on and writes something. 'You go this temple. It is the headquarters of Juna Akhara of Naga Babas. You know Burra Hanuman Ghat? This is the place. Tell the mahant I sent you.'

I tuck the paper carefully in my pocket. As I leave he asks if I like guava. He walks to the gate with me and as we pass the guava tree a fruit falls into his outstretched hand. He gives it me. He puts out his hand again and another fruit falls.

'Prasad, you take.'

I place them in my bag as carefully as if they were gold.

* * *

I walk back to Chitrakut along the dusty road. The sun is low and red across the fields and around me, workers are returning home, their day's labour stacked on a bullock cart, long horns pointing the way.

As I reach Ram Ghat, the main ghat here in this holy town, a mass of sound reaches me. I quicken my step to the sound of bells, long and melodious, and I arrive in time to run up the wide stone stairs to the temple. The lingams are almost ready for their salutations. A young man in a singlet and lungi is reciting mantras as he places flowers around the stones. Silence falls for a moment. The pujari, with his hand on his heart, sings mantras with the voice of an angel. The lamp is lit – a heavy brass lamp with a pyramid of tiny oil lights rising up in a cone of flame. He waves it in slow circles and the trail of light cuts the dark. His face is awash with gold.

Back at Yagna Veda, the preparations are in full swing for the bandhara to celebrate a great saint who died on this day. This I find out from Shastriji, who is watching the preparations. Seeing Shastri again is like meeting an old friend. His eyes twinkle and shine; the cloth tied around his head is faded and worn. I sit for the evening with him as he taps the rhythm with his stainless steel bucket handle and sings, as he always does, 'Sita Ram, Sita Ram,' over and over again.

*   *   *

From a pool of shade under a spreading tree I watch a swami recite his prayers. I have walked across the bridge to the other side of the river and look back at Chitrakut rising as if from the river herself. Just below me a howan, a fire puja, is performed by a pujari and a boy with a recently shaved head, with just a thread of hair at the back. The swami wears a buttercup yellow shirt and lungi and the boy is shirtless with a crisp, white, new-looking lungi. They sit on the ground and repeat mantra over and over, and the murmured sound reaches my ears like nectar. Like the gentle bleat of lambs in the English countryside, the sound of murmured mantra is the ever present, eternal soundscape of this landscape of the gods. The swami throws handfuls of offerings into the fire and soon the air is full of the sweet scent of sandalwood mixed with ghee. Across the water, pilgrims bathe at the ghats. The bright colours of the women's saris reflect in the still water, a polished mirror before me also reflecting the temples and buildings and steps that rise steeply in arches and lines, the colours pink and terracotta and white.

I rearrange my position, rub the cramp in my calf and remember the piece of paper I have tucked into my pocket from Naga Baba, my own invitation to the headquarters of his lineage. Here in Chitrakut it is Hanuman and Ram that listen to my prayers. Tonight I will take the train to Varanasi and I pray that Shiva welcomes me into his city. I wonder what I will find at the Juna Akhara of the Naga Babas.

At my favorite place by the river above Mcleod Ganj

With Papaji in a spontaneous moment outside
his home whilst buying guava

From left, Sundari, myself, Shastri the bhang wallah,
Sita Sharan, and Hania, at Yagna Veda

NagaBaba by his dhuni

Sitting by the Ganga at Benares

Babaji lighting incense at a small
shrine whilst walking in the hills

CHAPTER EIGHTEEN

The house of Shiva

*'For I have no bounds. I am Shiva. Nothing arises
in me. In whom nothing is single, nothing is double.
Nothing is, nothing is not. What more is there to say?
It is easy. God made all things. There is only
God. When you know this Desire melts away.
Clinging to nothing you become still.'*
The Ashtavakra Gita

Varanasi, also known as Benares, and originally named Kashi, is the city of Shiva. Sita has told me of a math, a building where sadhus stay, in Assi Ghat, the last in the long line of ghats that line the holy river Ganga as she flows through the oldest city in India. It is the obvious place to stay. An old swami bent at the waist lives here. He lifts his head in a permanent expression of surprise, his smile toothless and his eyes full of watery light. He clings to a thick walking stick and, as he passes, he pats me on the back as if I am a child. It is enough of an introduction when I tell him I am a friend of Sita, in my faltering but adequate Hindi. The building is single storey, terracotta red and encloses a courtyard with the temple in the middle. In old rusted ghee tins geraniums and marigolds burst with flowers. The room I am given has a kitchen area with a gas stove and one pot, a wooden bed with a thin mattress and a window that looks out over the ghats to the Ganga and the pale sky above.

The Ganga here is wide, a smooth silver stretch of sacred water. Assi Ghat is the northern perimeter of the city and the ghats fade away in the haze, a ribbon of jewels in the pink light. Rowing boats bob on the water's edge.

'Good price! You boat go, no problem.' 'Yes madam, boat!' Eager voices call from the river to me but give up when I respond in Hindi. I prefer to walk to find the Naga Babas at Burra Hanuman Ghat. Rose pink buildings rise steeply from wide walkways all along the ghats. Men bathe or offer prayers. Dobhi wallahs squat on flat rocks that jut out into the river, pounding clothes, rubbing and scrubbing in water that is murky and brown. Saris stretch out in the sun to dry, colourful stripes of blues, fuchsia pinks, reds and greens. Dhotis are held down with stones, the whites a testament to the miracle that anything can be washed in water the colour of mud. Trails of water arch and fall to a rhythmic thud thud thud as piles of Benares laundry are washed, dried, folded, pressed and returned.

Burra Hanuman Ghat houses an impressive temple with decorated pointed towers painted a deep pinky red. This is the ghat where Naga Baba told me to come. I have the paper he wrote on, tucked in the pocket of my robe, just in case I need more of a formal invite to this dwelling place of Naga Babas. The main headquarters of the Juna Akhara of Naga Babas is hidden in the alley behind. I step through a large wooden door to their world. In the dim light I can see the dhuni opposite the temple where sadhus sit. An old man wearing a long white shirt that reaches almost to the floor holds a large kettle and tin cups. He sees me and pauses. 'Aiyei, aiyei [come] temple looking, no problem.'

The temple is home for Hanuman. He is huge and orange and elaborately decorated with malas and jewels. He wears a crown and strings of beads around his thick neck. I am surprised to see Hanuman, expecting of course a lingam, the symbol of Shiva. A sadhu stands by the fireplace and comes to attend to temple business, giving me tilak, tulsi and holy water. I clear my throat and ask in my best Hindi:

'Mahant ji idder abhi? Meh Chitrakut se aiyer, Chitrakut Naga babaji bollo idder ana darshan kelier.' [Is the mahant here? I am coming from Chitrakut and the Naga Babaji told me to come here for darshan.]

He looks at me for a moment then beckons with his chin. 'Accha! Idder au.' [Okay, come this way.]

I follow him into the bare room with the dhuni in the centre. The light is dim, with no natural lights. Babas squat in a sort of circle, and most of them turn to look as I sit myself in their midst. I see an older man on the other side of the fire. The attendant is now serving tea from the kettle and serves him first. There are more sadhus than I first noticed, eleven I quickly count, and all eyes are on me.

The mahant has a shaved head and wears strings of rudraksha malas. The pujari offers a few words and he nods. 'Behtou, behtou, chai piou.' I respond by putting my palms together and bowing slightly. I wonder if I should actually touch his feet in respect but decide to simply stay where I am and sit. I take a beedi from the packet carelessly flung my way by a particularly gruff looking sadhu. Here I am – a western woman in the murky light of the dhuni. And the rush of excitement brings a smile to my face. I sit, smoke and sip my chai. I am struck by their beauty, these men who choose to wear little clothing and grow their hair to wild tangles. Some are young, others are old, their faces weathered, beards matted and dreadlocked, eyes slightly red. Strings of malas and roaming jutta. Beedis held in fingers with broken nails.

The mahant stares then motions to me with a nod of his head. 'Tum Chitrakut se aiya?' [You came from Chitrakut?]

'Ji. Nagababaji ashram gia.' [Yes, I came from Naga Baba's ashram.]

'Lingam ki darshan hai. Idder au.' [Come and have blessing from the lingam. Come here.] I am not quick enough and he repeats: 'Idder au!' [Come here!]

I jump to my feet and follow him out of the congregation and past the temple.

We bend our heads to fit through an opening. Inside is hollowed out rock, a cave. In a pit several feet deep is a rock lingam. The energy is palpable. It is like a hidden secret sanctuary shrouding this lingam, and it feels as old as the city itself. The air has a quality that suggests every particle holds the vibration of Om. I can almost hear the hum. I sit on the narrow ledge against the cold wall and the mahant nods. 'Ha, darshan miljaiger.' [Blessings will come.] And after planting his hand on his chest for a moment he leaves me. I stare at the lingam in the cave. It is roughly chiselled rock and smoothed to the usual oblong shape. No carvings, no snakes, just the shape of eternity: no beginning and no end. A pot and a brass tray with matches and thick stubs of incense are the only signs of puja. I notice too the lingam is marked with ash in three horizontal lines. The thickness of the air seems to fill my nostrils and hints at a fragrance I have sensed before, when sitting close to Papaji. For an intense, almost unbearable second, the point between my eyebrows feels pierced with energy then my body seems to slump. I bask in a state of deep meditation and slowly find my awareness returning to the fact of sitting on a hard stone floor and the energy all around me. Perhaps this is the darshan the Chitrakut Naga Baba intended. How extraordinary to have this experience with a rock – the undeniable presence … and how the mind, and the thoughts that bubble away in the background, vanish. How mysterious it all is.

Back at the dhuni I take my seat in the shadows. On the dhuni a tree trunk is smouldering away; a sadhu throws on a couple of sticks and a flame rises in response. I had no idea what I would find at the headquarters of the Naga Babas. I had given it no thought. What else but fire, chai, and a silence that brings a subtle sense of connectedness between every near naked sadhu in this dim room. We breathe the same air and wear a collective peace. The mahant stands and stretches before he walks out, his wooden shoes clopping on the stone.

'Kahan se aiya tum?' [Where do you come from?] the sadhu nearest me asks, wrapping his jutta into a knot on top of his head.

'Chitrakut se aiya, arjko.' [I came today from Chitrakut.]

'Tum desh, khya hai?' [Which is your country?]

'Humara desh England se.' I smile. England is more than a million years away from here.

The sadhus shuffle back to life. I have a feeling it may be close to lunch and decide to take my leave. 'Accha, chello,' I say to no one in particular. 'Om Namah Shivaya.' The sadhu next to me chants as I stand. Others utter 'Om' or 'Hara Hara Mahadev' – and I love it. The words, the curling sounds, send a thrill down my spine. Chitrakut Naga Baba's face appears in my mind and I can hear his chuckle. Thank you, I whisper, thank you. But these words do not fit. Om Namah Shivaya, Om Namah Shivaya, Om Namah Shivaya is all I need.

*   *   *

My room at Assi Ghat is the perfect base for my first visit in many years to the city of Shiva. The old swami at the math has what looks like six teeth and a shaved head with a little fuzz of stubble. He wears the usual orange lungi, with a woollen waistcoat over his bare chest. He is badly stooped and uses a stick. The temple houses a black stone lingam in a simple shrine with an intricate picture of Parvati and Shiva merged as one. Ardhanarishvara, the perfect union of ShivaShakti: male and female as one. As I look at the image, the one-breasted figure, I consider my connection with Babaji. When we make love it is as if our energy bodies meet, and there is no longer a question of he and I, our individual selves. There is a merging of souls to a place beyond duality. The thread of meditation that permeates Babaji's presence reflects in our union. It is the only relationship I want, and I like the secrecy, the tucked away places where our union takes place, with lots of space in between. I do not feel bound in any way. Surely this is the perfect relationship – one that reflects God and yet asks nothing of me. I can still portray myself as a woman alone, stride out on my journey with no one by my side, yet he is there when I return to the deodar forest, the mountains and rushing rivers, the high blue heavens and the fresh sharp air. And now I can fully immerse myself in the thrill of travelling to a place deemed holy, the hidden India my search is revealing.

*   *   *

Assi Ghat is the last ghat along the banks. From here on the river is met with sandy expanse. A group of kids play cricket, a woman walks with a basket of laundry on her head. I bathe wrapped in a lungi and quickly dip under three times. It is said that if you bathe in the Ganga here in Varanasi, your karma is washed away, purifying the soul and leaving a spotlessly clean temple for the Lord to reside in. It is easy to believe. I consider again the notion of presumption. What is belief? It is having faith. But faith in what? As a child it was about faith in a punitive God, who by the notion of sin controls the invidual by fear. Here in India my experience is presence. The presence of Papaji, the presence felt in temples, in all aspects of holiness that this land has revealed. Presence requires nothing but presence itself. Faith *is* the journey.

Pilgrims come from all over India to worship and bathe in the Ganga here. I head for Dasaswamedh Ghat, the main bathing ghat and centre of this immediate universe. An old man in swathes of white limps past me, waving a bowl of burning cow shit in his hands, chanting, calling to God.

Sellers work the crowd, with malas strung up each arm, thin beads at a cheap price. Ear cleaners ply for trade, their wooden box of tricks in one hand. Scrawny men whisper: 'You want change money? Good price, no problem.' Others with red eyes and hands in pockets murmur: 'Charas, you want charas? Best Manali charas. Good price. Two hundred rupees tola, madam.'

Boats below mingle in the shallows. Bright coloured sunshades splash against the brown. Bathers line the water's edge and ripples and drops of water glisten in the sunlight. Vultures circle in the blue above. A dark line of smoke trails in the smoggy air. Manikarnika Ghat is just downriver and the fires of burning bodies send death through the air.

I saw my first dead body as a student nurse. It was an old man, who had sighed deeply as we turned his body over. I still remember the sound of the sigh, as the last air rushed from his lungs. Nursing has allowed intimacy with death, and standing now on the banks of the river Ganga, with funeral pyres burning just downriver, I welcome the opportunity to witness the lap of death again. Indeed it was a death that opened my mind to vaster possibilities, led me to where I now stand.

Manikarnika Ghat is one of two burning ghats and a most auspicious place to be burnt. For a Hindu, Varanasi is the ultimate place to die and be burnt. Apparently one's liberation is assured. I feel no hesitation as I make my way through the crowded main ghat to take darshan from death.

On my way, by an elaborate Nepalese temple where a small boy stares out of a large cavernous window, I meet Surrendra. A banyan tree spreads its branches and the wall is the perfect height for sitting, so I sit for a while to watch the river, the smoke curling from the funeral pyres. Mostly I ignore the 'hello madam, which country? You want guide' from touts that hang around for western prey, but there is something about this man and the earnest way he approaches me; it's as if he has some good news he wants to share. He is older too, with a very long white shirt and a woollen waistcoat buttoned up.

'Suni, I am known,' he tells me. His mouth is red and half his teeth are missing. He has decided he is my guide. I know it's sensitive for a westerner to visit the burning ghats. I follow him past kiosks selling piles of powdered incense, red and gold cloth and other requirements for this last honour. Wood is stacked all along the gulis, or laneways, leading to the great fire. We emerge from the alleys onto the ghat itself.

'Morning time, cleaning time. Ghats burning twenty-four hours but morning time some cleaning.' Surrendra surveys the scene.

The idea of cleaning in India still makes me smile. I stand in a sloppy mix of dirt, cow shit, plastic, discarded banana leaves and clay cups. Three bodies on makeshift carriers lean against the steps by the river. The bright gold and orange cloth in which they are wrapped startles me. It is a far cry from the sombre black of funerals back in England. A fire is being prepared just beneath where we stand.

'This body now burning,' Surrendra tells me and I watch as two men carry a stretcher to where the wood is neatly stacked. The body is picked up by the shoulders and feet and looks quite stiff. It is placed on the wood and more wood is stacked on top of the body until I can just see bits of gold through the gaps. Another man pours something from a packet.

'Camphor?' I ask my friend.

'Ghee, this ghee.'

Then incense powder is liberally thrown in handfuls by one of the other men.

'This mother dying maybe. Old person, small like child. Old age small body coming.'

So far I see only men on the burning ghats. 'Suniji, women not coming here?'

'No, no, only man. Woman coming and crying, too much sad and then soul not able to leave happy.'

This body below me is likely a mother with five men in attendance. 'This sons?'

'Maybe. If no son then nephew job.'

A cow picks its way through the rubbish. Another fire is being prepared close to the water. The fire below us is ready to be lit.

'One flame, old old flame used for lighting every fire. No electricity, no light, only this fire for lighting every fire. This man now coming with grass.'

An older man with a red turban wound around his head and a lungi tied around his waist holds a wad of grass, alight at the end. He walks barefoot around the fire five times before setting the pyre alight. The grass has been lit from a fire that burns here day and night. It hasn't gone out for as long as this ghat has been here.

'You know why five times walking?' Surrendra is as absorbed in the process as me.

'No, why?'

'Five elements: air, water, earth, fire, prana. This body made up from elements, five time walking around then each one released.'

I imagine the process for this family, where such fine attention must in itself bring a sense of completion. In the west, no one gets dirty hands with death. Perhaps this is why we have such difficulty dealing with death. The second body burning before us is apparently that of an old person. Hindus believe the soul continues its journey into the great unknown and much care is taken to ensure the best possible migration. Already there would have been ceremony where the family sat with the body and made special offerings and gave last respects, as a priest recited mantras. Imagine if this happened in the west. Imagine if the body was brought to the home and goodbyes could be said. Instead the body is whisked away and shut tight in a coffin. The bodies of those who die of AIDS are locked tight in a body bag. I remember the many funerals I attended, the coffin and the tidiness of death I am used to. There is nothing tidy about death in this city of Shiva. It is here in all its certainty – bones and ashes that are thrown into the Ganga until nothing remains.

The fire has taken hold and the men stand to one side watching. The body is well and truly burning. The dark grey smoke wafts for a moment and I can smell the death in my nostrils.

'Smoke no bad smell? Body burnt bad smell yes?'

It's true; it doesn't smell too much like cooking flesh.

'This special wood. One type wood used and no bad smell coming.'

'Which tree?'

'This banyan tree.'

The same tree the Buddha sat beneath, the sacred tree of India.

I suddenly think of my own parents. I wonder how it will be for me when they die. What if something happened to them and I didn't even know? My letters or phone calls are often months apart. If something happened to me while I am in India would anyone bring me to these burning ghats, I wonder. I better make it known that is what I want. I double up inside at the unbearable realisation I would never see Babaji again. The ache in my chest is as real as a stubbed toe. Reason floods in, as it will. Very unlikely you will die, I tell myself. Of course, but one day I will. We all will, yet we live in a constant denial of our mortality. I pray that most of my life is spent here, in India, surrounded by lingams and statues of Hanuman. Surrounded by God. From the outside it may look like I have a life of little purpose, time to do as I please. Yet my search for peace, for abidance with God, is the only purpose of any relevance to me. In India it is easy to renounce the false riches of the west for this divine pageantry all around me.

'This fire looking?' Surrendra pulls me from my musing.

The group of men burning the old woman stand back now to watch from a distance. The flames are fierce and I can see an outline of an arm and then the torso, as the cloth has all burnt away. I look closer, yes, there is the head, and as I watch I can actually see the skull and fire seems to be coming out through the bones. It is quite fascinating. I have never watched a body burn before. The whole skull is a glow of orange and the flames devour the flesh in seconds. The outline of the body becomes more blackened by the minute.

Lined up on the steps are more bodies, wrapped in yellow and gold cloth that sparkles in the bright sun. Strapped on a bamboo stretcher they will have been carried through the streets, possibly brought on a truck from other cities. The bundles look so small, already diminished by death.

Two other pyres are now in flame, and three others are being prepared. I guess the cleaning time is over. Suni is already walking away and I follow him, past men sitting idle, another asleep on the ground with a newspaper over his face. We cross the alleyway leading onto the ghat and walk up under a stone-covered area. Here is the fire he wants to show me. The ash is piled high and the fire is fed with two big logs, more like tree stumps. The fire does feel very very old. I watch it but do not go close. This fire burns night and day and has burnt for thousands of years, according to Suni. These flames light every pyre here on the ghat.

I wander back to my spot overlooking the ghats. Three fires burn. Thick smoke rushes to the heavens. Boats glide by, bells ring out. A cow stands staring out to the river. I think again of my parents, how it must be to have a daughter well and truly flown away. And I am suddenly glad that my sister has resumed contact. Possibly there was a therapist involved but I am not sure now, as I walk back along the ghats to my room.

*   *   *

I stop in at the Naga Babas as I walk back home. It's late afternoon and maybe arti, evening worship, will be performed at sunset. I take darshan at the Hanuman statue. I can almost see a play of a smile on his monkey lips, his fingers move just slightly as he holds his sceptre.

A baba emerges as I stand before Hanuman. He rings the bell then steps into the shrine and offers me a spoonful of holy water. He doesn't speak, just nods, and I recognise him from the day before. I hear a 'Ho ho!' from the dhuni area and turn to see the mahant gestering with his hand:

'Idder au! Behtou!' [Come here! Sit!] I return his greeting with an Om Namah Shivaya and sit to the side, where I sat yesterday, as if this is now my place. Six babas sit around the fire and I am careful not to smile although I want to.

A pujari cleans the temple and Hanuman is being decorated with malas. Another is sloshing water from a bucket then sweeping it to the drain with a broom made of sticks tied together. From the open roof in the courtyard I can see that the sky is almost dark. I wonder where the day has gone.

Back at the dhuni a baba passes me a chillum and pats the floor near him. 'Behtou behtou.' [Sit, sit.] He is one of the wilder ones with red eyes and very matted dreads that flow in disarray around his shoulders. I settle in again with these men of little words, folding my legs beneath me and covering my shoulders with my shawl. I take a pull of the chillum and feel the hot smoke in my throat, the small head rush as tobacco then ganja courses through my blood.

The call to worship is from a conch shell. A baba stands and his jutta stream down his back to his red lungi tied tight around his waist. The mahant plays the damaru, Shiva's drum, and he turns it with his wrist so a small hard ball on a string flips from side to side. The sound is mesmerising. Cymbals, horns and bells add to the cacophony. It goes on for a long while. Other sadhus clap their hands, ring bells or bang drums. Plumes of sultry incense pour from copper pots and another pujari is smudging the whole place with a bowl of glowing sandalwood. The silence that follows, with the sudden absence of a heaving orchestration of sound, is profound. It reverberates through me, highlighting the sudden emptiness inherent in my own being, until someone coughs, another shouts 'Hara Hara Maha Dev', and the babas all erupt with their response: 'Hara Hara Maha Dev!'

I walk back along the darkened ghats. A young moon hangs with Venus by her side. It must be almost one year ago that I saw the same night vision with Babaji high up on the side of a mountain. My path is taking me to the heart of Shiva. In this last year I have received darshan from Arunachala, Shiva manifest. I have roamed high enough in his abode of the mighty Himalaya to touch the heavens. Fruit has fallen into my hands from a Naga Baba who has paved my way in Benares.

The sacred syllable of 'Om' is said to be a vibration, the original sound: 'In the beginning was the word'. Being here in Benares I sense how all matter is a vibration of the one. The stone used to build this city is still softly singing. This new-found love affair with Shiva banishes all idea of misery, all notion of one who suffers. I remember back to the retreat in Bodhgaya, when images and thoughts disturbed me beyond what I could endure. Where is all that now? I focus only on God, merge into the timeless space where duality has no place. Pray that the weeds of self-doubt have been plucked.

*　　*　　*

The next day it is already mid-afternoon when I again push open the heavy wooden door of the Juna Akhara. I wonder how many western women have sat at this dhuni, and I guess not many. I join the babas in their circle, squat with ease and take a beedi offered as the packet is thrown in my direction. I want to scrutinise them all but I keep my eyes downward, focusing on the fire, till one of them asks: 'Kahan se aiya, kisco desh tum?'

'Humara desh England,' I reply.

He doesn't want any more information so I ask something myself. 'App kitna sal ider rehtna?' [How long have you lived here?]

He doesn't understand but another baba repeats what I asked and he says, 'Kashi ek sal hogaya.' [One year.]

'Phele kahan?' [Where were you before?] I feel bold but I want to know something about their lives. I want to seize every moment. Others are engaging now, adding comments that of course I can't follow.

The baba speaks a rapid fire of Hindi. 'Dhiri dhiri,' I tell him. 'Me torra Hindi arti hey.' [Slowly slowly, only a little Hindi.] I must find a Hindi teacher. Maybe in the winter weeks alone in the ashram I can make learning Hindi my project.

'Accha,' he smiles. 'Phele gummne gaya.'

This expression I know from Babaji, and it means literally 'around going' or going to different places. An older baba with jutta almost to his ankles tells me: 'Idder, gurra sal hogaya.' He has been here eleven years. I want to ask what exactly they do but my Hindi fails me and we all end up laughing a little, except a fierce-faced sadhu who relights a beedi as he watched the action with a scowl.

Later, as the light changes with the late afternoon, I sit on the ghat and watch the Ganga slide before me. The steps are steep and the stone is warm. A sadhu washes two brass urns then turns and carries them, full of water, up the steps. A banyan tree, halfway up the ghat, shelters three men smoking a chillum. The smell of ganja wafts down to where I sit. A woman in a pink sari stands motionless on the steps. Three goats pick at plastic and stare out over the river. The light is low and rosy. Boats float down with the tide or row hard against it upriver. Another larger boat is packed with pilgrims and someone is leading a bhajan. The Ganga looks even wider now that the light fades. She curves around the wide arc of Benares and the edge of definition recedes with the day.

In India the line between real and unreal is blurred and not so easy to define. This is the beauty I see before me: men bathing in waters they believe to be sacred and in doing so creating the sacred; sadhus living in temples, doing little other than remembering their God; a dhuni burning day and night, the eternal flame igniting every heart. In India everyone believes in God. To not have faith is seen as a crisis. You can only be a Hindu if you are born one. So what about me? Born to Christians yet it is Shiva that is the focus of my prayers. As a child I felt I was an outsider, looking in to the Christian world of worship, ready to rebel as soon as age allowed. India, and this ancient custom of bhakti, devotion, unties me from my past. I recognise that this is where my soul belongs; where my longing for God, which has been with me all along, finally has a language to speak. I have found the God that is true to me.

*   *   *

Sitting by the mahant is a baba who I haven't seen before. He is not the sort of figure one could easily miss, even in a crowd. He is solid, sturdy, and covered with rudraksha malas. Malas cover his chest like a sash and on his head he wears a crown of rudrakshas wound around with a marigold mala on top. His upper arms are decorated with bands of beads and many more hang round his neck. Thick jutta fall to his shoulders and in his right hand a mala turns through his fingers. His body is smeared with ash and he sits in the half lotus, with one leg pulled up on the other thigh. He has an attendant by his side, a small man with a long white shirt. I sit in the shadows watching and the mahant nods again to me.

The baba with the malas is an imposing figure. He turns to me and speaks. 'This temple is one of the oldest in Kashi. Shiva himself allowed Hanuman and Sita to have his darshan on their way back to Ayodhya. Do you know this story? From the Ramayana.'

He emphasises the 'Ram' of Ramayana so it rolls from his tongue. And he speaks perfect English. I am so surprised I almost laugh. 'I know a little of the story.'

The mahant then speaks and I understand that he is telling the baba that the Chitrakut Naga Baba sent me. His look is intense as he seems to scrutinise me. I hope I am worthy of the invite.

'You are in Kashi; have you received darshan from Kashi Vishwanath?' He leans forward as he speaks; he looks quite young behind his thick wad of jutta and rows and rows of mala beads. The crown on his head looks heavy; there are so many rudraksha beads wound around.

'No,' I say and add, 'videshi [foreigners] are not allowed to enter the temple.'

'Yes, yes, but I will take you. This night at 3 am you come to my kuti and we will go.' His attendant explains where to find this baba. Clearly this rudraksha mala sadhu is his guru.

'This next door ghat, Dashashwamedh Ghat, tall steps coming, you know this place? Guruji here is living.'

I think I do know where he is meaning. 'I will find it,' I say. I have no doubt that I will go. After all, it isn't every day one receives an invite to the sacred lingam of Varanasi.

'Tikhai,' the rudraksha sadhu himself says. 'You come.'

The mahant nods again as I leave, then puts his hand up with his palm facing me and utters a low 'Om' in a soft deep voice.

In my room, I light a candle, heat water on the stove for a warm bucket bath and collapse on my bed. It has been another full day. The energy of the Naga Babas is filling me with a desire for worship, to be lost in the divine. It is as if my whole being from the moment I awake, to the moment I fall into sleep, is focused on the gods all around me. Nothing else holds even a glimmer of interest. This world of Naga Babas has opened its doors and let me in.

The lingam at the Vishwanath Temple is the site of the original manifestation of Shiva as he rose up through the earth as a pillar of light. It is the devotional heart of this city. Of course I must have darshan. To have darshan here is said to lead the worshipper on a sure path to liberation. Whenever I wake in the early hours is when I will set off to find the rudraksha baba. Alarm clocks are not part of my life. I do not even own a watch.

*   *   *

The earth and stone path is cold under my bare feet. The ghats are almost deserted. A figure sleeps on the steps, wrapped from head to toe in blankets. Outside a temple a sadhu sits but he looks asleep. In the dark, dogs run barking nearby but I keep my focus and walk quickly all the way, with my shawl covering my head. Nearer to Dashashwamedh Ghat, music plays from somewhere unseen. Lanterns sway, a boat rows on the water.

Benares never sleeps. Even at this early hour, sadhus walk down to the river with kamandal in hands, shawls wrapped against the cold. I guess it is around 3 or 4 am. A couple of dim lights beckon and as

263

I reach a big banyan tree I see the attendant looking out for me. He signals to me so I follow. The room is small with just a wooden bed on which the rudraksha baba sits, wrapping malas around his wrist, a small pile of them still beside him.

'Ha!' He speaks with a voice full of certainty. 'You have come.' He takes a thick string of rudraksha beads, big beads, and passes them to me. 'This mala you can wear.'

I like the feel and weight of the mala around my neck. I am wearing a sari as I guessed it would be the most appropriate. My shawl covers everything but my eyes. The attendant puts a dot of red between my eyebrows then a fleck of ash above.

'Guruji chello,' he says as the baba puts on a pair of the wooden shoes like the mahant wears. They have a wooden piece between the toes and look uncomfortable. He is naked except for the white loincloth. It covers very little of him. He stands and wraps a prayer shawl around his shoulders like a cape.

'Om Namah Shivaya,' he declares as he clops off down the steep steps.

The baba walks fast. I follow behind and he doesn't speak or look back until we head away from the ghats and into the laneways, known as gulis. As we come closer to the temple the tight alleys fill up with silent figures making their way for darshan. I expected it to be deserted. I wonder if it is an auspicious day for darshan or if this is the norm. The Kashi Vishwanath temple is also known as the Golden Temple as two domes are painted with gold leaf.

The queue for darshan stretches into the guli, even at this hour. The baba turns, nods to me and repeats 'Om' under his breath. I keep up the chant, preparing to enter the holiest place in this city. This is the most auspicious place of Hindu worship in all of India.

The baba is not queuing but pushing forward through the crowd until we are close to the entrance. A sign written in red letters explains the temple is off limits for any non-Hindu. I consider this for a moment. To be a Hindu one has to be born a Hindu and obviously I am not. Yet this culture – these gods and their worship – is my portal to the divine. Of this I have no doubt. And here I am, brought here by a sadhu who wears a thousand rudraksha beads. There is no time for anxiety about whether or not I am worthy, and I keep 'Om' under my breath, not wanting to miss my own possible salvation for the sake of creed.

A pujari stands at the narrow door and as we pass he looks at me. The Naga Baba is obviously known here and he barks something I do not understand. Keeping close to his heels I meet the pujari's look with the surety of my faith. I see the nod of his head and know I am through. I keep my eyes downward and 'Om Namah Shivaya' on my lips.

The temple is small, only lit with lamps. I stay close to the Naga Baba and follow him into the shrine with the lingam. The lingam is surprisingly small, surrounded by a gold yoni. A mala of yellow marigolds, red roses and bael leaf is wrapped around it. Above it a golden urn drips water. The air is thick and hot. A pujari beckons to me to receive a splash of holy water and as I place my hand before him he looks at me and mutters something to the baba. He frowns although it is difficult to see as the throng of devotees are pushing close.

The pujari gives rudraksha baba the tilak and a pinch of ash into his hand. He turns and dots the red then silver between my eyebrows. His finger is firm and precise and a dart of energy tingles beneath his touch.

It is over too quickly. I walk with the baba back to his kuti and sit a while in silence. I can see light seep in and shapes emerge in the dawn. I want to watch the sunrise over the Ganga and bathe in her waters at this auspicious time. This experience of walking in the night, following a decorated Naga Baba into the gulis of ancient time, has been the final gift from this city of Shiva.

'Bahut dhanyabad.' I touch his feet then start to take his mala off over my head. He raises his hand.

'This mala you take. You wear. Good karma for Kashi to bless you with darshan of Lord Shiva.' He looks at me with his eyes wild and piercing. 'Sometime you come, some yoga practising together.' He closes his eyes slightly. 'When Shiva and Shakti practise together then much powerful energy is rising.'

I keep quiet. I am sure it is true.

'Today I will go back to my guruji,' I tell him and he smiles. As I touch his feet again he rests his hand on my head and chants, 'Om.'

CHAPTER NINETEEN

Guruji

*'Keep quiet! Don't stir a thought. Look within.
There you will find your own True Nature,
where it has always been.' Papaji*

The afternoon train takes me back to Lucknow and it's late evening when the rickshaw drives past Papa's house. The pull to see him is immense but it is too late now, the house shrouded with darkness.

Before the first bird call, just as the mosque is calling all to the day, I ride my bike to his house. At the gate I find Kamal standing outside.

'Prem Kumari!' His greeting is warm.

'I know it's early but I want to give Papaji a Christmas card.' I hand him the card but hope I can see Papa myself.

'Wait!' says Kamal. 'He will be out shortly for his walk. Why don't you take a chai and wait?' He hands me back the card.

'Okay.' I turn to go. 'Can you lend me a couple of rupees?'

He laughs. 'This is the way to come to the Master, with empty pockets!'

I need only wait as long as it takes me to drink the chai. Papaji comes out through the gate, flanked by two of his attendants and a couple of other westerners who stay in his house. He greets me with a nod. I walk beside him, the card in my hand. He looks down at me smiling. 'You leaving?' he asks.

'Next week I will go to Dharamsala and take care of an ashram there for a month or so. The Babaji wants to go to Ganga Sagar.'

'He is Kali baba?'

'No, Papaji, he is a Shiva baba.'

'All Bengali babas are Kali wallahs.' He smiles at me.

I wonder again that he knows so much that I have never told him. In fact I have never really told him anything about myself. As I walk with him, the familiar feeling of expansive presence steals my mind and I am overwelmed with gratitude. Just being in his presence lifts the veil of separation. Back at the gate I hand him my card. 'It is Kamadgiri, Papaji.'

'Yes, yes, you been there?'

'I just came back.' He looks at me and I find myself asking what I have wanted to ask for some weeks. 'Papaji, can you give me a mantra?'

'Not on a Saturday.' He takes my arm and leans heavily on me as we walk up the path, through the front door into his living room.

'You sit here.' He points to the chair at the table next to his place at the end. I have been in Papaji's house several times before but I have never sat at his table. It is breakfast time and a couple of women bring plates of fruit, alfafa sprouts, toast and yogurt to the table. I eat next to him, in the intimacy of his home.

He takes fruit and drinks tea. Jyoti, the young Indian woman who helps look after him, rubs his shoulder. Others come, touch his feet then take a seat on the floor. Jyoti wipes his face like he is a child. He pulls his chair back and immediately two helpers are there, steadying him as he stands. He is an old man. What great compassion to allow us all to surround him.

I quickly fall at his feet. 'Thank you, Papaji.'

He nods. 'You come at lunch time.'

I do. I sit on the floor and eat chapatti and subze. The food is simple. I watch him, hardly blinking, afraid to miss even a second. It is Christmas Eve and the best present ever.

As he leaves the room he turns to me as I stand with folded hands, head bowed.

'You come tomorow for breakfast.' I look up just to reassure myself it really is me he is speaking to.

Christmas morning, again I walk beside him. This early morning walk is his ritual. He doesn't walk far but he loves to see the pigs sleeping in the slime and take in the smell of dawn. A woollen hat is pulled over his ears and he looks like the elderly man he is. Yet his presence roars all around.

There is a Bodhi tree in his garden and he folds his hands in prayer before it. It is a cutting from the original tree in Bodhgaya under which the Buddha sat. At the gate he turns to his attendant. She smiles at me. 'Papaji has invited you for breakfast with him. Come.'

I sit at the table again. Everyone is greeting each other with 'Happy Christmas' like a big extended family gathering. Papaji takes out his teeth after breakfast and his face loosens even more. He is fussed over constantly.

'Where is Prem Kumari?'

'Here, Papaji.' I step closer.

'You come at lunch time.'

People bring him presents wrapped in paper decorated with bells and Santa, and it seems so bizarre. He opens everything, joking with those close by, and the fragrance is of incredible love.

Lunch is over. He stands and I wonder if I should ask again. I want a mantra. Papaji is my guru and a mantra from my Guruji is the only way I will practise. Japa meditation is a powerful way of stilling the mind, of cleaning the thoughts. He is looking straight at me and I move closer.

'You tomorrow come. Come here again early in the morning. This is the procedure.'

I always loved Christmas. The town I grew up in won awards for the lights and decorations every year. Strings of candles, Santa, Christmas trees and stars strung across the streets, and trees entwined with hundreds of colourful lights. Our house had a tree with lights that twinkled on and off, streamers and tinsel and delicious smells from the kitchen as my mother surpassed herself year after year. The carols by candlelight, the church filled with tiny lights ... I remember the thrill to be out at night, wearing woollen hats and mittens, coats buttoned up against the cold, singing with triumph of angels descending from their realms of glory.

The air is cold and damp at dawn. Men cough and clear their throats, scarves wrapped around their ears. The street is almost empty. A group of rickshaw drivers huddle around a fire by the chai shop. Carts sit empty. I wait outside and it isn't long before the front door is unbolted and opened and Papaji comes out for his morning walk.

'Ah, she came!' is his greeting. I fall into step just behind him. I feast on the bigness of his form. He seems to grow even as I walk behind him and I can imagine him stretching to the heavens. The walk is silent today. His legs are bothering him and he takes Jyoti's arm.

After breakfast he takes my arm as I stand with my hands folded in namaste. He holds my arm so hard my hand is momentarily numb. He leads me in through the passageway past the kitchen and into his room. Jyoti holds his other arm and he sits down heavily on the bed. The room is small with two single beds. He tells Jyoti to go. She does and closes the door so I am alone with my guru. I sit on the floor, right by his feet.

He looks down at me with utter kindness. His eyes swim in pools of light. 'Now. You wanting a mantra?'

'Yes, Papaji.'

'Accha, very good.' He takes a pencil and paper and writes. Then he folds it carefully and gives it to me. I unfold the paper. Written in Hindi is 'Om Namah Shivaya'.

*   *   *

I leave on the night train. Nothing in me wants to go. These last three days of basking in Papaji's presence have been the icing on a very delicious cake. It is as if I have just sat down at the table of the King and after one bite I need to go.

It has been a rich two months since I last sat by Babaji's dhuni. I have walked high in the Himalayas, I have peeped behind the scenes at unchanged, unfiltered rituals, and witnessed worship and the ancient culture that is the heart of India. I have been taken for darshan at the Kashi Vishwanath temple. My Guruji, my Master, has pulled me to him. I am walking a path paved with gold and do not want to change direction.

As I rock with the clankity-clank of the train, I fall asleep and dream. I am watching Papaji dance with one of the men who helps in his house. They are dancing as a pair till Papaji lets go of his hands and turns to me. 'You know how to dance?'

'Yes, Papa.' He takes my hands but my feet are clumsy. 'Papa, I don't know this dance!'

He holds me closer. 'I do,' he says. I melt into him until there is no difference between him and me. I awake with the same feeling of overwhelming gratitude and a soft glow of gold in the rumbling dark.

I sleep again lightly, aware that I am asleep. When I finally wake to the sounds of a station and 'Chai, chai, chai' sung from the platform, it is as if the light has gone out. A dull grey veneer covers the world.

It is cold and the sun is pale. The bus ride takes forever; a truck is overturned and the road is blocked. As usual people sit and watch and nothing moves for what seems like hours.

It is already mid-afternoon by the time I reach McLeod Ganj. Prayer flags greet me and I notice the absence of westerners at this time of year. The mountains are grey and bare. There is no snow yet but it is cold. Even some monks wear beanies. Everywhere is parched and at the chai shop I am told it hasn't rained for months. I search myself for the excitement I know I feel to be seeing Babaji again. I gaze at the mountains. But it is a blank canvas that has lost its charm.

CHAPTER TWENTY

———∾∾∾∾∾∾∾∾∾———

Winter in the hills

'A Karma Yogi performs action by body, mind, intellect and senses, without attachment or ego, only for self- purification.' The Bhagavad Gita

The path through the forest is fragrant and familiar. The gate creaks as it opens. The garden is neat and mostly empty. The growing season has come to an end. I am waiting for the tingle of excitement but it doesn't arrive. As I swing my bag to the ground and poke my head around the door, at last I feel it: warmth in my stomach, a tremble in my heart. There he is, the same as ever, sitting by the fire.

'Prem Kumari come, accha! Accha!'

I kneel beside the fire and he touches my face just for a moment. 'Namaste, Babaji. Namaste.'

'Chello chai piou, journey tikhai?'

No one else is staying at the ashram and the stage is ours. I try to be enthusiastic but the truth is I am not. I just can't quite be here, as if some part of me is missing. I watch from the sidelines, unable to fully inhabit myself.

After a cold bucket wash, clean clothes and chai I feel more present. I tell him about the trip to Chitrakut and that I am learning the Hanuman chalisa.

'Bahut accha. Hanuman chalisa saying, then much power coming. Mind clean hoijayaga.' He gazes at me long and hard. 'You jutta growing. You sadhu looking now!'

Where does the light go that shines from your eyes? I almost ask. His beauty parts the grey that has misted my vision; then the grey falls again. I hope that after a good sleep I will wake to my usual sense of joy. I realise how high these last weeks have been, as if a subtle lightness filled my being.

'You night time travel so early sleep is good.' Babaji is burying the embers with ash, piling it high so they will still be hot enough to relight in the morning. I think for a moment of Varanasi, of the fire by the burning ghat that burns day and night.

'Babaji, have you been to Varanasi?'

'Ha went. One month two maybe stay. Bahut powerful place. Bahut shakti.'

'I went just last week. Spent time at the burning ghat.'

'Burning ghat sitting good. After clean cloth putting? This place you know bhuta? Ghost? Death place many ghost sitting. You woman also. Some protection needing. Mantra speaking.'

I remain quiet. The mention of mantra again removes me slightly, returns me to Lucknow, to Papaji's house, the intimacy of sitting at his feet in his bedroom while he wrote out the words. So precious to me! I have folded the paper and placed it in my passport. And no, I hadn't put on clean clothes although I remember now how good it felt to discard the clothes at the end of the day, already dark after arti with the Nagas. The smell of the fires, of death, had penetrated and I remember washing my hair and wrapping it in a gumcha cloth for the night. I have heard too about the ghosts at burning ghats, and how the Aghoras, another sect of sadhus, who like to dwell in burning ghats and graveyards, use a human skull as an eating bowl. The Aghoras stretch the limits by meditating and performing rituals amidst the smell and decay of death.

Babaji pours hot water from the kettle and we take it outside. It is freezing. My breath crisps like icicles against my nose.

'Cold too much. Beedi no smoke, sleep going,' Babaji mutters, wrapping a blanket around his shoulders. We stand side by side in the darkness.

'Tikhai, Kumariji, tikhai?'

I am not sure how to answer. I follow him into his room. Something has changed and I do not know why. I have only been away for a couple of months yet I am rearranged since we last were together; the pieces of me have fallen slightly differently. I know now that this relationship has changed something for Babaji and the knowing leaves me uncomfortable. I sense his wanting, his absolute delight in my return.

He lights a candle and the cold contracts me further. I have forgotten the words and there is no one to prompt. I do not know how to navigate. I decide it will be fine once I am alone and I can lose myself in taking care of the temple. I suspect all I need is a good sleep. Babaji is murmuring 'Om' before his altar, then he unwraps his shawl and climbs under the blanket.

'Thundi hey, Kumariji, au.' And he pats the mattress, telling me to come. No point wallowing in thoughts. It is cold so I also unwrap my shawl, leaving my clothes on, and lie next to him as he blows the candle out, the suggestion of light remaining from the oil lamp always burning on his altar.

*   *   *

Babaji wakes well before the first rooster. I lie in a half sleep realm where thought remains dormant and I rest for a moment with the awareness that sleep now retreats and the phenomenon of the waking state dawns. I hear him repeat his japa meditation, sitting before his altar in this room. Darkness still enfolds and when the rooster summons all in hearing to the prelude of another day, Babaji rises. After a few louder 'Oms' strung together in a song, he heads out of the door for his ablutions. A tap releases cold water for his bath and I hear the toilet door, at the bottom of the garden, creak on its hinges. I rise as light begins to give definition and begin my day too. As the first ray of the sun touches the mountain I join him by the dhuni. He uncovers the still glowing ashes from the night before, placing sticks to feed a flame that smokes for a moment before leaping in an orange streak. Babaji sits silently, watching the flame, reverent and still. He smooths and tidies the ash in the fire place, then places the stand over the flame, substantial now with a larger piece of juniper wood giving ample flame, and puts the kettle on for hot water. The flame throws vague warmth in the chill. Winter's bite in the mountains is sharp.

'Babaji, I walked up high in Nepal. Trekked to Muktinath but I had to turn back. It was so awesome being up there.' I want to share some of my adventures over these last few weeks. Babaji has brewed chai and I savour the warmth of the small steel cup in my hands. There is a sense of separation between us, of not quite reaching each other, and last night we did not make love. He has pulled back to stand as a mirror to my own withholding.

'This no good alone going mountains. You woman, woman staying with man better.' His displeasure is obvious. I have never heard him speak like this before. It is as if my own energetic confusion has thrown him off too. Scrambling to safer ground I tell him more of Papaji and how grateful I am to have met him.

As always when I speak of Papaji he replies: 'Guruji meeting then sub se best karma. Guruji meeting sub kuch hoijayaga. Guruji kriper hai.' [Meeting your Guruji is good karma. Meeting Guruji everything comes good. This is Grace.]

The energy smoothes and we fall into silence. Babaji toys with the fire but the crack between us is there. I sit by the fire and all I see is Papaji as his face plays in the flames; fleeting images, but his face is undeniable.

After kidgeree for lunch we search for the sun and sit on plastic chairs by the temple. The warmth is a treat after the forgotton cold of these mountains, now winter breathes her chill. Babaji oils his hair with coconut oil, rubs his arms and legs and wide cracked feet.

'Winter time and dry coming.' Then he turns to me and smiles deep into my soul. 'Tikhai, Kumariji?'

And in a sudden rush I remember the first time he turned and looked at me like this, with a question and answer all at once. It was the day after Diwali when he had rested his hand on my head for a moment and the energy had coursed down my spine and back up again.

'You bedroom going,' he says as if asking and commanding all at once.

He joins me a few minutes later and I am lying on the bed waiting for him. His fingers, as they run themselves slowly down my face, leave a thin trail of coconut oil. 'You cloth out taking. Pant off taking.' And he too takes off his waistcoat and his t-shirt and then his lungi. I want to pull him to me, climb on top and find his hardness, but I lie still and enjoy the warmth creeping between us. His hands grasp my body, mould me like he does the dough. He enters me and holds his body above me, looking down into my face, my eyes, not moving, until with exquisite slowness he thrusts a little deeper … and I fear I may crack apart for wanting all of him.

*   *   *

The sun already filters through the deodar forest, leaving our seats by the temple in shadow. Babaji sits there again anyway so I join him, after pulling on my own woollen waistcoat.

We silently smoke a beedi, re-order, and I find the edges of my lips want to curl up and smile. As I do I notice that I begin to relax, tune in to the surrounds – the small wren sitting on the edge of the branch nearest my chair and the way the beedi smoke curls in the shadows … and how much I would like to smoke a joint.

'Joint banau?' Babaji asks, as if reading my thoughts. I smile wider and look at him. Falling back in. Yeah, a joint will be good.

'Charas hai?' I ask.

He walks to his spot on the verandah and pulls out the makings from under his cushion.

277

And after rice is eaten, with a little curd, dishes washed, fire tidied, kettle on to boil, the effects of the smoke long gone, I find again the nagging disquiet. As if now night has fallen it too has descended in me. I don't want to be here. Again as I look at the fire it is as if every flame forms a brief vision of Papaji before reaching up to be swallowed by the darkness.

'Kumariji, now you here my heart too much good feeling. Ganga Sagar no going, maybe next year going.'

'Tikhai, Babaji.' I feel a sudden relief as I realise I can stay a few weeks, then return to Lucknow. I already know what I will say, that it is too cold for me and anyway surely he will understand this desire to be with my guru. 'Tikhai, Babaji,' I say again.

In Babaji's room I pause to find my night eyes and cover myself under his blankets. Rough woollen blankets that tickle slightly against my neck. We find each other easily in the black dark, the oil lamp a pinprick of light, fully dressed until the warmth of us under the blankets allows the first shedding of clothes. As layer by layer is removed, his hands explore every inch of me and he holds my face and whispers 'Om' as he finds my inner places. I stay as still as I can, folding into the smoothness of his skin, the tightness of his muscles, the tickling of his beard and the fragrance that is him: coconut oil, incense, wood smoke. His malas brush against me as the weight of blankets presses him deep inside. Making love banishes my doubt, removes the question to be here or not. It is a sublime dance our bodies are performing and we are becoming experts.

He doesn't ejaculate. He never has. 'This liquid out going then power out going. This sex energy sub se good energy. Me keeping inside then this sex living inside here!' He rubs his chest, leaning slightly closer so I can see his smile and the almost white glint of teeth in the pearly light.

This intimacy under the cover of dark is irresistible, the energy undeniable. When I am apart from him, sexual energy just doesn't come into my picture. I have no interest and certainly no attraction to any other man.

*　*　*

The day is brilliant; sunshine pours through deep blue skies. We sit on the verandah enjoying the pools of warmth that fall low across the garden.

'Babaji, I want to take a walk. Head up the mountain a little way, stretch my legs after train and bus ride.'

'Accha, walking tikhai!'

What I really need is time to figure out what is going on. I cannot lose the image of Papaji and I am not in peace. My bargain to stay a few weeks feels impossible. I want to return to Lucknow now. It is as simple as that. But here I am, sitting in a little ashram nestled in a forest with mountains rising behind and the air sharp and crystal clear, my luminous sadhu lover by my side. These last few weeks have immersed me in sadhu ways, opened doors to ancient worlds that resonate deeply within. Now I am here, in this ashram that is home, with a sadhu who is available to me, for my questions, my intrigue. More than this, with whom I share an abiding connection. Why can't I just surrender to being here? Papaji is not going anywhere and after a few weeks I can be back in Lucknow.

Walking will be good. Time to sort myself out and resolve this inner conflict.

At the first ridge the uncared-for Durga shrine sits and the valley falls away. I climb straight up the mountain, off the path and find a spot to sit. The ground is rock hard and awash with tall golden grass amidst shrubs with tiny purple flowers. I spread my shawl on the stony earth, taking off my shirt so I am wearing just my t-shirt. The sun lulls me for a while to rest. I whisper my mantra, tasting the sound, the roundness, and the way the words roll off my tongue. After a moment I am cross-legged, no matter that the ground is hard and stony. I recite 'Om Namah Shivaya' over and over again, turning my mala through my fingers. I open my eyes and gaze at the valley below. An eagle soars above, circling in the blue, and a birdcall stings the silence. Vague sounds of the village drift with the breeze ... a dog barking, women calling far below.

I have a handful of almonds and a packet of beedis in my pocket. I also have a joint I rolled this morning. I make myself comfortable on the stony ground, resting against a rock. A gentle breeze brings the fragrance of sun-baked earth and the sky is cloudless. Above me it is so blue I can almost touch it. I feel my body relax even with the hardness behind my back and the stone beneath me. A settling. Yes, it was good to come up here and take time alone. The sun feels good and I plan a trip to the valley behind; maybe Babaji would like to come to our place by the river. How freezing it will be! No plunging in this time.

I light the joint, throwing down the match as I always do. In an instant there is a flame that spreads before I can think. The grass takes hold, and suddenly a ring of flames surrounds me. I stamp at them then swipe with my shirt. As quick as I can beat at a flame another springs up. The breeze takes hold and the flames become bigger; the heat pushes me back until all I can do is retreat. The fire rushes upwards as I stumble to the path and watch in horror as smoke pours black against the heavens. Shock holds me spellbound, paralysed with dismay, as I watch flames burst into the blue.

I run further up the path, passing no one. I climb a little way off where I can't see the flames and fling myself against a rock. I have no idea what to do. My heart thumps, panic rises in my chest.

Thoughts fly through my mind, *How can I get help! How can I ever face Babaji again! I never should have taken this time alone!* I keep repeating to myself this is a careless accident but am unable to listen.

It's late afternoon by the time I can bring myself to walk back down. At the temple a group of villagers watch the fire. It is burning wild and free. They look at me and I am filled with fear, convinced they know it has been started by me. I join in with 'Khya hogaya? Kitna agni?' [What's happened? How much fire!] 'Barish nahi bahut din.' [Many days no rain.] At the chai stall by Tushita more locals and a westerner watch the fire. From down below it looks even more extreme. A whole side of the mountain is burning and the smoke billows high in the sky, a black eruption against the blue.

The milkman and Babaji stand in the garden. I am heavier than lead. Everyone watches the sudden show. The fire claws the mountain in a swirl of smoke, the orange glow of flames more vivid with the evening light. I stand in silence too and watch it with them until the milkman heads on home.

We sit by the dhuni and Babaji is staring at me. I can hardly speak but I have to. 'Babaji, this fire. I started the fire. Threw down the match as I lit a smoke and flames leapt in a moment.'

'You this fire making?' His look settles to a frown. He stares at the fire and I want to cry. It takes every ounce of myself to hold on. 'You this fire doing then puja making, trees hurting, many animals suffering.' This simple fact that something can be done is a relief.

He takes the kettle off the stand and places the stand to the side. He pulls wood from the woodpile then builds the flame to a neat triangle of fire. He sprinkles water and lights incense.

'Tum idder behtou.' His tone commands and I respond, sitting opposite him, rather than in my usual spot to one side. He rummages around in his wooden box, the same one where he kept his opium piece the time he hurt his leg and where he keeps his chillum. From a paper wrapping he tips dried herbs into a bowl.

'Garden me, ek pati. Tulsi, malum hai?' I nod. I know the leaf he means. 'One handful bring.'

I step into the almost dark and find the plant. I break a branch and the sweet fragrance of tulsi is released from the leaves crushed between my fingers for the puja. The dark sky hosts an orange light show and if I hadn't been the cause I might find it stunning.

Babaji mixes the dried leaves with a sticky black resin. I think it is frankincense. He also has spooned most of his ghee into another katori and I make a mental note to buy more ghee tomorrow. Bowls now arranged he wraps a shawl tight around his shoulders.

I have attended fire puja before, but not with the same significance. What we are offering to this fire before us is for my benefit as much as for the suffering of the animals and plants. It strikes me suddenly that of course there is no difference. The fine web of interconnected being is burning very bright.

We sit by the dhuni all night and most of the following day, fasting, not even drinking water. Every now and again he throws a mix of herbs into the flame with a spoonful of ghee and a sprinkle of water. As he does he utters 'swaha' which means 'I offer'. I do not know what mantra he is saying and I do not ask. Babaji is calm. Whenever I tell him of my distress he responds with, 'All is karma. Not your hand doing this or that. Not your hand.' But it doesn't help. 'Fire coming nature way of cleaning.' His main concern is for the trees and animals that are suffering. After hours of the hypnotic repetition of mantra and battling sleep, I find it impossible to think any more. I am just part of this scene, sitting by the fire very late into the night. I am sure at times I do fall asleep, still sitting, only to waken back to consciousness. All of it feels like a continuation of the dream, as Babaji keeps his vigil, muttering mantra, throwing pinches of herb, keeping the fire fed, coughing from time to time. By the time the birds begin their dawn serenade I feel refreshed and at peace.

The fire burns for two days. An ugly swathe of black leaves a scar as far as I can see up the mountain. Smoke still trails in thin lines, silvery and sparse. It is the third morning and time has lost itself, blurred to this immediate experience of now. Sitting by the dhuni for so long has been tapas – a practice that involves austerity. I feel clear and precise, like a definite footprint in virgin snow.

Sitting now on the verandah Babaji brings chai. I sip the milky sweetness and it could be as it always has been between us but it is not. I know he feels it too. It dangles between us like a knife that cuts a cord.

'Babaji, I have to go back to Lucknow.'

'Tikhai, Prem Kumariji, tikhai. One, two day resting, then chello.'

A long sigh escapes from my lips as I close my eyes.

That night Babaji lights candles, illuminating the gods on his altar. He takes several sticks of incense, lights them with a candle and places them in a holder on the floor. Every night we have shared this bed, a mattress on the floor with a lungi as a sheet and coarse woollen blankets to cover us. Seven nights I have been here, two of them spent sitting by the dhuni performing puja. Shadows seem to reach forward and dance on the walls as an audience. Babaji sits by the altar, only his shadow moving. In the flickering light he looks as dark as the moonless night outside.

After a moment he joins me on the mattress, leaving the candles burning. As always, we lie side by side in silence. Our breathing synchronises and I can feel the energetic pull to him that my body knows. I remember so well our first loving, up in the cave where I poured my soul into his. Our union has remained, as soul lovers demand. He takes my hand. I turn to him and run my fingers up under his t-shirt, trace the tight contour of his chest. He pulls away then stands, pulling his t-shirt over his head, unwrapping his lungi. He stands for a moment by his altar, then takes his malas off and places them by the small Shiva lingam. I have never seen him without his malas.

He throws the blankets back and watches as I undress. Our eyes remain locked, and naked we sit facing one another. The candlelight is perfect. In all our previous unions we have never kissed. I have presumed it is just not something that sadhus do. In fact I have never been a big kisser myself, not enjoying sharing saliva and tongues. I've told myself it's probably a hangover from a past life as a Hindu. But now I want to kiss him, I want it all. I find him with my lips and he responds, cautiously, unsure; then he gets the hang of it all and the energy is sudden, animal almost. I am a concubine, Eve seducing Adam with the juiciest fruit of all. Released from his malas and the weight of blankets, we love as if it will be the last.

*   *   *

In the morning the trail of smoke is barely visible. We spend the day mostly in silence, sitting close to each other, meditating. He looks at me and his eyes fall quickly away, to the empty trees, the barren garden.

'Kumari, you stay and my wife living is better.' His eyes fall to the floor.

Tears actually slide down my cheeks and I can see a ring of damp on my thigh where they pool. All rules are broken now as I slide close and rest my damp face against his rough waistcoat. I can hear his heart beating through the wool.

He pats my head, fiddles with a tangle in my hair.

'Jutta hey, Kumari. Tum sadhu log. Guruji hai, Bhagwan ki kripa hey.' [Dreadlock you have, you are sadhu. You have your guruji. That is much grace from God.] It is a moment of exquisite tenderness and I

283

want this. I want this simple love. I want his company, this life. Perhaps it is possible to put it on hold, to leave it on the back burner while other pressing matters are taken care of. Only time will tell.

'Babaji, why don't you come to Lucknow, meet my Guruji?'

'Me no interest going. All is karma, Kumariji. This my place, this quiet place ashram caring only for garden, foreigners staying. Day coming, night coming. You here is good, you no here is good.' I know this is his truth. The moment slips away.

As night falls we eat a little kidgeree, neither of us hungry. I wear sadness like an unwelcome gift. The night is cold but I wrap a couple of blankets around me and sit outside on the verandah watching the black sky as thousands of stars are revealed in points of light amidst the pine trees. The flames from the fire now subdued, but in the day light a line of smoke still rose to the blue empty sky above.

Babaji joins me and we sit close. I remember suddenly the small piece of charas I have had since Nepal and find it in my money belt. I roll it up and we smoke, oblivious to the cold snatching and freezing in our breath.

'I love the night, Babaji. The world disappears and God can reign undisturbed.' I feel a sense of destiny like never before. 'Babaji, you know you make the best chapattis ever?'

'Accha?' he says. 'Kumariji, you sometime still come here, tikhai?'

'Tikhai, Babaji.'

Sleep eventually pulls me and I am the first to snuggle under the blankets fully clothed. It is not long until a rooster crows and a thin slither of moon pauses as dawn breaks.

*   *   *

At satsang house I am greeted with surprise by everyone but Papaji, who nods to me as he passes on his way out of satsang. 'You came back?' He laughs then turns to Bharatmitra, his attendant: 'She went to take care in the mountains but has come back instead.' He chuckles again and grips hard on my arm so I walk a little way with him until he lets me go.

CHAPTER TWENTY-ONE

The temple

'The root of meditation is the form of the Guru.
The root of worship is the feet of the Guru.
The root of mantra is the word of the Guru.
The root of liberation is the grace of the Guru.'
The Guru Gita

I want my own home. I want to live alone.

I find a house to rent in the lanes near Papaji's house. It has a high wall and gate with a front garden, a verandah and a courtyard inside with a grille covering the opening to the sky. Stairs lead up to the flat roof. A buffalo family lives in the vacant lot next door and Janaki lives a couple of minutes' walk past the mosque towards Amrapali market.

The day after I move my few possessions into the house, Papaji leaves for Haridwar. It is unexpected but apparently he wants to go to the Ganga and Haridwar is an old haunt of his. I am completely unfazed by the fact that I have returned from my commitment in Dharamsala and he is leaving. It doesn't matter: this is just what is happening.

I unpack my box of belongings, make an altar in my bedroom and sit the lingam I bought in Chitrakut in the centre. I wash it carefully and place marigolds around the base. The courtyard is perfect for a dhuni. I can cook on a fire and keep things simple. The space under the stairs to the roof is an ideal spot to build a temple. I can see the finished vision very clearly in my mind. I may not have stayed up in the ashram but I want to bring this aspect of ashram life here. It is how I want to live: to focus my days on temple business.

From the buffalo woman next door I buy a mound of cow shit to mould the fireplace. I have no problem mixing it with earth as I have often watched Babaji mixing earth and cow shit into a wet paste. I smooth the sides till a round fireplace sits in the courtyard. The mixture dries out, leaving a golden-brown, earthern centrepiece. Wood wallahs are easy to find. I buy five rupees worth of wood, which I tie on the back of my bike.

For the first fire I invite Janaki. I keep it burning late into the night to build up the ashes and for the simple joy of watching a flame. I use dried cow shit as well as wood, another offering from the holy cow. I buy ten pats for two rupees, already dried and shaped from the buffalo woman next door.

I sketch plans for the temple. I want to raise the floor and decide bricks and cement is the way to go. For the next ten days I lose myself in the ancient art of temple building, making my own shrine. I fast during the day, taking only kidgeree at night. This is a retreat styled by and for my very own self. I mix the cement and pour it, all by hand, laying the bricks until I have a slightly uneven but quite functional floor. I paint the walls deep blue with white pillars and arches lined with a gold border of 'Om'. The lower half I tile white; in the tile shop I find pictures of the gods: Shiva and Parvati, and a Ganesh to sit to the left. On each wall I paint a big red Om. 'Om Namah Shivaya' chants softly under my breath.

The base of the lingam, the yoni, I model with cement. Shiva's bull, Nandi, is often found in Shiva temples and I fashion one also from the cement. The nandi looks more like a puppy lying at his master's feet, but I know what it is and that is all that matters. I haven't realised cement is so harsh on the skin and my fingers quickly become raw and painful at the tips. Penance I decide, although for what I am not sure.

In the evening I light candles and let the magic move in. The walls of the courtyard are a warm earthy brown and on the back wall, with the buffalo family on the other side, I paint a Shiva. He has big eyes and neat tilak and piles of jutta with the Ganga flowing from his locks. Snakes and strings of rudraksha malas wrap around his neck. He holds one hand up with Om painted on his palm.

I have the recurrent desire to go to Papaji's house, even though he isn't there. One morning I do, and knock on the gate.

'Hi, Prem Kumari, have you come to help clean?' It's Sally, the young Australian girl.

'Yes,' I reply, and why not? She and the swamiji have been left behind to take care of the house. Swamiji is in his eighties and has been a devotee of Papa since 1985.

'Swamiji, I am building a temple in my house.' His face is almost covered in a bushy white beard and thick eyebrows, and his orange scarf is tied over his forehead. His hair is thin and fluffs around his face and his bright eyes are slightly hooded.

'A temple? For which god will you be welcoming?' His interest is immediate. 'Shivaji, the temple is a Shiva temple. I will go to Benares to find a lingam. I want to make puja.'

'Very good! A temple for Master! What mantras will you be reciting?'

Good question. I do know a few mantras but I really want to get it right. I know how important the sounds and rituals are. 'Can you tell me appropriate mantras?'

'Yes, yes.' He is excited and sings for me and shares stories of temples and people he has known. I go the next day and the next. The energy in Papaji's house is precise, as if his fragrance has been left behind. My favourite job is to clean all the ornaments on the cupboard in the living room, little statues of the gods, photos of temples, jars of Ganga water. With Papaji absent I take my time and study things closely. On the walls are old photos of him and one in particular throws me back into a place of feeling sure I have known him before. He is wearing a yellow t-shirt and a white dhoti, and I guess him to be around forty or fifty years old. He stands in front of a temple and has tilak on his forehead.

At 10 am we have tea, sitting at the table, before I return home. I continue with my project. It is obvious that Hanuman needs to be here, so I paint him on the wall opposite the temple. He comes to life with the stroke of paint, his lips gently curled, big eyes slightly downcast, hands together in reverence. Yellow flower malas adorn his shoulders and on his head is a crown inlaid with jewels and stones. On the yellow background I write Ram in Hindi, in tiny red letters.

From a mattress and a pile of cushions on the floor I survey the scene. The temple to the left tucked in under the stairs, white pillars against navy blue background, gold edging and red Om signs. Shiva on the wall opposite me, his hand in a blessing, the gold snakes glinting in the light. Satisfaction creeps around and settles with a smile on my lips. The dhuni still smoulders from making chai, the thread of smoke adding another perfection. Now Hanuman is here – serene and silent – to complete the picture. Only the lingam is missing.

*   *   *

The ball of red sun peeps over the horizon. The Ganga spread like glass, already a smudge of pink. Dawn is alive in this city of Shiva. The guli I have emerged from spills out to wide steps. A row of Shiva lingams sit in little shrines but the singing I hear comes from a small temple. I follow the voice; inside the small temple a pujari sings to the goddess. I know these mantras from my time spent with Sita. This pujari's voice is strong and harmonious. I stand and wait, watching the sun reflect in a swaying line of gold on the water below. Monkeys chatter in the huge banyan tree and I notice another lingam tucked into the roots. The pujari finishes his puja and gives me a dot of red on my forehead. I feel dressed now that tilak is in place.

A boy runs up the steps to where I stand. 'Boat? You want boat?' Below me boats are moored in an abstract collage. I have time on my hands until the market opens. I follow him down to step carefully onto the wooden boat. He rows out into the water and tells me his name is Vishnu.

Men stand waist-deep in the water. Hands are folded in prayer and they cup water, pouring it slowly to the rising sun. This is the time of day when the Gayatri mantra is recited and I do the same.

Om bhubhavur swaha, tat savitur vyrenyum bhargo devasya dhimihi, dhuoyo nah praschodiyat.

Orange marigolds drift and leaf bowls float by with a candle still alight. The boat removes me from the action yet allows me to absorb the scenes around me. I have been in India four years now yet Benares still has the capacity to awe me with its rich undiluted culture. The energy is immense as a steady flow of humanity offers prayers to their holy river. Shiva is praised in an endless chorus of worship in this city that is his own.

Further upstream the pilgrims thin out. Women wash children, scrubbing their faces, while others jump and splash about. Teeth are cleaned, bodies soaped. Boats pass with Indian tourists who wave and call, 'Hello, madam!'

From the river the architecture is more noticeable. Old buildings with elaborate arches, crumbling walls and faded paintwork look like the remnants from the Mughal Empire. Flowers drift by, the odd log. I notice a larger object and stare. As it passes the boat Vishnu tells me, 'Body, body.' And so it is. A man with a shaved head, wearing just a loincloth, floats by face down. His shoulder and arm that are exposed to the air are already decomposing. The slight stench catches me a moment after the body floats on downstream. It is definitely macabre. It is one thing to see bodies burning, yet to see a near-naked one float by jolts me. Life continues all around regardless. Children shriek as they jump into the river. Men clean teeth a few metres from decaying corpses. Madness? It just is as it is.

Smoke rises again. The other burning ghat is coming into sight. Four fires burn. A cow picks through rubbish and as we row level to the pyres I see a man washing the bones from a recent cremation. Black ash swirls in the water. In Benares death is a raw reminder of the way we all will go. The transience of life has never been more apparent.

We are almost at Assi Ghat, and I wonder if I could call in on the old swami at the math where I stayed, but decide not to. Vishnu turns the boat around and we drift back with the flow of the river, the sun already warm.

'Thank you, ji,' I tell Vishnu, as I climb from the boat back onto the old stone ghats busy with morning pujas and pilgrims, and the endless, never ending hum of worship all around.

*   *   *

Mid-morning the market is open. A sweet shop makes especially good kirkadoms, a Benares speciality of crumbly white balls with a liquid inside that explodes sugary sweet. They will be perfect for prasad. I buy a brass bell and a couple of pots with a brass spoon for giving water.

At the Khadi Bhawan I buy several metres of my favourite silk. It is cream and rough to touch but I know after a few washes it will be soft and supple. The tailor will make it up into a long robe, all I ever wear nowadays. Apparently silk has a great vibration for meditation. Presumption again? Truly it is all presumption – any idea, any belief, any notion at all. As Papaji tells us, it is better to keep quiet. Now to find my lingam.

'You come my factory, many lingams you will find,' the man in the shop tells me. I follow him down tight alleyways, squeeze past a cow and almost bump into an old woman pushing a cart overflowing with garbage. The shop has a huge lingam sitting outside. Two big Hanumans rest side by side against the wall and a man squats, chipping away at stone. Inside is my idea of heaven. Murtis are everywhere. Shiva sitting cross-legged, Hanuman kneeling in prayer, Krishna playing his flute. They are all painted and their faces are enraptured.

'Behtou, behtou.' A young smiling face welcomes me. I sit amongst them all. This is his family business. He tells me his job is to sculpt and paint the faces.

'Kitne sundar,' [How beautiful] I tell him.

Many lingams to choose from, but the choice is easy. My eyes rest on a bluey silver lingam with a natural tilak marking in red. The markings are in the tilak pattern of Shakti worship. Perfect. Shiva Shakti in one.

'Ardagh hai?' Vinod wants to know. I do not know this word. He points to a yoni and is concerned I am taking a lingam without its companion.

'Yoni hai, phele banayega,' I tell him.

'Madam, this word is not correct. The word is Ardagh, the Parvati.'

I practise it a couple of times. Vinod is charming and brings me chai, his large eyes magnified behind his glasses as he passes me the cup. I could sit all day surrounded by his gods. I take the lingam and wrap it in silk. I bathe it in the Ganga, keeping, 'Om Namah Shivaya' constantly in my mind. I fill a jar with Ganga water to take back to my temple.

Business now complete, I walk up the river, through the mingling crowds to the Naga Babas' dhuni. A baba sits in the entrance and he lifts his hand in greeting. 'Ho ho.'

I reply, 'Om.'

The dhuni is busy; the mahant is speaking. He has seen me and raises his hand in recognition. I join the group of sadhus, sitting with my bag to one side. I wish I could understand his words. After he falls silent some of the babas leave, touching his feet as they go. Some have shaved heads, suggesting a recent initiation.

'Maha Dev, Maha Dev!' The mahant nods to me. I touch his feet then show him the lingam. He takes it in his hands as gently as if he is holding a new baby.

'Kis kaam lingam kelier?' he asks. [What is the lingam for?]

'Meh mandir banayea humara ghar. Varanasi jana lingam milgaya.' [I'm making a temple in my house. I came to Varanasi to find a lingam.]

'Accha toh lingam pourana whalla ragdo darshan kelier.' [Okay, so put this lingam with the old lingam for darshan.] So I do of course, placing my lingam, still wrapped in the silk, in the pit with the stone one inside the cave.

I spend the afternoon between the ghats and the Naga Babas. As evening paints colour in the sky, the call to arti resounds with three long blasts on the conch shell. The ringing of bells crescendo until all I experience is sound. The mahant holds the damaru high, his head thrown back, eyes closed. The damaru is Shiva's instrument, said to produce the primal sound of creation that vibrates the cosmos into existence. The temple erupts with singing – these wild men with only loincloths covering strong brown bodies, singing their praises to God.

*   *   *

I am wise now to travelling with no reservation. I push to the front of the queue as I discover women are allowed to do, so seldom would an Indian woman be travelling alone or buying a ticket alone. In the past I have had men touch my breast or brush too close to some part of my body. Recently at Lucknow station, jammed in with the crowd buying a ticket, the man behind me stuck his hand between his legs. I am over it. I have absolutely had enough of any hassling from men. The ticket costs forty-six rupees and is for the unreserved carriage.

As the train pulls in I find the first-class A.C. compartment and jump on board. I wait by the doorway, watching the hustle as chai wallahs scurry up and down and porters with cases stacked high jostle through the crowd. As the train pulls out I find an empty compartment. It has a door that locks and two berths, like the first-class non-A.C., but the window is tinted and cannot be opened. There is a small stainless steel sink in the corner and the floor is clean. The bunks are wide and padded, not torn or stained, and I settle myself down to await the ticket collector. It isn't long before he comes, and I have left the door open.

'Ticket, ticket.' He is looking at his clipboard with its list of seat reservations.

'Sir, I was very late to buy a ticket at the counter and the unreserved carriage was full of men and I felt very uncomfortable.' I pull my shawl further over my head as I talk.

'So, sir, I have found this empty quiet place to sit where no one will disturb me. I can pay the difference of the fare or maybe I can give you two hundred rupees?' I speak with innocence but he knows I am offering him baksheesh. He nods his head and pockets the rupees. Then in Hindi I thank him and tell him that my heart is now happy with the arrangement. Covering myself with the shawl I sleep soundly until Lucknow looms in the dawn.

*   *   *

Swamiji is full of support for the inaugural puja. The day after I return from Benares, with the lingam still carefully wrapped, he comes to my house and is pleased by what he sees.

'Bahut buriya, Prem Kumari.' He instructs me on the right mantras, repeating them with me until he is satisfied the sound is correct.

'Mantra is sound. The sound has a vibration and each word must be correct.'

You are my Mother, my Father you are. You are my friend my companion. You are my learning, my wealth you are, you are my all in all, my Lord of Lords.

'Baal pati you can find in Bhootnath market,' he says to me. 'Baal leaf has three fingers, if you like. They represent the three gunas: sattva, tamas and rajas. We pray to be even beyond the sattvic energy that you must be. Only a sattvic mind can truly worship. And the time must be right. Usha, usha is the congregation of night and day, when you will sit and meditate doing a little pranayam. Sundia, just after sunset, when the arc of the last sun is in the western sky, this is the time for puja.'

Swamiji has cataracts and the pale line of his eyes mist easily. He fades to silence as if he too contemplates his words. He has bad knees and I bring him a chair, the one from the verandah by the front door. It is the only chair I have. After a while he wipes at his eyes and continues with his list: 'Saffron, incense, chandan powder.'

The following day is the new moon. It is one month since I returned from the mountains. Papaji is still in Haridwar. All afternoon I slowly stir rice in simmering milk, spiced with cinnamon, cardamom and a little nutmeg. Just as the rice is almost cooked I add handfuls of sugar, raisins, cashew nuts and almonds.

The flower wallah is curious when I pick up metres of malas. 'How much flower mala are you buying!'

'For puja,' I tell him. I take yellow and orange marigolds and several rose malas. The fragrance surrounds me as I walk home. The pinks and reds spill in pools of petals as I take them from my bag.

Hania and Shobha have just returned from Brindavan, Hania's old haunt where Krishna played with his gopis. They come bearing sweets from Mathura, the birthplace of Krishna, and many stories of their stay in the Neem Karoli Ashram there. Janaki is of course here and Uma, her daughter, is over for a visit and has been helping me with the preparations. Tall stems of gladioli sit at the feet of Hanuman, candles burn and incense pours from the four corners. The dhuni is surrounded with flowers and sprinkled with rose petals. The ash is neatly raked and a fire all ready to light.

Swamiji sings mantras as I bathe the lingam. I offer sandalwood oil and rose water. Mantras slip from my lips as easy as a kiss. Shadows dance and stars shine through the open roof. The fire is lit and the gods bow down to receive our prayer.

I feed everyone khir and much later I sit alone in lingering candlelight. The temple is a tangible mass of solid energy. This is my home.

*   *   *

'Allaah Akbar! Allaah Akbar!' The mosque crackles to life through loudspeakers with the dawn call to worship. The imam pauses to clear his throat. 'Allah Akbar!' welcomes me to the day. The family next to my wall are already up, the woman's voice harsh in the quiet. I hear a low call from a buffalo and the stomp of a hoof against the packed earth ground. The grandfather, with his hacking cough, spits and clears his throat. Sounds and smells reach me through the musty dawn as day shifts nearer and birds join the prayer.

I wash the lingam and on the yoni, the ardagh, I place fresh flowers then I wave a burning stick of incense in slow circles before carefully placing it in an incense holder to slowly fill the room with its fragrance. I take my rudraksha mala, waiting for the call from the mosque to quieten. I picture the white tower of the minarets, a finger pointing to the heavens, and rest a moment in the silence that follows a call to god.

I repeat the mantra 108 times, as many beads as there are on the mala, fingering the beads with each 'Om Namah Shivaya'.

Then I meditate. Papaji has said that the mind is like an elephant walking through a bazaar. The keeper gives it a stick to hold so it cannot grab at the fruits. So it is with japa meditation. It seems that the conditioned mind has its own life, as the ebb and flow of thoughts, weighted by emotion, linger like clouds passing the sun.

It is still dawn as I remove the flowers from the temple then pour water over the lingam. I wash the floor and sweep the water away. I place fresh flowers and light incense. I sweep the floor of the courtyard before lighting the fire to boil the kettle for chai. Cleaning the temple keeps me focused on what I want: the simple act of surrender.

*   *   *

Papaji returns from the trip to the Ganga and I want to continue cleaning in his house. I dream that I am asking him if I can come and help. He says yes and then hugs me very tight.

That morning I go early and am invited in. Papaji is sitting at the table reading letters. He takes his glasses off and looks up as I enter. I touch his feet then ask: 'Papaji, can I come and help clean in your house?'

'Yes, yes,' he says, hardly looking at me. Then he adds: 'You come Sunday and Wednesday.'

Satsang is five days a week. Silence takes on another quality like the changing light of sunset. He jokes, tells stories and always his eyes sparkle with a radiance that infects us all with his love.

'Samsara, let me tell you about samsara. This is the story of samsara.' He chuckles to himself before continuing. 'There is a well, a long deep well and at the bottom in the pool of water are crocodiles snapping their teeth. A man is hanging on a vine holding on tight, just above the mouths of these crocodiles. But he is content because dripping from somewhere above is a nectar, like honey, and he has his mouth open to receive a tiny drop every few seconds. He hangs there with the crocodiles below, holding on to the vine, happy to receive a drop of nectar. But high above are two rats gnawing at the vine with their sharp little teeth. These two rats are called day and night. You cannot escape from time. So make use of this precious birth where your desire for freedom has brought you here, to Lucknow. One instant of a second – that is all it takes. To know your Self.'

Janaki, Hania, Shoba and I often eat lunch together. I cook because I love to. I make a big pot of kidgeree and before we eat we offer a plate to the temple, to Hanuman, and then enjoy our food as prasad. Sometimes I make chapattis and whenever I do, I can see Babaji's hands and the way they mould and shape the dough. My chapattis are good but not as good as his.

Janaki has planted salad greens in her landlord's garden so now we enjoy lettuce and arugula with tomatoes and cucumber from the market along with grated beets and carrots. Hania likes to cook too and invites us all over for samosa and puri and carrot halwa. Within the circle of sisterhood, women connecting, sharing ourselves, my need for company is more than nurtured.

In the late afternoon the call to prayer rings out from the mosque. I coax the fire to a flame for a chai before a trip to the market to buy flowers. It is my neighbourhood now and I'm met with 'Namaste! Namaste!' as I ride my bike to the market. The wood sellers offer me chai if the old mataji is there, squatting over her fire in their shack with the blue plastic roof. I play with the kids as I tie up my bundle of wood – a little girl with huge brown eyes and her baby sister who she carries around on her hip like a grown-up.

Every evening I buy a litre of milk from the family next door. Just before sundown, locals gather at the wooden bench, middle-class neighbours from the road that runs alongside the Muslim village. They stand to one side to avoid the mud and chat amongst themselves, waiting for the steaming frothy buckets of milk straight from the buffalo. The men milk the animals, pulling their teats as they squat barefoot in the mud, with the silver bucket between their legs, calling 'hup hup!' to their animals as they snort and stamp their big feet. Their fleshy pink mouths slobber and steam in the cool of the evening.

As the sun retreats to light other worlds, I sweep the temple, replace the flowers from the morning with malas of yellow, light the candles, refill the oil lamp that burns all the time and offer incense to all the deities. Swirls of smoke pour over the lingam. I ring the bell, pausing a moment as the sound lingers, calling a silence in respect of prayer. I sing first to Ganesh then to the lingam and when I am finished I wait, watching the way the gold Oms glint in the candlelight and the Shiva on the wall beside me seems to receive my prayer. The passage of the moon, a constant companion on this journey, represents the ebb and flow of this world of duality.

*   *   *

Wednesday and Sunday become the highlights of my week. Papaji is always in his room when I dust the knickknacks, the statues and photos and jars of Ganga water. Around 11 am he comes and sits at the table, reading the newspaper or letters he has received. People write to him from all over the world. Sometimes people come to see him, an Indian family or Indian devotees living elsewhere. He has his regular visitors and they sit with him at the table. Papaji is a fan of cricket and if a game is on he loves to watch. I often sit on the floor towards the back of the room and watch him, an old man sitting at his table with friends around, watching sport, rubbing his shoulder and helping himself to the nuts in a bowl before him. Yet his presence remains as tangible as ever, and I settle into myself, close my eyes and meditate, bathing in his grace.

Satsang, sanga – company of the wise – Papaji's home and my temple and all its requirements, bring a routine and a purpose. It brings a sense of belonging, to community, to environment. It brings connection with myself.

*   *   *

By the end of February the days are warm and the sun rises with a hint of orange. March takes hold and the days of shawls and blankets at night are gone. Again I have to consider what to do about my visa. I have no desire to go anywhere, to travel any place other than to Papaji's house and satsang. Certainly, I have no interest to go to another country. I have heard that it is possible to get a five-year visa so I decide to go back to England and trust that I will be given what I want. I also have virtually no money and plan to stay a couple of months to work and visit my family. Also, I recently met a man who is now in London. Tony is a western baba, you could say, with Jamaican blood and dreadlocks piled on his head. Our attraction was immediate.

March 27 is my birthday. In the evening I hear a knock on the door and in comes Chandi Devi, one of the women who spends her days in Papaji's house.

'Prem Kumari! Papaji has heard it is your birthday. He has a gift for you, come come!' I go with her up to the house. Papaji is watching cricket on the TV.

'Ah! It is your birthday?'

'Yes, Papaji.'

He nods to Jyoti who leaves for a moment then returns with a present wrapped in paper. I open it and inside there is an orange shirt.

'I used to wear this. Now it is yours.'

I take the shirt and unfold it. An orange shirt, the colour of the rising sun that sadhus wear, and one that my guru himself has worn. Can anything be more perfect? I fall at his feet awash with gratitude. He chuckles as I try to thank him. 'You eat, sit here and eat.' He points to the chair next to him so I sit. An overwhelming sense of presence emanates from him, and all I want to do is fall to his feet in gratitude. Jyoti brings me a plate with a few sweets, the best possible birthday cake. As I leave I tell him my plan. 'Papaji, I am going to go to England for a couple of months to get a five-year visa and work a little.'

'Five-year visa? Very good.' And he shakes his head slightly with a small smile, his eyes twinkling like the night sky. 'You then come back here.' It isn't a question and in any case, there is no doubt.

'Yes, Papaji. I come back.'

'Who is looking after your temple?'

'One friend will stay and take care.'

'Accha. Tikhai. Chello.'

*   *   *

April brings heat and temperatures near forty degrees. It is time to go. In Delhi I book my ticket to England for the following week. I want to spend some days in Rishikesh by the Ganga before I leave this sacred land. I follow my inner voice and unexpectedly meet up with friends in a crowded market street. This voice is new and is accompanied by a thickening in my breath, a subtle change in my perception and the undeniable feel of presence. Papaji has said, 'I am with you wherever you are' and I know this to be true.

Before I leave for the station to travel to Rishikesh, my friends and I sing the Hanuman chalisa together three times. I am running late now and am surprised to see it is already dark as we pile out onto the street. After quick goodbyes I take the first tempo that stops on the busy street outside. On the handlebars are pictures of Hanuman and a little statue garlanded with flowers. The tempo driver turns to me as we drive off and says: 'My guruji is Hanuman.' In a beautiful, sweet voice he sings the chalisa. I am beyond delighted. Just before the station he stops suddenly, jumps out and touches my feet. 'You are Deviji!' His eyes are bright and shining.

New Delhi railway station is vast and the chaos outside blocks the road. Taxis, rickshaws, people on bikes and others mill in the dark around charcoal burners by the rows of food stalls. The driver edges the tempo in through the crowd, pumping at his horn, the sound lost in the shouts and chaos.

He tells me, 'Jinta mut karo ticket miljaiga saat number counter.' [Don't worry. You will get your ticket counter number seven.]

I touch his feet. 'Ram Ram, ji, Ram Ram.'

CHAPTER TWENTY-TWO

The Ganga

'Self is what gives breath to life. You need not search for It. It is here. You are that through which you would search. You are what you are looking for! And that is all it is.' Papaji

Haridwar is one of the seven sacred cities in India. It is considered the place where illusions are left behind before embarking on a pilgrimage to the 'char dhams', four sacred places high in the mountains. I've visited the Ganga here several times and to dip in her holy waters is always a pilgrimage. From the train station I take a bus to Rishikesh. Hania has told me of an ashram that is a perfect place to stay: Phool Chatti, on the banks of the Ganga several kilometres from here. It is possible she will also come for a few days. I hope so, as I set out for the walk.

The river is wider now than when I last saw her an hour or so back. The neem trees fade out and jungle reaches down to the road. Thick vines twist in the trees and I have heard wild elephants live in these forests. The road rounds a corner to reveal a smooth arc of river. A low, whitewashed wall with a gate strewn with pink climbing roses welcomes me and I guess this is Phool Chatti. There is a sign on the gate in Hindi and I read each letter, spelling out 'Phool Chatti', which means garden of roses. I walk through the gate under a fringe of pink into a courtyard. A dog sleeps under a bush and when he hears me he lifts his head and barks three times. A moment later a woman glides down the stairs from a top floor room, her dark orange robes vivid against the white. She is pulling a scarf over her head and walks quickly, with purpose. I guess she must be Lolita. Hania has also told me of her.

'Namaste!' I call as she reaches the bottom step. She looks young, a teenager even and her face is pinched in a scowl. I wonder for a moment if I am at the right place. Lolita greets me with a nod.

'Namaste, Lolita? I am a friend of Hania and have come from Lucknow. I would like to stay a few nights. Do you have a room?' As I ask for a room I pause, realising I want to be completely alone for a night or two. Maybe it is her unfriendly manner but something compels me to say: 'Actually I want to spend a night alone further upriver. Would you have a blanket I could borrow?'

I am surprised by what I am asking but suddenly I want this – I want to have some time alone by the Ganga. With my days in India suddenly numbered, I want to seize every possibility.

'Tut, ashram coming and blanket taking.'

Lolita is the first woman sadhu I have seen who is young. A large nose dominates her face and her eyes are wide and shaped like almonds. Her hair is thick and shining black, hanging to her waist. I catch the vague scent of sandalwood. She has the air of a princess, and I see no one else in the ashram.

It's hot, early afternoon, siesta time. She may have been sleeping and the dog barking woke her up. She disappears into the room to the side. The low roof of earth-red tiles and whitewashed walls remind me of a Spanish hacienda. Bougainvillea trails through trees, a deep red in the green. Lolita brings back a blanket and doesn't smile as she folds it up and gives it to me. 'You this blanket bring back.'

My thank you is genuine.

I go along with my feeling to find a place by the river and make camp for the night. I fold the blanket over my shoulder and head back to the track I noticed by the river. I follow it over a rushing stream until it ends on a stretch of beach. The Ganga glides by in strokes of shimmering green.

I press on upriver along the beach. The sand ends with a tumble of boulders and I climb easily, scrambling over stones, rocks and boulders until again the banks of the river are soft sand. I climb through low, twisted trees, spurred on by the thrill of finding myself alone in nature with the Ganga flowing free beside me. I don't know how long I walk for but long enough to feel as if I am in the middle of nowhere. The banks are steep now, covered in tall, wispy grasses that catch the light in delicate bells of gold. I scramble up, climbing higher, away from the water, and then down again, until a narrow ledge almost defeats me. I inch my way along with the bag tied firmly over my shoulder, holding on to the rock cliff until the ledge widens. Below is another stretch of beach strewn with boulders. The ledge narrows to nothing and the rock face is sheer. I hang there for a while, wondering what I have got myself into. I throw the bag down then jump, landing with a bump and falling forward onto my knees, laughing. On my knees by Ganga Ma!

An indent of sand surrounded by high rocks beckons. The grasses sway in the breeze and somewhere beyond birds call and shriek in the thick jungle of green. Shadows stretch as I make camp. All along the beach are pieces of driftwood smoothed and worn. I drag the bigger pieces to my camp, leaving grooves in the otherwise virgin sand.

In my bag I have my kamandal, another long shirt, a pair of old leggings and a change of trousers, a thick shawl, my woollen waistcoat and a couple of lungis. I also have my toothbrush and toothpaste, some coconut oil, a couple of broken cigarettes with a tiny piece of charas and some matches. I also have the blanket.

On the banks of the river opposite, a group of monkeys play in the rocks, others swing down through the trees, and I am thrilled to be the only guest at this show.

The Ganga is wide and calm, her waters swift and smooth. The great snowmelt in the mountains above has just begun. I plunge in, gasping with the cold and strength of the current. I swim a little upstream then glide down, finding my feet again on the sandy banks. I plunge under three times and let the cold flow through me.

I light the fire and sit to watch the day depart. A flock of birds flit low over the water then turn in perfect unison in an arc of white. The sun is almost gone, only the light left to linger. Streaks of pink fade to dusk and the veil of night ripples around me.

I build up the fire and it dances on the rocks in ripples of orange. I find a wild delight to be here, alone with this world. I have eaten nothing since three samosas at Haridwar railway station. I have no food with me so part of my night by the Ganga is to fast. I have already filled my kamandal with her water and let the sediment settle. As the flames settle too I rest the kamandal near the heat to warm the water. I drink the gritty water in long gulps and I am satiated and satisfied. There is a fire before me and beyond that is the Ganga herself. The night sky is alive with the play of stars in a moonless heaven.

*   *   *

I wake, damp and cold, from my bed – a lungi beneath me and the blanket and shawl covering. Night is still the queen, and a waning moon rests above the horizon. The coldness surprises me after the heat of the day. I pile all the big pieces of wood on the fire and watch it blaze, warming myself until the stars slide to the west and a crack of light appears in the east. I sleep again and wake to sunlight, warmth and a pair of little wrens flitting and darting in the grasses behind my camp.

It is obvious I will not go anywhere. I want to spend a whole day on this beach. After a morning bath I build a sand lingam, smoothing the yoni and shaping a snake curled around the base. I like the image of the snake, the mastery of desires that keep us caught in the illusion of samsara. Ha, I laugh to myself, how desire has arisen! I could not have been more surprised to find myself lovers with another man so soon after returning from the mountains and the fire and the winter that was not to be. After Tony and I met outside satsang house, he ate lunch by my dhuni, and not so many days later I found my fingers entwined in his dreads as he lay beside me, the perfect package. He looks like a baba, has a fire of devotion, and as Papaji said to me 'he is a beautiful man'. Then our nights in Delhi before his sudden return to London. But is this samsara? Or only when I suffer? *Do not be attached*, I tell myself, as I realise how much I am looking forward to seeing him when I return to London. He will meet me from the airport.

I busy myself collecting wild flowers for an offering to the lingam, and smile at the perfection of a flower growing wild by the Ganga, its unsmelt fragrance only for God. I light a stick of incense and settle in to my surrounds.

My quiet is disturbed by the sounds of people. At first I am not sure where the voices come from but then as shouts and calls come closer, I run behind a boulder and watch as two rafts come tearing downriver. Whitewater rafting on the Ganga! I had no idea – and it is the last thing I expected. In an instant they are gone; their shouts echo and fade in a moment, silence returned.

I drink a lot of water, throwing out the sediment in the bottom of the lota, refilling it and leaving it to warm and settle in the embers of the fire. I have fasted before but never with just water. Numerous times I have only drunk the water left after cooking potato and eaten beetroot with turmeric and cumin as a short cleanse. Often on a Monday I drink water during the day then eat a little kidgeree with ghee and pink Himalayan rock salt in the evening. Monday is Shiva day and traditionally a fasting day.

I finish adorning the lingam with the wild flowers and lie in the shade of a rock, watching the water flow by. Even the birds rest in the noon sun. Finally a gentle breeze ruffles the surface and I wade in and stand waist deep in the cold, milky water. I think of Babaji up in the mountains and his way of saying, 'All for time pass, Kumariji, all for time pass,' and my heart aches.

Suddenly, taking off in a plane and leaving this country seems a huge task. I know I will return, of course I will. Then doubt slides in. Why return to England at all? But as quickly as it comes I remember Papaji's blessings for this trip and his words as I left: 'You take five-year visa very good. I am waiting for your return.' I had fallen at his feet as I always do and he had held his hand on top of my head for longer than usual.

*   *   *

I sun myself in the fading warmth as the day slides away to evening. Cicadas sing in shrill cadence for the passing of the light. I wake again in the cold early hours. I pile wood on the fire as ghostly pale flecks of moonlight shine like ice.

Sometime in the morning the rafters career past again, their voices giving me enough warning to make myself scarce. One of the men points to my fireplace and camp but the river allows no time and they are gone.

Silver white sand spills through my toes. Electric blue dragonflies dart above the green water. Sun-bleached driftwood is strewn all around and I gather up the bigger pieces to take back to camp. Boulders tumbled from the grassy wildness provide generous shade in which to watch the river slide by. I feel so at peace; gratitude bubbles up like a song in my heart. Bow to God in gratitude and find all of creation is doing the same.

The hot sun parades above. I dip in the Ganga and dry in a moment, spread out on the sand, pressed between this warm earth below and a vast blue above. Beside me glides the Ganga. All through history renunciates have removed themselves from the world, vanished into the wilderness to commune with God. His voice is strong, amplified by the silence.

Living wild always brings chores. There is a big log that I want to try and pull back to camp. Yesterday I sat for a while leaning against its warm smooth wood. I walk up the beach – 'my' beach as I think of it now – and I stop still in my tracks. In the sand are big prints, cat prints. A leopard or even a tiger. I am sure they were not here yesterday. They look so fresh I glance quickly around. What is that rustle just over in the tall grasses? Nothing – and I let my thumping heart settle. My whole system is on high alert and adrenalin courses through me.

I follow the tracks off the beach to the rocks where the jungle spreads up the hillside. The prints are definite and neat, a few centimetres deep, and in places even have little pointy bits where I guess the claws have indented. I sniff the air, like an animal myself, but there is no trace of cat smell. Would I know what a tiger smells like? I wonder. Somehow, I am sure that if he is close there would be a scent. I stare into the green tangle of grasses then into the forest. A flock of parrots take off in alarm, their red wings beating in a whirr as they mock my fright. A small shiver plays down my spine and I collect up my wood bundle, leaving the big log where it is. At the safety of my camp I jump at the sound of the wood falling from my arms. I sit, cross my legs and focus on my breath. The high alert has calmed but I still have an undeniably nervous feeling in my stomach and find myself glancing up the beach. Only hours before my aloneness had thrown me into absorption with the surrounds, a simple surrender to the oneness of nature. Now my aloneness is stark and vulnerable.

A cramp in my thigh presses me to move. Stretching my legs, I consider my options. I could easily return to Phool Chatti but I am not sure if that is what I want. I lie back and lose myself in the sky, not a cloud to be seen. I really am not in a hurry to head back to civilisation. My breath responds with a long sigh and I spend the afternoon sitting, my mala resting in my fingers. *Om Namah Shivaya. Om Namah Shivaya. Om Namah Shivaya.* I have seen tiger prints in the sand. It doesn't need to be anything more than just that. *But what if he comes again?* a small voice asks. I check again within myself. Do I want to stay? I have no interest at all in sacrificing myself for a tiger's dinner. I stay quiet for a moment and the same response comes: I want to stay. I trust that means I am not in danger.

Now that I am staying I gather a bundle of grass to sleep on to see if that keeps me warmer in the night. Before sleeping I pray to be protected from harmful thoughts, that my heart be a constant companion with God. And please don't let the tiger eat me!

In the early hours, thoughts of the tiger grip me, but there is no fear. I build up the fire and listen to the silence but the only sound is the faint whisper of water as she glides ever onwards.

Another day awakens. Monkeys chatter and parrots fly through the patchwork of greens. I lie for a long time watching the jungle. Intricate patterns of light play in the trees and leaves as big as plates spiral downward in flecks of red.

I check for tiger prints but find nothing new. The old prints are big, bigger than my outstretched hand. I guess she came to drink and I wonder if tigers sleep through the night and roam in the day or sleep in the day and drink by night. I light the fire early – there is no shortage of wood – and imagine cooking chapattis on the hot embers. Then I imagine Babaji being here and his deft creation of chapattis. He would be in his element here. Just like I am. Hunger is there, niggling at my stomach, but the lightness of being is far from unbearable. Perhaps tomorrow I will leave. I imagine for a moment how good the dhal and chapatti will taste for dinner at Phool Chatti ashram, how sweet the chai will be.

Sleep comes early and stays till the cold pulls me awake in the early hours. There is no moon; a long while later she creeps over the hill behind, thinner now, almost a crescent. I watch the stars tip and the blackness soften to navy; somewhere a bird calls and day begins again. I walk to the river and squat for the longest time, watching the water's surface as the mist hangs inches above her with a smudge of silver, the stillness of dawn magnified a thousand times.

I throw more wood on the flames and bask in the warmth, meditating until the sun brings her morning glory and stretches of light fall across my lap. Breakfast is warm water from the river. It tastes silky and specks of sand stick on my tongue.

My attention is pulled up the beach and I follow my senses. There, in the sand, are fresh prints coming down from the jungle and following the river upstream to the end of the beach. The prints backtrack then disappear again to the grass and forest.

'Wow!' I exclaim to the sun and sky. 'A tiger!' I have no idea if I should be scared but this time I am not. I have passed a night sleeping on a beach about thirty metres from a tiger and lived to tell the tale. I have enough wood to keep the fire burning all night. Maybe at sunset she will come to drink again, her stripy orange form gleaming against the pale sand. Or maybe it's a leopard!

Wasn't this the day I was going to return? Four nights I have stayed and yet still I want to stay. It seems unnecessary to head back just because I have seen tiger prints further up the beach. They haven't come my way, after all. I remember my fright when I discovered them a few days before. Perhaps fasting has left no energy for fear. And I do feel diminished, noticeably so, yet lighter in my being. I know enough about fasting to guess the dull headache I have is a normal response and I also know that tomorrow I could feel quite different.

The sun lowers in the sky, throwing strands of diamonds to sparkle in the water. I collect flowers for evening puja. Amongst the grasses are a yellow wild flower that looks a little like a daisy and a bush with tiny purple petals. I fill my lungi with the colours and turn to see two men climbing over a boulder. One is Indian and one is western. The Indian guy has a gun slung over his shoulder. They are as surprised to see me as I them and after a moment of staring, the westerner, who is obviously American, speaks for us all. 'Hey! What a surprise! What are you doing here?'

I place my bundle of flowers to one side and offer a namaste. 'I am spending the day up here, quiet with the Ganga.'

They are friendly and curious and so am I.

'We are tracking a tiger. It has been spotted by villagers further upriver.'

'A tiger? Are you hunting it?'

'No no,' the American assures me. 'I am a hunter but not for the kill. This friend here is a tracker and we want to see if we can spot it.'

He looks like a character from an Indiana Jones movie. His shirt is unbuttoned and his chest has lines of sweat running to a hairy stomach. He wears solid boots with socks scrunched around his ankles and as he speaks he takes off his hat, a wide-brimmed floppy canvas one that has seen better days. He wipes his head with a red bandana and his pale hair is flattened with sweat against his head.

'It's been quite a walk up through that jungle.' He looks wistfully into the forest, shielding his eyes with his hand, and points to a rocky outcrop in the distance. 'That's where he has been hanging out. Reckon he is a big cat too.'

'How do you know that it is male?' Suddenly this tiger is my tiger, but these guys are obviously on to him.

'By the size of his prints. Must be a male.'

At that moment the older tracks are seen and they talk in excited voices as I watch in amazement. It is suddenly so bizarre to be up here on the banks of Ganga Ma with an American hunter and his tracker.

Of course I have to ask. 'What do tigers eat?' I join them by the water.

'Small animals they find up in the forest. Deer, wild pig.'

'So he's not coming to hunt down on the beach?'

'Sure no, they only come to drink after they have had a good feed. They never drink with an empty belly.' The American sits in the shade of a rock while the tracker measures the prints and checks around in the tall grass. 'So what exactly are you doing up here? It's a bit remote, ya know.'

What can I say? I pause a moment then figure I may as well be honest. 'I came up here for a couple of days' quiet. I like to be alone in nature. It's awesome to sit by Ganga and receive her darshan.'

His eyes pierce me again. 'Mmm. I always like to be out in the wilds, even as a kid, with nature, wildlife. This is where you find God. Not in the religion of today in old churches stuffed up with bad attitudes.' He chews on a fingernail and looks upriver, as if worried he has revealed too much.

He pulls out a handful of dried fruit wrapped in a plastic bag, unties the bag and offers the fruit to me on his outstretched hand. I look at the dried dates and raisins. His hand is deeply lined and calloused, the middle finger stained brown from nicotine. I really don't feel hungry.

'No, thanks.'

He shrugs and throws the lot into his mouth, chewing slowly.

'Are there many tigers still in this area?' I ask. 'Do they really only come to drink with a full belly?'

'Scared of the tiger, are you?' He chuckles. His smile is warm.

'I saw its prints yesterday and last night I can't say I was scared, but hey, I did find myself thinking about it. I just built up the fire. I am sure no tiger comes near fire.'

He looks at me again. His eyes are blue, very blue. 'That's right. Used to be many tigers but now they are protected. Reckon they still get hunted though.'

His friend comes to join us. 'We must think about keeping on. Not so much day left and I want to get up on the ridge. This is a big cat and I am wanting to see him.' He looks tired and excited at the same time.

The American reties his bandana, takes a long drink from the water bottle fixed onto his belt. 'Watch out for the tiger, hey!'

I smile and add my own goodbye. 'I hope you don't find him!'

I watch them head off along the beach then up through the grass until they disappear, and the silence settles again. My mind is busy. It takes a while to empty itself, but the main thought that stays is that the tiger is no threat to me. I pick up the flowers and head back to camp. Day is already painting the hills a soft mauve and I sit behind the lingam and watch. Sudden thoughts of Babaji sprinkle through my landscape. I rummage in my bag and find the broken cigarettes and piece of charas. In my money belt I find a few loose papers and roll the whole lot up. Then I sit back against the rock and light the joint, drawing the smoke deep into my lungs as my head spins for a moment with the smoke and days of not eating. Take me, I whisper, as if my lover were near.

*   *   *

Every evening the monkeys on the banks opposite come down to the water to drink. I wave to them and they sit up on their haunches, staring across the wide curve of water, the babies tumbling and playing along the bank. The last rays of light linger for a moment then fade as the world dims to black. Flames send orange sparks to fly in the darkness. I pile on more wood and sit watching the night show in the heavens.

I wake again with the cold air damp and black. I wrap the blanket around me, pull a heavy log onto the fire and blow the still-glowing embers to a flame. This rhythm of sleeping early and then waking in the early hours rewards me with the black night sky alive with stars. While living on my boat I would sit out on the bow for the pre-dawn silence. In London the sounds of a city are never far away. But in that pre-dawn time there was a pause, as if the city itself were holding its breath before the mass of population awoke, crowding the ether with thoughts. Now as I sit before my fire, with the gentle crackle of wood and playful light of the flames amplifying the blackness around, I find more delight in the heavens, which I have never truly appreciated before, than the vast silence. I lie back on the cold damp bed of grasses with the heavens above me and watch the nightscape shift and change … creeping towards the west as a million stars cavort across the sky.

Dawn uncurls as the thin arc of the moon rests above the trees. Three birds fly in a line upriver; patchy silhouettes reveal tree-clad hills and a deep orange throws form to lacy spirals. Light pours in and colours emerge. I shake off the blanket and await the sun.

It's time to go. I spread the blackened wood over the beach and cover the fire with sand. The lingam will be taken when the Ganga's waters rise with the churn of snowmelt from high above.

I walk back along the beach and at the base of the rock wall realise I have a problem. I can see the ledge above but there is no way I can climb up to it without footholds. I sit down and think about what to do. The answer is obvious. I will wait until the rafters come by – as they have done every morning – and hitch a ride with them. I figure it will be easiest to get their attention from a vantage point where they can see me from afar, to give them time to manoeuvre close to shore.

I walk back past the camp, past the tiger prints still there in the sand, mingled with footprints from me and its trackers, and climb up on the boulders where I can see upriver. I wait until I see the first boat rushing into view and I stand and wave and wave until they see me. Sure enough the first boat steers into the shallows and lands on the beach. The leader jumps out as I run up. He is looking concerned and pleased at the same time.

'Can I get a lift downriver? I can't walk back the way I came.'

He wears shorts and a life jacket and baseball cap. His English is perfect.

'Jump in!' And I do. The boat is full of Indian students having a whitewater rafting experience and they are delighted to find a western woman suddenly in their midst. I laugh with the wildness of suddenly taking off through rushing currents, swirling white as we career downstream.

'What is your country?'

'What is your good name?'

No one asks me what I am doing sitting by the river. We laugh and shriek as I hold tight to the side of the raft.

So the Ganga herself takes me back and on the beach at Phool Chatti I recognise people I know sitting by the water. The migration away from the heat of Lucknow has begun.

'Here, this is where I want to hop off.' The crew navigate in to shore and with a quick thank you I jump off and wade through the shallows to the beach.

'Prem Kumari!' Hania laughs with her surprise to see me emerge from a raft. I break my fast with a feast of mangoes here on the beach, the fleshy yellow fruit melting in my mouth. Juice runs down my chin and the sweetness explodes on my tongue.

Women, nature, silence. In two days' time I will be on my way back to England.

*　　*　　*

I'm back in Delhi, just for the day. The air is thick and turgid. As night falls I step into a narrow laneway to a little temple. It is a Durga temple and there she is, riding on the tiger. The pujari ties a red thread around my wrist and I pray it lasts until I am back in this land once again. As I emerge from the laneway onto the crowded street, the same rickshaw driver from the week before stands by his rickshaw.

'Deviji! Aiyae! Kahan jarre tum?' [Come, where are you going?]

'Biasaab, humara desh jana raatko. Airport jana.' [I am going to my country tonight. I am going to the airport.]

I had planned to take a taxi but I have plenty of time. His name is Krishnan. Of course he sings the Hanuman chalisa as we drive through the evening traffic to the airport, the whine of the rickshaw and the smokey polluted air rushing all around me. I sing with him softly, holding the words like precious gems.

In the process of building my temple in Lucknow

Janaki and I singing by my temple

With Papaji on my birthday

With Hania dipping in the Ganga just after returning
from camping alone by the river Ganga

CHAPTER TWENTY-THREE

Paradise lost

'Do not run away from grief, oh soul. Look for the remedy inside the pain. Because the rose came from the thorn and the ruby came from a stone.' Rumi

L ondon is cold: eleven degrees, with a chill in the damp wind that freezes my skin. At the airport it is a reunion straight out of central casting. Tony, with his long dreads and flowing robes, and me full from Ganga's darshan, silk robes and hair piled on top of my head. Orange tilak still smudged on my forehead from the Devi temple I visited before leaving for the airport. I emerge from customs, prayer shawl billowing around my shoulders, to his embrace.

Tony lives in Brixton and I rent a room across the road from him in the converted attic of a terraced house. There is a park up the road with a walled garden – an oasis of colour as spring bursts before me. Mauve wisteria hangs from wooden trellises and the cherry trees cascade pearly pink blossom. A bench in the park has a recent inscription: *Kumari, a being of radiant light.* Tony is as surprised as me. 'I have never seen this before! This must be for you.' The bench becomes ours and we visit every day. The evening before I leave to visit my parents, I sit in the kitchen while Tony cooks rice and peas. A photo of Papaji is on the table and a small statue of Ganesh. As I contemplate what a wonderful re-entry it is into my homeland, the small voice of guidance speaks loud and clear. *This relationship is now over. This is as far as it will go.* I brush it aside, impossible to believe.

*   *   *

I see them standing in the milling crowd of weekend travellers before they see me. How small they seem, a little lost even as if it is they who return from distant lands. Then I am waving through the clean tinted window, from my comfortable padded seat, as the bus pulls in and they see me, and my throat tightens with joy and apprehension. This childlike man, waving like a schoolboy, who is now walking towards where the bus will stop, is the same man I have had such outrageous ideas about. *How could you? It cannot be true*, whispers my mind, and as I step down to their greeting I am sick with worry that coming to England has all been a mistake. By the time we have driven to their home through the English countryside I have convinced myself all is well. Their happiness at my return softens me and I counsel myself that all is fine and anyway I have so much to share, stories to tell. After a week of squeezing myself into the mould required to be the daughter once again, I return to London, intent on working.

There is a shift between Tony and me that I can't quite put my finger on, and one morning soon after I have settled into the attic across the road he tells me. He has a partner of some years and she lives here in Brixton. She is far from happy with my entry onto the scene. I gather my things from his bedroom, dress in remarkable speed and leave.

I stay three months in England, working night after night at St Mary's, often on the ward where I used to work. I give myself to the task as best I can. Now I feel a detachment to the suffering before me, a detachment that does not always feel comfortable. I perform my duties with utmost care, but I keep myself somewhere in the background. I do not share readily of myself, and cannot begin to even imagine how to explain to the staff who knew me before what it is that I am doing in

India. I savour the night shifts, when most patients sleep, their stories of who they are tucked up with them. In the early hours when one calls out, I attend to their needs as quietly as I can. This life does not entice me back, nor open doors I may want to search behind. The contraction within me spins me in a tighter cocoon as I bump noses with my more fragile self once again.

Tony does not simply vanish like the blossom falling in the park. We continue to be lovers, and I believe him when he tells me it is over with Rosa, yet I am unable to stay present. Often I watch myself fly from my body as we make love, and I struggle to find a way back in. From a relationship that felt bathed in glory I fall back to earth.

I long for India, for the mountains, the ashram, and Babaji's glance. For my temple, my refuge and, most of all, for my guru. The last months in India my experience was rose-coloured and glorious. Focused on puja, the rewards for me were evident. I felt limitless and expansive, the fragrance of God constantly in the air. Back in England, the weeks pass by and that energy slowly seeps from me, leaking little by little, bringing me back to earth.

No temple bells ring out in the dawn. No images of Ram around me, no passerby bowing with folded palms to the Hanuman murti adorned with flowers. I gaze when I can to the night outside, never really dark yet the moon traces her passage regardless.

*   *   *

Tony and I continue our dance. He comes and goes, pouring wine into my soul, and I cannot resist his infectious love and tight tight embrace. His heart is full of bhakti and our connection, in spite of the drama, is laced with the grace and fragrance of Papaji. We meditate together and Tony is known in his community as a man of God. Friends come and sit with him and he always has an open door to anyone in need.

I work for a stretch on the special care baby unit, for babies born with HIV. They are tiny scraps wired up to machines. Sick babes, some born riddled with cocaine or methadone from their mother's addiction.

One night, as I take my break at 3 am and boil the kettle to make a cup of tea I won't enjoy very much, I know it is time to return. I think of Sita and the way she would always carry her cup and cloth and travel aids. It is here in this country that I need them. I bring my own mug as the shared ones in the staff rooms are usually stained from someone else's coffee, and I want to cover the chairs before sitting.

*   *   *

Before returning to India I spend more than a week with my parents. Always keen gardeners, they have a reclaimed plot. Lovingly tended, it is filled with lettuce, greens, carrots and a magnificent display of sweet peas showering colour and fragrance. I think of the sweet pea as the emblem of my mother. We pick runner beans for dinner on the patio and walk all day along rivers that burble and glide through meadows awash with wild flowers.

I had forgotten how lovely England is. She wears her transition of spring to summer with poignant beauty. The countryside is a feast of green. Russet buds enticed by a warming sun open to leafy splendour as horse chestnut, oaks and copper beech stand as the giants they are in fields of pastel. Daffodils give way to bluebells that carpet the woods with mauve, and the days stretch longer with the call of a barn owl haunting the twilight skies.

'Darling, you look so beautiful.' Dad trots down the stairs for breakfast and tries to kiss me on the lips. He always wants to kiss me on the lips and this morning it freaks me out. I turn my head away and confusion causes him to frown. It is here again – the tinge of nausea, the quiet disquiet of high alert.

The next morning I wrestle with the ironing board, trying to fold it up. I hear his footsteps coming up the stairs. 'Hey!' I call out. 'Can you give me a hand with this?'

'Oh yes, I'll come and give you a bang!' he says, almost at the top stairs now.

In an instant I am gasping for breath. The airing room is small, enclosed. I'm hot and cold at the same time. My breath is sharp and my throat seems to suddenly close up. I don't know how I manage to speak but I hear the words forced out. 'Oh it's okay, I have managed now.' I rush to my room and sit on the mattress on the floor that is my bed. The breath is doing its own thing. I feel like I inhabit a wild crazy monster of a body and it is more than scary. I stare at my photo of Papaji and very gently it tips forward, then back, then forward again and back.

Downstairs Mum and Dad are eating breakfast. I sit at the table too but this is hardly a breakfast conversation. 'You know, I have to ask you something. Did anything happen to me as a child? I mean did anything inappropriate happen to me?'

Their faces are blank suspended.

'Look, I just keep having images, memories. I don't know, I don't understand.' My voice trails away.

My father returns to his porridge, moving his spoon around the bowl.

My little piece of safe ground is rapidly vanishing. All around is a quagmire of sharks. Mum's eyes glaze over in a way that scares me again. Dad continues with his porridge. I have no idea now what to say. I have felt such anxiety to speak these words, to make them concrete after so much confusion. And I might as well have mentioned the weather.

My mother wipes her nose then blows it loudly. 'Will you have cereal for breakfast, darling?'

I do not know what I find more shocking: my own admission, my father's complete absence or the way the next scene rolled in as if indeed we were discussing the weather.

Later she wants to bring the subject up again. 'Was there something you wanted to talk about, darling?'

'Look, no, not really, Mum. No. It's fine.'

I'm fine I'm fine I'm fine. My mantra all my life.

*   *   *

I have heard that Birmingham is the place to obtain a five-year visa. I wear my long silk robes and pile my hair on top of my head. Tease the dreads out to fall in untidy strands. I dab my finger into the ash from Naga Babaji's dhuni and trace it across my forehead. I carry a small silver container with ash inside that he gave me and I know it is a blessing.

The consulate general happens to come from Lucknow. 'Lucknow is my home town!' he exclaims. I charm him with Hindi and he repeats what he first told me: 'We do not give five-year visa.' He smiles as he stamps the approval for a five-year visa. I need not return for five years. I am going home.

*   *   *

'What happened to you, Prem Kumari?' Bharatmitra asks me the first day I am back. 'You look like you were run over by a bus in England.' He gives me a hug.

I think that being run over by a bus may have been the easier option. At least it would be clear, certain. There would be no doubt.

I am struggling to manage the confusion I feel about memories that cannot possibly be true. It's as if two parties within me are sparring for their voices to be heard. Why should I have reacted to my father like that when he walked up the stairs? Why am I now remembering standing as a child at the top of the stairs in the house in Seaford – I must have been four or five years old – watching him as he came up the stairs towards me, a twist of coldness jabbing me in the guts. As he strode up the stairs I did not like him one bit. And even then I felt ashamed, that I was unclean in some way. *You're crazy*, the other voice whispers. *How could you think such things? What kind of a person are you?* And it is true; it does not make sense. My father is respected, a loving, good-natured man, Christian to his core. He tends to his garden and takes long walks in the countryside. My father, my dad, who I adored.

Then the other voice again. Why had he been lying on my bed one evening when I was thirteen, after seeing me with my boyfriend outside the school disco, standing arm in arm. 'Necking,' he had said, 'must not happen.' No boy should be allowed to touch me. Yet as he spoke, he was himself stroking my thigh. Running his hand slowly up and down. Lying so close to me. And why does my throat tighten, then fill with the salty taste just for a moment, as an icy cold panic sweeps through my body?

I hear myself talk to Janaki about it all, yet I feel removed, slightly to the side. I hear the words but cannot identify with the speaker. I do not talk about it all; I could not admit half of what is going on inside of me.

*   *   *

The monsoon is ferocious this year. The streets run with rivers of slime and my dhuni is covered with plastic as the rain gushes into the courtyard. I surrender to a gas cooker and eat buttered toast most nights for dinner. One late afternoon soon after my return, my back gives way, the old injury returned. For several days I can barely walk. I am overtaken with anguish. I feel as if I am pinned to the mattress on the floor where I spend hours lying flat on my back. In a moment of almost panic, when the confusion invites a host of voices declaring my damnation, I slam my hand against the floor. Hard. I want to slam it again and again but I catch hold and a second later I am flooded in shame. *How crazy are you? What a stupid thing to do. What kind of a person does something like that? You're just a fraud. Hiding away in some temple thinking you are all holy. Gone too far this time.*

I'm visited by friends and I accept acupuncture and massage, I accept all the help I can find to fix my back. I try to speak of my upset, the complete and utter turmoil that these ongoing thoughts have brought, this constant sparring within: *Did he or didn't he? You're making it all up, just nonsense.*

I emerge on my feet a week or so later to another monsoon deluge. At least the heat will ease. The noise of the air cooler drives me crazy. It's a basic contraption that roars away all day outside the window but the cooler air cascading from the whirling motor is worth it. This is the first year I have done anything mechanical to counter the heat. Perhaps next season I will indulge in air conditioning.

Sudden sunshine brings steamy air almost too thick to breathe, then another downpour from the heavens. Finally, the moody, menacing skies, heavy with grey, recede and I too expand with a little more light.

I spring clean the temple, light incense, and sing prayers to whatever God is listening. Shiva is my ishta, my personal deity, yet performing puja twice a day no longer enthrals me. I feel like a tired parent, bored now with the duties of mothering, yet to even consider this boredom is sacrilegious. My ingrained fear of a punishing God creeps out between the cracks. I feel vulnerable and shun company, feign retreat. The truth is that to let anyone close to me is too hard. There is so much I want to share, to talk about, yet my mouth feels strangely closed.

'I'm worried about you, Kumari dear. You are not yourself ever since your back went out and you hurt your hand. You are just not yourself.' Janaki has brought a pot of kidgeree around and even a jar of ghee. I find it unbearable almost that she knows of my demons and keeps on loving me regardless. 'Look, my friend Justin who is here, you remember, you met him yesterday?'

'Sure.'

'Yeah, well you know, he is a psychologist. I think you should speak to him.'

A few days later I go to his air-conditioned apartment. I sit on the floor on a rug. He sits up on the large daybed. He is from San Francisco and has kind eyes. His hair is quite long and looks silky and soft. So does his beard. I guess he is a man who grooms himself well on all occasions.

'Hey, sit up here too,' he insists.

And that's when I lose it. It's as if a stranger inhabits me and I flirt a little and take his suggestion of joining him on the daybed as a sexual advance. I know that was not his intent and my shame knows no bounds. I turn inside out with embarrassment. I see myself at thirteen, trying to seduce Adrian, the twenty-year-old student with eyes made overly large through his thick glasses. I had gone to his flat to ask questions for a homework project and had done my best to come on to him. On Justin's daybed I cower in my shame and loathe myself.

'What's been going on, Prem Kumari? Janaki mentioned she thought it may be good to chat.' He seems oblivious to my internal distress. I pull myself together for a moment at least.

'Well, look, I have all these memories and I think I was sexually abused but my mind keeps messing up.' The words rush out in a hiss and the relief is huge.

He looks at me with such compassion I feel even more unworthy. Can't he see how fucked up and weird I am? His voice is soft. 'It's a very brutal thing to happen to a child.'

But that's it. I can do no more. Just admitting these words sets the jury off with such intensity it is like loudspeakers in my head. Instead I just sob and hate myself. No, I won't speak another word.

CHAPTER TWENTY-FOUR

Prayer

'This place where you are right now, God
has circled on a map for you.' Hafiz

New moon in October heralds Navratri, nine days of worship to the goddess. Navratri is also known as Durga Puja. It is time out to honour the goddess in all her forms. The shops fill up with statues of Durga, while lights and extra flower malas sit at the flower wallah. The collective focus on worship re-inspires my own and I look forward to celebrating. After all, it was back in Chitrakut a year ago now that I first learned the Devi puja, the verses in praise of the goddess.

Swamiji is keen to assist. 'Ah, Prem Kumariji, to worship the goddess is to understand the very basics of this creation. Yes, we have our Lord Shiva residing over all but even he, in all his greatness, will be nothing without the goddess. You see the goddess is the very essence of energy. Do you see? You must understand – everything is energy. To think even of God requires energy. Energy is the basis of this world, of this existence. We have sattva, rajas and tamas – this is everywhere to see! Tamas is inertia, that is dullness and slothfulness, ignorance also. With rajas we have action, activity and when out of balance it brings passion and indulgence. Then we have sattva. Sattva is calmness, purity, a mind cleared of thoughts.'

Swamiji pauses for a moment. He frequently becomes teary and stops mid-sentence, as if tasting that of which he speaks. 'This is why we must only take sattvic foods and keep away from bothersome people that disturb our quiet. Sattva is a natural state but must be cultivated in most. This is why we meditate. We repeat the name of God to remove negativity, the tamasic tendencies. This is why, Prem Kumari, we are so very lucky to meet the Sat Guru, Sri Poonjaji. The one manifest outside ourselves to reveal our true self, here in our heart.' His milky eyes water and shine; his hand is firmly on his heart. I feel ashamed that only a few weeks ago I had considered ending my practice. Here is a man in his eighties with sore knees and cataracts inspiring me, but more than that he believes in me. I cannot let him down.

'Now the great Devi, the goddess we will be remembering in these nine days, is the expression of the whole universe where nothing is devoid of consciousness. Not one aspect of creation can be without consciousness. Which is why we say here in India, that the goddess is mother of all the universe.' He takes my hand in his. 'You understand, Prem Kumari? We must understand!'

I nod. But do I understand? Since my minor breakdown I hold on even tighter, yet it all can seem so pointless. Self-doubt is a weed that can quickly infest a recently flowering garden.

'Now, each day you must eat no grains, take no dairy. A little black tea with sugar is allowed.'

Janaki is also celebrating Navratri and we eat lunch together. Potatoes, carrots and beetroots cooked with turmeric and cumin. We squeeze lemon juice and add ghee. In the evening I eat nothing and for breakfast fruit. As each day passes I feel more and more myself again as my attention is tuned to worship, thoughts filled with the goddess.

On the last day a feast is prepared. I will take the food as prasad to Papaji. From early morning I cook: chick peas in gur, to make a very sweet offering, and puris, which I carefully tend as they burst golden in hissing oil. I wrap them in a cloth to keep warm, while I stir the savoury spicy channa dhal.

Papaji plays with me as he eats. 'Come, come.' He beckons me to the table. I sit on the floor and watch him eat one chick pea at a time. 'Oh, these not cooked?' I laugh as he feeds me with his fork.

Worship dissolves separation, the faulty belief that there are two. The gratitude I feel for Papaji showers me. Is this the revelation of faith that the Bible speaks of? That when there is faith and earnest worship, the fruits fall to our open hearts?

*   *   *

Soon after Navratri is Diwali. Firecrackers explode late into the night and the houses are lit up with fairy lights. It is the closest thing to Christmas as Lakshmi is celebrated. I feel the goodwill, the welcoming of this goddess home. The return of the light as the moon yet again begins her cycle. I sit once more in a place of reverence, of kindness with myself, and whether I will or not return to talk to the psychologist no longer becomes a question. I think much of Babaji and ponder a quick visit. I let the thought settle and it is clear I will not. I send him a card and a package with incense and almonds. I wonder sometimes whether our connection will take hold again. I imagine passing long years with him in the mountains, or travelling together to places of pilgrimage, yet I have a feeling this will not come to pass. I feel him often, as if he were here, sense his subtle fragrance of juniper and coconut oil.

*   *   *

Winter throws muted shades. Evenings become cold and the days shroud with haze. The sun once again recedes behind a smoggy skyline. Another year comes to an end and the illusion of time visits for a moment.

A local man, not more than a teenager, has hassled me too many times as I walk through the village to the market: a jostle from his elbow or walking behind me, just too close. I am on my way to buy dhal and gur just after siesta time and the sandy street is empty. The mosque calls out for afternoon prayer as he walks towards me. He passes, and faster than I can respond, he reaches out and grabs my breast. It hurts and I have had enough. The outrage fuels my actions. I wait a moment then turn and follow him. He enters the mosque and I cover my head and follow him in. Inside the mosque a line of men and boys stand with their hands folded in prayer, facing a wall. I see him washing at a row of taps. Heads turn to stare. Before he has a chance to even see me I push his head hard into the tap and he stumbles backwards. He looks startled, angry, and I vent my fury, my rage. He stands stumbling, a little off balance. Then I see he is only a teenager. I slap him hard three times and walk out as quickly as I entered.

Outside I am mortified. I know the elders of this mosque; we nod and greet each other almost every day. It is absolutely forbidden for a woman to enter the house of worship. I continue on to the market, adrenalin still pumping, finally calming down as I order a kilo of rice and a little cumin.

When I return past the mosque, the elders stand outside. 'I am so very sorry to enter the mosque,' I explain in Hindi.

They are full of smiles. 'Madam, we are very sorry. This boy is no good. After you his father also is beating!' A group of the women stand around and as I finish my conversation they ask me to eat with them, gesturing with their hands. I feel like a hero. Finally I have made a stand.

As I sit under the smoky night sky on the roof of my home, I reflect again on the triumph I felt as I slapped the boy's face. And the intensity of the rage, the overwhelming torrent that for a moment allowed me to believe I could pummel him to the ground. I remember the time I was fighting with my dad. Play fighting, he had said. It was the annual family holiday to Criccieth, a beach mission on the sand and ice creams. He and I were alone in a room and I had brought my knee up to his groin with a swift and forceful jerk. He had doubled over in pain. 'Never ever do that to a man again,' he had said through clenched teeth. My mother had been in the kitchen and I had left the flat, walked to the seafront and stared out over the green-grey water. I remember the shame but I remember too the sense of injustice. But I cannot remember what happened in the moments before I kneed him. The glory of being a hero rapidly fades.

*   *   *

February brings Shivaratri, the night of Shiva and a big festival in India. It is the night of the black moon and Shiva is worshipped in style. Of course I want to celebrate in my temple and I invite Papaji to come. Ever since the Durga festival last October I have returned to my temple life with full enthusiasm. It is the only way of living that makes any sense to me. I have learned the Hanuman chalisa by heart now and I find chanting a soothing balm. Sometimes I wonder where life will lead me. For sure I will not return to England; more and more I see myself living in the hills with Babaji, quietly passing time. After my experience with Tony in London the simplicity and uncomplicated nature of Babaji and his life in the ashram, is even more appealing. 'All for time pass' he so often would say. Keep your thoughts on me, Krishna tells Arjuna in the Bhagavad Gita, and hence be in peace.

Papaji is enthusiastic. 'Yes, yes, of course. Shiva temple so Shivaratri we will celebrate together.'

At the end of my lane a big ditch is being dug. It has been left as a ditch for days now and I am concerned that the van that Papaji travels in will not be able to pass. I ask the driver to come and check it out before the day. He drives the van over no problem. 'We are all looking forward to coming tomorrow to your house. Papaji has been talking about it today.'

'How many people will come?' I ask, realising I will need to prepare more prasad than I thought.

'Well, we never know with Papaji!'

True, I think, as I busy myself with preparations. The day before I clean and scrub and on the day itself I fast all day, as is the custom. I sit for hours by the dhuni stirring a big pot of khir, with nutmeg, cinnamon and a pinch of saffron. Raisins plump up as they soak in the milk and the almonds and cashews soften just enough. Later in the day there is a power cut. I light a myriad candles and decorate the temple.

I wash the lingam with milk and offer ghee, sandalpaste, bael leaf and many sticks of incense before arranging the strings of rose malas for the lingam, marigolds trailing everywhere. Janaki is here of course and a couple of friends I have invited. The power remains off. We are all ready, dressed in our finery, tilak in place.

'Prem Kumari!' It is Chandi Devi, at the door. 'Prem Kumari, we cannot drive the van over the blockage at the end of the lane! Papaji says you must come to the house. He is really cross.'

I have no time to think. I take my shawl and call to Janaki: 'Take care of the house!' I go with Chandi up the darkened lane to the van. I sit behind Papaji.

'Why do you not tell us we cannot drive to your house? I cannot walk this far. You should know this!' He is almost shouting and everyone is quiet. I sit behind him in absolute bliss. It all seems a big joke, so obviously a play, words spoken, activities performed. As Rumi says: 'There is field out beyond you and I, I'll meet you there.'

At his house the living room is full. I sit at the back and remain in a deep state of meditation. Everyone is eating, but I cannot even consider food. Eventually Papaji stands with his helpers at his side. He is an old man and clearly in pain as he takes a moment to get his balance. 'Where is she? Where is Prem Kumari?'

I push through to the front and he takes my arm, leading me through the door.

'Now we will go.' There is a flurry of activity. 'Where do you want to go, Papaji?' Bharatmitra, his main attendant, asks.

'To Prem Kumari's house of course!' he bellows, still holding my arm. Again we pile into the van and we drive over the ditch all the way to the gate.

The house is in darkness. The power is still off in this street. Janaki and the others are singing as I rush in, the candles burnt almost to nothing. 'Papaji is coming now!' I say and there he is, walking in. He sits on the chair just by Shiva painted on the wall. He has taken out his teeth and his face is old and soft. I can barely speak, let alone sing. Swamiji rings the bell and puja begins. Papaji nods as I sing to him, offer the flame to him as he sits on the chair before me, wearing a woollen hat and sweater.

Kabir, the great saint of Kashi, was once asked: 'If God and the Guru were to stand before you, to whom would you bow first?'

'To my Guru,' he replied. 'As he is the one who has showed me God.'

My words are a whisper as I sing, sitting at my Guru's feet. 'Tva meva Matar, cha Pita tva meva, tva meva bhandhu, chaska tvameva.' You are my mother, my father too.

We eat the khir. I would have preferred to serve it warmer. Papaji stays a little while, listening to our bhajans and watching me intently. The air is charged with love. He holds tight to my arm as he walks out into the black night. 'Chello, chello,' is his response as I fall at his feet, there in the dark, muddy laneway.

The house is empty now. Candles still burn. I feed the fire and boil milk. The sudden silence after the party is like the pause between breaths. The night for Shiva wraps around me like a spell. I roll a joint. Cross my legs. Build the fire up some more. I sit until my eyes are too heavy and slip away to bed to sleep the few hours before dawn emerges all over again.

The very next day it is clear that I will not perform puja any more. As much as the desire has been there – for a year almost exactly – now it is not. The same, small voice suggests that I offer flowers and keep the temple clean, but the time for puja is over.

It is April and the temperature is already more than forty degrees. I do not want to spend the hot season in Lucknow. Janaki is staying up at Phool Chatti and I decide to join her. There is an American woman living there now who runs an outreach program for the villagers in the nearby hills. I decide to go and help.

CHAPTER TWENTY-FIVE

ShivaShakti

'Whatever is destined not to happen will not happen, try as you may. Whatever is destined to happen will happen, try as you may to prevent it. This is certain. Therefore the best course is to remain silent.' Ramana Maharshi

On the bus from Haridwar to Rishikesh I see a westerner on a motorbike. Not an uncommon sight, of course, but I notice his white-blond hair, his brown leather jacket and his casual smile as he negotiates his bike past the bus. I decide I don't like him.

When I reach Lakshman Jhula, the idea of walking to Phool Chatti ashram with my quite heavy bag is not appealing. I hear a voice: 'You need a lift?' It's him. He is going to Phool Chatti.

Karlo is part of the scene at Phool Chatti. He has a small stone house in the garden. It isn't very long before we are lovers.

*　　*　　*

After another monsoon in Lucknow, I give up my precious home. I set sail with the winds. In mid-April Karlo and I arrive in Gangotri on the back of his Enfield, having driven through snow falling like a magician's trick. Gangotri is high in the Himalayas and the end of the road. Later when the thaw begins, we trek to Gomukh and the source of the Ganga. We stay in a tent where a sadhu lives and he cooks rice and dhal on a kerosene stove. We walk up over the glacier that is the Ganga's source to Tapovan. Tapovan is the seat of heaven and rising above this grassy meadow is Shivling. I could remain here forever. But life keeps turning. Karlo is due for a trip to Europe.

'Let's spend some days in Mussoorie before I go.' Karlo is always planning, always looking for fun. 'We can stay in a fancy hotel, live it up for a few days before I go.' He likes to party. His body is loose, lean and supple. He has the pertest nipples of any man I have known.

Walking in the forest far from the bustle of town we find a cottage for rent nestled in the greenery. I'm not ready to return to the heat of Lucknow. I love the forests, the serene silence. The cottage reminds me of England. It's stone with a slate roof and even has a bathtub in the kitchen, a bedroom with curtains at the window and a western-style toilet off the bedroom. In the living room is a loft with a steep wood ladder. It is set in the grounds of a large rambling guesthouse clearly influenced by the Raj, home to a group of American language students studying Hindi at the nearby school. The guesthouse is just one of several elaborate houses, surrounded by manicured gardens amidst the pine forests that open to reveal vistas of the higher Himalayas.

I watch Karlo drive away, until the 'thut thut' of his Enfield fades. I savour aloneness, sip at it bit by bit, day by day. I walk often, gazing out to the horizon of peaks, hazy in the midday, pristine against a purple evening sky. That's where we have been, way up there in those white worlds. In the evening I cook rice and dhal and the silence shouts. I pull the curtains, check the locks and fall early to bed.

I settle in. I am glad Karlo is gone. Being with him had thrown up parts of myself that I would rather not see. He smoked a lot of charas and would disappear into himself. I felt lost and dark and self-critical.

After some days alone I am still searching for a sense of ease in my own company. I try to write a script for my own character but can't quite find the lines.

One day clouds cover the mountains. Grey mosaics mottle the sun. The air is hushed, trees forlorn. The forest breathes a fragrance that only deodar can. As the first drops fall I abandon the idea of walking. I hurry home, build the fire, and listen to the distant shudder of thunder creep nearer until it crashes above. Rain drums on the slate, lightning flashes, illuminating all in silver-white. Thunder claps so loudly that I jump again and again. As darkness engulfs the house, I read in bed but I'm distracted by the storm, by the slight gap in the curtain. I try to fix it but it just doesn't quite close. Giving up on the evening, I turn out the light and watch for a long time as the storm swirls outside, crashing and pounding, illuminating ghostly shapes for a moment before plunging to black again.

I'm woken by a smash that sounds like glass. The skylight in the living room must have blown in. I lie alert in the dark as the storm rages all around. The rain will be coming in. Nothing in me can bring myself to climb out of my snug cosy nest. *It's not the skylight*, something whispers, but I won't listen and I don't care if the rain comes in. Another crash and smash, but this time a torch light flashes in the living room. I'm up in a second and I turn on the light. There is glass all over the floor; the pane in the door is completely broken and the freezing night air blows the rain in.

Half the door is broken, leaving plenty of room for a hand to reach in and open the lock. If I was vague with the script before, now I am clueless. Panic screams through every cell in my body. I have lost the ability to respond. Desperate to pee, I run to the toilet. As I pee, another lightning flash illuminates the window. And then I see him, a man pressed up against the outside wall, watching me.

The scream that erupts from me has lain dormant for millennia. In a moment all returns to blackness and I rush to the door. I must get there first. I stick my head through the broken pane, the sharp shards of glass underfoot, and scream to the night. The rain slashes, the wind is freezing and still I scream on and on until I am just a mess of terrified quiet. No one will come. No one has heard. Do I run to the house or stay here? Run? No way! Alone in the forest on a black, stormy night with a potential attacker? No, stay, stay. I pull two chairs up against the door and grab a knife from the kitchen. I snatch up a candle, a smoke and the book of talks by Ramana and climb the ladder to the platform loft. There is enough room to sit and sit I do. I can see the door from here and my eyes never leave it.

Fear has rooted in my gut like a strangler vine. It's twisting tight and I can barely breathe. My hands shake as I roll a smoke. The knife is just by my side. And then it is as if the firmanent rips. I can feel a tangible sense of my psyche rearranging itself. *No one will believe you.* It whispers then creeps louder, like the sound of hooves galloping on a frost bitten earth. *Don't tell anyone. Do not tell. No one will believe you. You bring this on yourself staying alone in the forest. This is your fault.* And on they come like a hunt moving in on the fox. *Go early to the town, get what you need and fix it. No one needs to know. No one must know. They will not believe you.* The voices slide away but the crack remains.

Some time later the storm abates, moves away, and only rain falls. As light shuffles the blackness I hear a bird. My foot is bleeding; a sliver of glass is embedded in my sole. I pull it out and feel nothing. I take the knife and climb down the ladder. I pull the chairs away and open the door. I run silently through the forest, knife clenched in my fist, and pound on the door of the house.

This old mansion house in Mussoorie houses a different India than I am used to: American language students, fresh from college and a wealthy Indian family on holiday from Delhi, with two glamorous daughters and their handsome husbands. One is a pilot, the other a businessman. Everyone is concerned as I am ushered in and immediately taken under the wing of the household. 'I heard all that screaming in the night. Woke me up. I presumed it was a local family, domestic issues you see.'

There is no room free so I share with Mary Jane from Kentucky who is here to learn Hindi as part of an aid outreach job she has in Uttar Pradesh. I fit in as best I can although I feel like a stranger in their midst. I pull myself together, trying to banish the recurring image of his face leering through the window, caught in that crack of lightning.

Nothing happened, I tell myself. *Nothing happened. It could have been so much worse. Just get over it.* At night I wake from sleep and my heart literally pounds in my chest. A cold sweat tingles on my forehead. Fear has to be tasted to really know it.

*   *   *

Some weeks later I walk the streets of Delhi. I hear temple bells ring, smell frying spices, watch the cows chew on piles of garbage and walk amidst the chaos. It is a welcome distraction, moving from the chaotic inner to a preponderously chaotic outer. I rejoice, my heart sings once again. I wait in the smoky early morning for the express train to Lucknow.

Back in Lucknow I take on the home of friends returning to America now their baby is growing. Before they leave I stay in another friends home to look after Sasha, their dog, while they holiday in Goa. For two nights I will be responsible for two houses. Raman comes to my rescue. I first met Raman years ago in Delhi. I had been bitten on the leg by a street dog in the early hours as I walked from the train station to find a hotel. Later in the day I had met him and his wife. I was touched at his presence and care as I told him of my upset following the bite, which ensured that our meeting stayed in my memory over the years. Raman spent years travelling with Papaji in India when Papaji was younger and before his limited mobility kept him in Lucknow, when the crowds arrived. Raman told wonderful stories of living with Papaji in Haridwar on the banks of the Ganga, staying for months here in Lucknow in the small house near Hazrat Ganj.

'I'll stay and look after the dog; you settle in to your new home,' he told me.

The first night after I move I dream with vivid intensity. I dream that I am in the other house and it is being attacked by a group of monkeys, so violently and aggressively that the building crumbles around me. The monkeys change into men and I see Sasha lying in a pool of blood. I scream over and over, 'Oh my God! They have killed Sasha.' I wake to the black night, alert and anxious. It is 3 am and sleep does not return.

In the morning I go to satsang early. A friend who lives close to where Raman is housesitting walks towards me.

'Prem Kumari,' he calls, 'something has happened to Raman.' He helps me stand my scooter as he tells the story. Last night, in the early hours, a man broke into the house. He entered the bedroom where Raman slept and as he sat up, woken by a torch beam, the man had hit him three times with a crowbar. 'He crawled to our house, blood everywhere. He is hurt bad. He is in the hospital; he wants to see you. He could have been killed.'

The clinic is down the road. I wait as he is being sutured, tears coursing down my cheeks. When it is finished I am taken in to where he lies on a table. A big wad of bandage covers his head.

He has ten stitches in his head, another five in his leg and a further seven in his foot. If the iron bar had landed inches to the right he could well have been dead. Raman smiles at me; his eyes are bright yet his face very pale. The relief that he is okay, the absolute wanting to care for him, leaps from within me and reaches out as I take his hand. He squeezes it tight. 'Prem Kumari. I am so glad it was me not you.'

Our bond is cemented. How could it not be? Later I go with Janaki to clean up the mess. At the front door is a smear of blood and the trail leads to the bedroom where he slept. On three walls of the room blood is splattered from floor to ceiling. A sense of dread, of extreme and loathsome vulnerability, grasps me as we clean the blood from the walls and take the bloodied sheets from the bed. The energy lingers with a malevolent presence and I shudder to think what could have happened if it had been me sleeping in the bed. Or what could have happened if the intruder had come a night earlier.

*　　*　　*

I busy myself with making a home. On an empty wall I paint another huge Hanuman and resume my practice of puja and prayer. I have my altar in the living room and every day I clean and wash and offer flowers and incense. The world and all its dramas laps too close to my edges and I know deep down inside myself that my connection with the Divine, with God, is amplified in the silent moments. I renew a commitment within myself – that the purpose of my life is to wake up to the truth of reality – and I know that for me devotion is my path. Every day Raman visits with a rose. *For the goddess* he tells me.

The winter months pass and Papaji shows signs of his age. He is eighty-six years old. He walks slowly, leaning heavily on the arms of his attendants, and often he responds with 'Sing! Sing!' to earnest questions. Regardless of the frivolity, his presence pervades. I no longer help with cleaning in his house, and haven't for almost a year now. If I feel the urge I walk to his gate; I am mostly invited in and sometimes I am not. It no longer matters to me. I feel him as a texture in my breath, a sudden swooping in of presence and I know his words are true. *I am with you wherever you are.* I help with the videoing of satsang and watch him from behind the lens. I experience myself retreating above it all, then up and up until satsang house is a tiny speck in a vast world. My time in India is drawing to a close. Here in Lucknow I become just a little bit more western. Respectful of Indian culture, my shirts now reach just to my thighs and I no longer wear a sari.

I want to visit Babaji. It has been two years and three months since I have seen him. Occasionally I have sent him a card and twice he has replied with a postcard of Shiva. Written in Hindi of course, mostly quotes from the Bhagavad Gita and notes on what is growing in the ashram garden.

Have I chosen to stay away from him and if so, why? Yet the idea that I have chosen this or that simply is not true. My path has evolved and I have walked ahead. What is life but a book written by the hand of God?

* * *

Mountains in early April and winter is still evident as the snowline slips away to leave a landscape birthing spring. Trees, barren and still, unfurl fingers from the ice to stretch upwards towards mountains adorned in white. As I push open the gate I am struck by the sense of sanctity. Nothing has changed. The temple hangs in the still air and the cold holds the silence. Not a murmur, not a sound. No sign of smoke curling from the roof, no white cat walks down the path. On the verandah the hessian sack pillow sits in the same place against the wall, his coconut bowl by the side. Inside the dhuni room the fire is smoothed. Wood is neatly stacked against the wall. Everywhere is tidy, almost bare. I sit down on the step. I do not have to wait long. I see the top of his head then the gate opens. He sees me the moment he steps through. We meet by the temple. He looks smaller than I remember and a few grey hairs mix in his beard that has grown long.

'Babaji, Babaji.'

'Oh ho Kumari come. Kumariji come.'

His voice is rich and deep yet trembles for just a moment. He drops his bag there on the path and holds my face, full of tenderness. *I didn't know I love you this much*, my heart shouts out and I close my eyes and let the emotion ride. He smells just as he always did – the sweetest mix of incense, coconut oil and wood smoke.

'Kumariji, Kumariji.' He holds my face again. Our foreheads touch then he stands back with his hand on his heart muttering, 'Hari Om Hari Om.' As quickly as it came the display is over. He picks up his bag. 'Kumariji here stay?'

'Yes, maybe one week stay?'

'Chello me chai make.'

We settle back in just like that. The dhuni has never gone out. The wooden box of treasures sits by his seat. The rusted jar of chai spices – cardamom, cloves, bits of cinnamon bark – is the same. Most of all: Babaji. I watch him play with the fire, notice his wide brown hands. The firelight catches in his beard and he has two patches of grey. His eyes are the same dark pools; he shyly glances up at me and I cannot take my eyes away.

At night we eat kidgeree with dollops of ghee and pink Himalayan rock salt ground in the mortar and pestle. The plates washed and stacked to dry and with the fire burning freely, we sit silently, absorbed by the flame. I realise how much of a teacher Babaji has been to me. His life as a renunciate portrays the truest sense of renunciation: that of one's mind. No attachment to outcome, to any agenda. He lives his life uncluttered by thoughts, untroubled by the world. He always told me: Tat Tvam Asi. Thou art that. He gave me the answer to the question of Advaita: Who am I? But as with all things we have to find out for ourselves.

We sit late into the night. I have no desire to break this spell. Outside the moon is almost full. Her light falls silver through the window. I remember the night we sat offering puja after the fire on the mountain. Grass has already grown covering the scar that remained all winter. The terrain has shifted; day passed to night to day again under countless different vistas yet I, the one experiencing, has remained the same.

In the morning, I hear him wake and begin his routine. Coughing, clearing his throat and the low mumble of mantra. I join him at the dhuni for black tea. The milkman is yet to come.

'Today walk going. River place going. Wood taking and little leg stretching?'

I smile. I taught him this expression – 'stretching my legs' as I used to say when I wanted to walk in the mountains all day. 'Sure, Babaji.'

I wait on the ridge, watching crimson folds in the eastern sky turn to gold. It is a repeat of years before. We meet at the Durga shrine, still in the same state of disrepair. The path has collapsed in places and we walk over a landslide. Finally the roar of water fills my ears and then the sight: pristine magical nature. I cross the river first over the familiar boulders. The water is freezing. The spray sprinkles on my cheeks in tiny needles of ice.

Babaji spreads the blanket he has been wearing tied around his waist, over the flat ground. The rock overhang provides a roof and the fireplace of blackened stones is still here. I stand again by the water watching it swirl until I can hold myself no longer and return to the fire and to him. He sits on his haunches watching me. I sit by his side and he faces me then pulls me to him. He holds my hand in his, traces the lines on my palm with his finger.

'Babaji, can you read palms? Can you tell me my future?' I'm half playful and half not. Perhaps it can all be known simply as this.

'Future khya hai? Future I don't know. You God looking bas [enough].' He follows the lines a moment more then lets go my hand. And he holds me tight then tighter. The sun rises high enough to fall around us from above. He pulls back his lungi to reveal his readiness. I wrestle my trousers away and give myself to him, with only the elements to accompany.

That night we sit by the fire. 'Babaji, you have charas?'

'Small piece hey. Chillum piou?'

'Chillum ney, joint tikhai.'

'Accha banau.' He rummages in his box and pulls out a matchbox with charas inside.

'You make, Babaji, then it is prasad.'

'Kumariji, you your country going and one husband take. You children coming and home life better.' I let my eyes fall to the fire. He crumbles the mix and speaks again. 'This your hand lines speak.'

Caught in this spell, the world outside and my life in years to come hold little interest. Right now, being here with Babaji is enough. I know my time in India is drawing to a close, for now at least.

More than seven years have passed since I witnessed Henry's passing. I left my life of the known, my boat and my job, my identity as a young English nurse, to search for the presence revealed as the thin veil between life and death lifted. That India would hold me for so many years, imparting her jewels of ancient wisdom, I never could have guessed. My destiny is unknown. I followed my heart and the blessings have been immense. India has swept me away and allowed me to emerge again, has given me the experience of her gods, of worship and devotion to the divine in all the manifestations, and has blessed me with Babaji, who sits before me now, quietly reading the Bhagavad Gita. I have met my guru, the one who dispels the darkness of ignorance and shines a light on my own self. The presence of God has revealed itself within my own heart, giving me the platform to live my life wherever that will be. Papaji's presence is with me wherever I am. The presence of Papaji, the presence of my own self – there is no difference. As a bhakta, a devotee, I can only bow to the feet of my beloved Guru Dev.

I remember when Henry told me, 'I chant. I sit still. I remember again that peace is all around me, always, no matter what the circumstance. Life can throw many challenges – better to be prepared in your mind.' I cannot deny the confusion about my father – whether he was inappropriate sexually with me or whether I am simply making it up, elaborating on something that possibly happened and making so much more of the story. And if so, what does that say about me? What kind of a person would create such stories? Whatever the truth, it has left a deep disquiet that needs healing. And what does it say about my father if indeed what I sense, what I remember, what I feel in my body, are true? The split between myself as an expression of the divine, and the poisonous self-doubt that draws me into my own personal samsara, is too easily triggered since the storm-ridden night in Mussoorie.

The moon slips to a shadow to emerge one evening as a thin smile in the west. I watch her slide slowly beyond the horizon as night takes hold. It is time to leave.

Back in Lucknow India bears down on me and I long to be able to walk unseen, unnoticed, another white face among many. I cannot handle any more having eyes follow me, leering looks wherever I go. I need a holiday in the west.

In August 1997 I visit Raman where he lives in Australia. Three weeks later Papaji dies after a short illness. His health had been deteriorating over the last year. What was a planned visit, a holiday from India, now becomes unending. It will be ten years until I step on Indian soil again.

राम राम राम राम राम राम

CPSIA information can be obtained at www.ICGtesting.com
Printed in the USA
LVOW07s1047310814

401727LV00003B/621/P